VERSIFICATION

MAJOR LANGUAGE TYPES

VERSIFICATION

MAJOR LANGUAGE TYPES

Sixteen Essays

Edited with a Foreword by

W. K. WIMSATT

New York
Modern Language Association
New York University Press
1972

Library of Congress Catalog Card Number: 72–89366

ISBN: 8147–9155–7

Manufactured in the United States of America

CONTENTS

For Maynard and Florence Mack

FOREWORD

> The essence of rhythm is the fusion of sameness and novelty . . . A mere recurrence kills rhythm as surely as does a mere confusion of differences. A crystal lacks rhythm from excess of pattern, while a fog is unrhythmic in that it exhibits a patternless confusion of detail.
>
> —Alfred North Whitehead, *An Enquiry Concerning the Principles of Natural Knowledge* (Cambridge Univ. Press, 1919), p. 198

> The variations necessary to pleasure belong to the art of poetry, not the rules of grammar.
>
> —Samuel Johnson, *A Dictionary of the English Language,* London, 1773, end of the "Grammar"

Every feature of a poem is both an act of knowing and responding and at the same time a thing known or knowable. The knowing and the response absorb the thing known. It is no less true that they are involved in it, reflexively, and for critical purposes they resolve into it. We can hold these aspects apart if we wish. We can call the thing known the "objective correlative." Or, with an opposite emphasis, we can stress the fact that since the poem is a mental transaction, everything in the poem is something that happens to or inside the reader.

It is never really helpful to clear understanding, however, to speak of any given feature of a poem as if in some very special way (more than other features) it is a happening inside us, an agitation (or an ordering) of our impulses. Meter, or more inclusively verse, is one feature of poems which has sometimes been conceived in that way, as a kind of game played with the reader's expectations and disappointments, or perhaps a form of hypnosis, or a rhythm of his feelings or of his verbal and mental responses. "Metrical organization," we are likely to be told, "occurs not in the physical signal but in the pattern constructions of the listener." We substitute the experience of the verse for the verse itself. We give up the verse and fall back on our responses.

But versification also has this peculiarity: that of all the features of a poem it offers itself as perhaps the clearest and most firmly definable objective correlative of our responses. In a closely allied way, it develops the most specific patterns of any part of poetic study. It has the most technical aspirations. It is codified in numerous grammars. It is a part of linguistics—both a minutely charted and a conspicuously public study.

The authors of the sixteen essays which compose this volume show themselves, one and all, writers of a grammatical bent. The aim of the volume is to expound, not how readers at various times and places have been affected by verse, but what the poets have written. The collection gives a comparative sketch of select Western and Eastern systems of versification as widely separate in time and place as the parallels of Biblical Hebrew, the tones of Medieval Chinese, the alliterative stresses of *Beowulf,* the Tuscan hendecasyllables of Dante, the alexandrines of Corneille and of Hugo, the "sprung rhythms" of Hopkins, the syllables of Marianne Moore. What lies between the rules, says a wise contemporary French critic, is more important than the rules. Yes, but what lies between lies there not in spite of the rules but in peculiar ways just in virtue of them. Versification is a signal instance of the enabling power of shackles in art.

The rules, however, have never been the object of an easy harmony of opinion among the experts. Some differences appear even among those who participate in the present co-operative enterprise, at a few places where their concerns overlap. The editor of such a collection will perhaps be tolerated if he intrudes some proemial reflections upon aspects of the problem—illustrated mainly in the field of versification best known to him—under these five echoing heads: verse and SENSE, meter and LOGIC, MAKING and BREAKING meter, counting SYLLABLES, measuring ACCENT.

I. SENSE

A coin in a parking meter works in two ways: one emblematic, as a coin of the realm, representing the price demanded for parking; the other physical, as a piece of metal the size and shape necessary to work the machine. The relation between the two functions is a cold one. It will serve by contrast to point to the peculiarly intimate and warmly colored (if "conventional") relation which prevails between the physical and the symbolic sides of language (*signifiant* and *signifié*). The two sides of language are blended in a system so spontaneous, so tacit, so pregnant, and so pervasive, that they are normally experienced as an identity. They constitute a reality. Like language features at any other level, versification (so far as it is a physical or phonetic fact) is perhaps definable apart from any explicit meaning, but in the act of poetic knowing, it is inextricable. Verse is never anything we encounter independently of the meaning of versified language. It is certainly never anything that we experience as a *value* apart from that *meaning*.

If rhythm, as Whitehead asserts, is a pattern of likeness and difference, then we can adopt the working conception that verse is an artifice of systematic sameness which, running along with several kinds of difference in a poem, makes the rhythm; it enables the framing of special differences at various levels. But sameness too is a manifold. How many kinds of sameness may not, in complex instances, be claimed for the verse? Most likely, for ordinary purposes, we think of meter as a matter of syllables, and of stresses, quantities, or tones. Whatever the language, some marked phonetic or physical and immediately perceivable recurrent quality seems part of the essential device. But patterns of sound have meaning, and even syllables and accents in themselves have their meanings or potentials of meaning (morphemic and phonemic). And we remember the striking intrusion from the East into our prosodic history, the verse of the Hebrew Bible, where the recurrent sameness lies very conspicuously, not in syllables, accents, or any small phonetic elements such as "feet," but in the syntax and the semantics of parallel clauses.[1] Here meaning asserts itself massively as a metrical component. The versification consists in a series of parallel assertions.

In a somewhat similar way, we can cite refrains, anaphoras, and other elements of parallel sense from folk poems of our own more immediate heritage. And from literary poems. The intricate variation in the order of a certain set of six line-terminal words in the successive stanzas of an Italian or an English *sestina* is a metrical matter undetachable from the arrangement and rearrangement of meaning. The sonnet-wreath (*sonetti a corona*) invented by the *cinquecento* Sienese *Academia degl'Intronati* consists of fourteen sonnets linked in a closed circle by the repetition of last lines as succeeding firsts. A fifteenth, "master" or "base," sonnet consists of the fourteen last-first lines, in order. Versification imposes and participates in a fantastically severe requirement of coherence, closure, and thematic summation.[2] An English couplet realist, the Reverend George Crabbe, wrote a long poem, *The Parish Register*, divided into three parts: I. Births; II. Marriages; III.

Funerals. By a certain indulgence of the extrapolative faculty, it might be possible to say that the persistently recurring events of each part of this poem are a kind of versification, an overriding feature of the more minutely measured syllabic-accentual meter.

II. LOGIC

I have read that a certain whimsical small-town bartender had a habit of accumulating tips in a quart jar. Nickels, dimes, quarters, fifty-cent pieces, silver dollars, paper bills were dropped into the jar until it was full. This bartender then took it to the bank and wrote out a deposit slip for "one quart of money." If measured on a scale running from what is in a sense most simple, logical, and artless, to what is most highly sophisticated artificial, and even "counterlogical," verse shows a tendency to develop towards something like the status of a quart of money. In the most ancient kind of poetry represented in this volume, that of Biblical Hebrew, the verse, as we have just noticed, emerges as a sequence of parallel masses of meaning. This is a highly logical verse. (Its emotive quality seems closely related to its very reiteration and insistence.) Elements of counterlogicality appear, of course, even here, in features such as those that analysts following Bishop Robert Lowth distinguish as "imperfect" synonymy, "compensation," "stairlike" progression, chiasmus. But for a plenary example at the counterlogical end of the scale, let us turn to some more minutely segemented sort of verse—for instance, the English iambic pentameter. It is true that in certain lines of Milton and other Renaissance writers, this verse may approximate a kind of extension or subdivision of Hebraic paralleling:

> Of hand, of foot, of lip, of eye, of brow.
>
> (Shakespeare, *Sonnet* CVI)
>
> And swims or sinks, or wades, or creeps, or flyes.
>
> (*Paradise Lost* II.950)

Or, to iron out that second example slightly, suppose:

> And creeps, and crawls, and walks, and runs, and flies.

Or, for the ultimate reduction:

> And walks, and walks, and walks, and walks, and walks.

But we know that the formula was not like this.

Of Mans First Disobedience, and the Fruit
Of that Forbidden Tree, whose mortal Tast
Brought Death into the World, and all our woe,
With loss of *Eden,* till one greater Man
Restore us, and regain the blissful Seat,
Sing Heav'nly Muse . . .

"True musical delight . . . consists onely in apt Numbers, fit quantity of Syllables, and the sense variously drawn out from one Verse into another . . ." The relentless, though highly abstract, parallels of Milton's iambs (or Shakespeare's, or Pope's, or Wordsworth's) carry the poem along in a steady equal march; at the same time, and in the same words, the poem is marching, semantically and syntactically, in a varied sequence of *other* paces. There is no simple physical analogue, of hobbled runner or acrobat in chains, that can express this.

III. MAKING AND BREAKING

In a good book on the development of English prosody during the latter half of the sixteenth century, John Thompson has argued that the fourteeners and the poulter's measure (twelves and fourteens) which achieved a kind of dominance for a while, in works of Surrey, Googe, Turberville, and Gascoigne, were precarious meters; they tended to fall apart if even very slight liberties (in the interest of sense) were taken with their extended phonetic structure. So, when they did keep themselves going, they encouraged or even demanded a degree of inflated sense, garrulity, gabble. The writers seemed at moments resigned to a flow of nonsense. The iambic pentameter line, as developed largely by the succeeding generation of dramatists, was a much more freely manageable instrument. It had its limit of tolerance or snapping point, but on the whole it was more resilient. It became the standard English line.

Contemplating that idea of the English pentameter, I think of something as incongruous as a modern synthetic substance known as "silly putty." This embodies three qualities in a kind of physical paradox. A lump of it may be kneaded and shaped in the hand like putty or dough. (Verse, whatever else it is, is a manipulation of linguistic givens. It is an extra-canonical, somewhat variable, arrangement of canonical features.) But in the second place, silly putty is elastic, to the extent that a lump of it will bounce if dropped on the floor. (Most living verse, and notably the expressive iambic pentameter, tolerates a considerable measure of dislocation, and reasserts itself; it springs back towards its norm.) But then thirdly, a piece of silly putty, if hit sharply with a hammer, will shatter like glass. (There comes a point in the distortion of the single iambic line when it breaks—it ceases to sound like a line of the kind it is supposed to be. Or at least such has been a usual view with prosodists of the conservative tradition.)

That paradoxical account of the sophisticated iambic pentameter may be a good way to distinguish it from the jog-trot fourteener. But perhaps an adequate definition of a meter involves more than a definition of a single line of that meter? Read the first ten or twenty lines of *Paradise Lost,* and we establish the meter of the poem. We notice perhaps a few instances of the main kinds of permitted substitution or "complication": the inverted first foot, the elision of the extra syllable. Nothing in this highly characteristic passage, however, could have prepared us for the Italianate multiplication of trochees in a few lines of the poem such as the following:

> As a despite don against the most High. (VI.906)
> Spirits odorous breathes; flours and thir fruit. (V.482)
> And dust shalt eat all the dayes of thy Life. (X.178)
> Burnt after them to the bottomless pit. (VI.866)[3]

A given line may not by itself sound to us iambic. We may prefer to call it "unmetrical." But this may not mean very much. Each of the very few anomalous lines in *Paradise Lost* is part of an immediately iambic context—and of an overwhelmingly iambic long poem. It is carried by its context. The tenor of poem and passage is as much a part of the rule as the nearly, but not quite, absolute prescription that can be drawn for the individual line.

IV. SYLLABLES

"The presence of syncope (the omission of presumably supernumerary syllables: *ev'ry, nat'ral*)," writes a contributor to this volume, "is generally a signal that a fairly strict accentual-syllabism is the prosodic vehicle. For this reason, if for no other, it is obvious that none but authoritative texts should be used in prosodic study." No seeker after the truth will object to knowing the veritable texts. Yet in this innocent enough, this unexceptionable, ideal lies the occasion for a perhaps too simple appeal to history. Linguistic historians incline to tell us that the poets and their friends really did drop these syllables, as well as certain others involved in such elisions as *th'immortal.* In poets of the romantic age, on the contrary, we find the full spellings restored. And this is taken as illustrating a fact about English speech in that age and also as showing in romantic poets a less finicky rule for number of syllables. It would appear to be true that fashions in spoken compression may change, and no less, fashions in prosodic extra-syllabism.

But an underlying structural situation embraces both the syllable actually elided or syncopated and the *extra* light syllable of the fully pronounced word—in English syllabic-accentual verse from Chaucer to Tennyson. We are inquiring about matters of degree, rather than of structure or principle, when we ask whether extra syllables *were* actually compressed. And an opposite kind of situation can be encountered. In his book on *Shakespeare's Pronunciation* Helge Kökeritz argues, from the tilt of the word "cardinal" as it appears in some passages of Shakespeare, from the spelling in some passages—and from Henslowe's spelling—that Shakespeare said "car'nal."[4] "Upon my soule two reverend *Cardinall* Vertues: But *Cardinall* Sins and hollow hearts I fear ye" (*Henry VIII* III.i.103–04). For the pun, the syncopated pronunciation was necessary. But for the meter, a more basic thing was the structure of the word (*cardinal—car'nal*) and its role in the line. It is a fact that Shakespeare *often* too used the two-stress trisyllable, as need arose in the meter of his history plays. "Good Father Cardinall, cry thou Amen . . ." (*King John* III.i.181).[5]

Consider the following two lines from *Paradise Lost:*

> *Lethe* the Riv/er of/ Oblivion roules . . . (II.583)
> And where the riv/er of Bliss/ through midst of Heavn . . . (III.358)

It happens that Alexander Pope, in a well-known *tour de force* of metrical demonstration in his *Essay on Criticism,* invents a negative or counter-example of close relevance to our purpose.

> These Equal Syllables alone require,
> Tho' oft the Ear the *open Vowels* tire. (ll.344–45)

It seems not likely that Pope is reporting that he and his friends were in the conversational habit of collapsing their speech in slovenly expressions like "tho'ft," "th'ear," "th'open." In that case the vowels would not be "open." The hiatus (or the "gape," as the sixteenth century would have said) would be closed. And this line would have only seven syllables. The point of this invented illustration is that these adjacent vowels in actual speech offer some degree of invitation to a closing or elision, but that, though the demand of a metrical line may confirm the invitation, it may, on the contrary, and in this instance does, cancel it. There is a clash of invitations. (This would be a clumsy line, in Pope—if it were not an autonymic stunt—or in Milton[6]—and no less in Wordsworth or in Keats.)

> Not so, when swift *Camilla* scours the Plain,
> Flies o'er th'unbending Corn, and skims along the Main.
>
> (ll. 372–73)

V. ACCENT

Using mainly the example of the kind of verse in which most of the poems I enjoy most spontaneously are written, I have been devoting this Foreword to a sketch of a few central distractions that often seem to defeat efforts for clarity in prosodic discussion. And now one more, a quiet difficulty, but the most pervasively encountered of all. I suspect it must have analogues in many other meters and languages. I have in mind a sort of double rule, or the co-operative claim of two closely connected principles (one as it were a phantom, or ghostly paradigm, lying inside the other). To these I assign the names "rule" and "norm." An automobile driver can drive steadily down the middle of the space between a white line on his left and the edge of the road on his right, thus observing not only a rule but a kind of norm implied by, or enclosed in, the rule. He can invoke a momentary suspension of both the norm and the rule if he veers to the left and crosses the line to pass another car. Or he can violate both norm and rule by crossing the line and driving in the left lane. Or fourthly (and this is a matter for the metrist to ponder well) he can stay *entirely within the rule* and yet drive *eccentrically* if he drives along as close as possible to either the line or the edge, or if he weaves back and forth between them.

What is bad driving may be good verse. I have argued in other places my not entirely original view that the accentual rule of English iambic meter is (with due allowance for a few recurrent modifications) that of a *relatively* strong stress on each second part of a foot, that is, on each even-numbered "position" in the line.[7] The operative system of stress values is binary. (As in classical Chinese verse, syllables of phonemically even tone alternate, in dual opposition, with the several kinds of tonally changing syllable; and, as in classical Greek verse, three kinds of *short* syllable are set against a yet greater variety of *long*.)

> / . / . \ / /
> When to/ the ses/sions of/ sweet si/lent thought
> / . / . \ /
> I sum/mon up/ remem/brance of/ things past . . .

The abstract stress rule is realized in the verse elastically, with undulations. One need not accept just the theory I am proposing to conceive a rather level or "neutral" realization of the iambic line.

> / / / / /
> The cur/few tolls/ the knell/ ŏf par/ting day.

An excellent opening of a very quietly level meditative poem. And thus Gray's *Elegy* mainly pursues the "even tenor of its way"—its variations and its tensions arising more in syntactic and semantic shifts than in departures from its metrical norm.

But variation and "tension," we know, are important things in poetry, and notably in its rhythm (its movement broadly conceived) and even in its meter (its movement narrowly conceived). How can the meter, precisely, involve tension inside itself? Not by the rules being broken—a broken rule produces no more tension than a broken rubber band. Only through some sort of internal complexity or duality of principle. The "modifications" or recognized and permitted "complications" provide one sort of local tension. They can be emphatic, vibratory, expressive.

> / / / / /
> Wondring/ upon/ this word;/ quaking/ for drede.

But the issue is more pervasive. It is within an ambit inside the sheer meter itself—the regular meter—that we must discuss that further kind of dynamic difference which I have especially in mind.

> / . / . \ / /
> When to/ the ses/sions of /sweet si/lent thought . . .

> / \ \ / \ / / /
> Rocks, Caves,/ Lakes, Fens,/ Bogs, Dens,/ and shades/ of death.
> (*Paradise Lost* II.621)

> / . / / .
> Immu/table, Immor/tal, In/finite.
> (*Paradise Lost* III.373)

Ten monosyllables (eight strong stresses) against three polysyllables (three strong stresses)—the bare jolty landscape names against the Latinate theological dignities—each sequence contained, however, within the unmodified measure of the pentameter.

It is a remarkable feature of these two so different sequences of words that each *is* an iambic pentameter. These are parts of a large contrast, the diagram of the meter and its norm against the cosmos of the poem's sound and meaning. The contrast involves more than the meter. Yet it is a metrically generated contrast. If a word were not a polysyllable, it could not have both a primary and a secondary stress. If it were not a major monosyllable in a series, it could not have a strong stress stronger than an adjacent stress. If these words were not parts of a meter, the degrees of their stress could not be forced so closely upon our attention. The cosmic contrast shades intimately into and works out of the insistently fine contrast between various degrees of stress (within the limits of the binary rule) and the level norm that is always at least intimated by the rule.

The editor of a cooperative enterprise such as the making of this book has necessarily enjoyed the aid and abetment of numerous persons. In the blazon of my indebtedness, I am happy to list:

1. The sixteen contributors, each of whom showed himself first nimbly responsive and then enduringly patient. That statement, taken collectively, involves a paradox that will not be explicated here.

2. The successive members of the Modern Language Association Committee on Research Activities, and especially Joseph A. Mazzeo and the two chairmen, James Thorpe and Winfred Lehmann.

3. The Executive Secretary of the Association, John Hurt Fisher; and the Assistant to the Executive Secretary, Walter S. Achtert; and the copy-editor, Donna Walsh, whose hand appears in every paragraph.

4. The experts in prosody who accepted invitations to read and criticize the several papers. Those who are willing to be named are, in the order of the papers as they appear in the volume: Craig La Drière (Elements of Versification), James J. Y. Liu (Chinese), Howard S. Hibbett (Japanese), Gerald F. Else (Greek and Latin), Victor Erlich (Slavic), Calvert Watkins (Celtic), Einar Haugen (Germanic), Dante Della Terza and Paolo Valesio (Italian), Tomás Navarro (Spanish), Pierre Guiraud (French), Edward Weismiller (English and the Foreword), Calvin S. Brown (music and verse).

5. Friends, learned and genial, who at various stages of the planning and work, gave invaluable advice. I must be overlooking some. But let me name,

roughly in the order in which I remember consulting them: John Hollander, Victor Erlich, Roman Jakobson, Gene M. Schramm, Howard Porter, Henri Peyre, Sheridan Baker, Lowry Nelson, Thomas M. Greene, Warren S. Smith, Dorothee Finkelstein, John C. Pope, Maynard Mack, Seymour Chatman, Samuel Levin, Richard S. Sylvester, Marie Borroff, Traugott Lawler—and Craig La Drière and Edward Weismiller. The last two, especially, cannot be thanked enough. Each, in the fullness and finesse of his learning in areas of comparative prosody, came in with extraordinary generosity and conscience to aid the closing phases of the work.

To all these benefactors I wish to express my warm appreciation and earnest thanks.

W. K. Wimsatt

Silliman College, Yale University
1 March 1971

NOTES

1. John Lotz (below, p. 114) shows a form of Uralic folk verse adding syllable-count to semantic parallelism.
2. See John Lotz, *The Structure of the* Sonetti a Corona *of Attila József*, Acta Universitatis Stockholmiensis, Studia Hungarica Stockholmiensia, 1 (Stockholm, 1965), pp. 1–4. Cf. John Donne, *La Corona.*
3. This line may be said to exhibit the sequence "pyrrhic" and "trochee," xx/x (in positions 5, 6, 7, 8), without medial pause. Edward Weismiller (see below, p. 215) believes this is the only type of irregular line employed by Renaissance writers of iambic pentameter which actually threatens the iambic meter. This line invites a reading as four feet instead of five; the last six syllables tend to group themselves as two anapests.
4. *Shakespeare's Pronunciation* (New Haven: Yale Univ. Press, 1953), pp. 29, 63, 97, 299, 371.
5. Bartlett's *Concordance* lists 74 occurrences of *cardinal*; of these, 52 are two-stress trisyllabic.
6. Edward Weismiller brings to my attention the following two instances of isolated hiatus in *Paradise Regained*: "And o're a mighty King *so oft* prevail'd" (III.167); "Against *the eastern* Gate of Paradise" (IV.542).
7. A. Bartlett Giamatti, below pp. 148–49, discusses the less prescriptive stress patterns of Italian verse, deriving from the fact that the unstressed Italian vowel has much greater clarity and shape than its English counterpart. Cf. p. 177, the French syllabic system.

A NOTE ON THE TERMS

VERSIFICATION, VERSE, METER, PROSODY

Versification (rather than *verse*) in the title of this book aims to accent an interest in structure and analysis. The essays use the terms *versification* and *verse* almost interchangeably, according to the relevant emphasis. *Verse* and *meter* too appear as almost, but not quite, interchangeable terms. The term *verse* ordinarily embraces not only the elements of line, syllable, and prominence (see below *prosody*), which establish *meter*, but also such supporting features as alliteration and rhyme and such larger boundaries as stanza. For some purposes, on the other hand, it may be convenient to consider any or all of these latter as parts of *meter*, not additions to it. *Meter* (in the more limited sense) is ordinarily taken as the main principle of *verse*. It is in any event the most debatable aspect. According to one musically oriented distinction the name *non-metrical verse* may be granted to simply syllabic verbal measures, the term *meter* being denied on the ground that they lack regular accent and hence "pulse" (see p. 241). The classical term *prosody* once had great prestige and convenience for verse study. But it has been pre-empted by modern linguistics and, along with another term, *suprasegmental* (favored by American writers), is used today to refer to phonetic features—chiefly stress, tone, quantity, juncture—which occur along with, and give inflection to sequences of, the minimal segments of sound called syllables (see pp. 19–20). The prosodic features of a language, along with syllables and with syntactic frames, are the aspects available for the making of verse.

THE AUTHORS

JOHN LOTZ. ELEMENTS OF VERSIFICATION

John Lotz was born on 23 March 1913 in Milwaukee, Wisconsin. After attending elementary and secondary schools in the United States and in Hungary, he studied at the University of Budapest as a member of the Eötvös-Collegium, with fields of specialization in Philosophy, German, Hungarian, and English, and received the Doctorate of Philosophy in 1935. He taught Hungarian and Linguistics at the University of Stockholm and at Columbia University during the period 1935–68, becoming Professor of Linguistics at Columbia in 1956. He was Director of Research in the Uralic and Altaic Program of the American Council of Learned Societies, 1959–65. From 1967 to 1971 he was President and Director of the Center for Applied Linguistics, Washington, D.C. His publications include *The Concept of Time in History* (Hungarian), 1936; *Das ungarische Sprachsystem,* 1939; and numerous articles in English, German, and Hungarian on general linguistics, phonetics, metrics, and Hungarian language and literature. In collaboration with the Haskins Laboratories, he has directed and produced X-ray motion pictures, with sound, concerning aspects of the speech event in several languages. Besides the introductory essay "Elements of Versification," he contributes to the present volume a three-part article on Uralic Verse.

HANS HERMANN FRANKEL. CHINESE

Hans Hermann Frankel was born 19 December 1916 in Berlin, Germany. He attended the Gymnasium at Göttingen. He graduated B.A. from Stanford University in 1937 and continued his studies at the University of California, Berkeley, where he received an M.A. in 1938 and a Ph.D. in 1942. He taught Spanish at the University of California, Berkeley, 1938–42, and 1945–47. While working with several U.S. Government agencies in San Francisco, Washington, and New York during World War II, he learned

Chinese, and became Associate Professor of Western Languages at the National Peking University, 1947–48. After a period of research and teaching in history at the University of California, Berkeley, 1951–59, he has been Assistant Professor of Chinese at Stanford University, 1959–61; Associate Professor of Chinese Literature at Yale University, 1961–67; and Professor since 1967. He was married in 1948 to the Chinese calligrapher Ch'ung-ho Chang, also an expert in Chinese musical drama, and now Lecturer in Graphic Design at Yale University. He has published several articles on Chinese literature and has in preparation two books on Chinese poetry.

ROBERT H. BROWER. JAPANESE

Robert H. Brower was born 23 March 1923 in Cambridge, Massachusetts. He received a B.A. from Harvard University in French Literature. Trained as a Japanese language officer during World War II, he received a Ph.D. in Far Eastern Languages and Literatures from the University of Michigan in 1952. He taught for three years at the University of Minnesota and twelve at Stanford University before returning to Michigan as Professor of Japanese in 1966. He is co-author with Earl Miner of *Japanese Court Poetry*, 1961, and *Fujiwara Teika's Superior Poems of Our Time*, 1967, as well as author of numerous articles on Japanese classical poetry and literary criticism and translations from the Japanese. For the past several years his interests have been concentrated on the poetry and poetics of the twelfth and thirteenth centuries, and he is preparing a literary biography of the great seminal figure of the age, Fujiwara Teika (1162–1241).

PERRY B. YODER. BIBLICAL HEBREW

Perry B. Yoder was born 7 June 1940 in Portland, Oregon. He attended Goshen College, Goshen, Indiana, receiving a B.A. in 1962. From 1962 to 1968, he did graduate work at the University of Pennsylvania in the Department of Near Eastern Studies, specializing in language and literature, and during the academic year 1965–66 studied at the Hebrew University in Jerusalem, Israel. He received a Ph.D. at the University of Pennsylvania in 1970; the subject of his dissertation was "Fixed Pairs and the Composition of Hebrew Poetry." Since 1968 he has been Assistant Professor of Religion at Bluffton College, Bluffton, Ohio. He is at present engaged in a computer-assisted analysis of Hebrew prosody.

A. THOMAS COLE. CLASSICAL GREEK AND LATIN

A. Thomas Cole was born 22 August 1933 in Chilhowie, Virginia. He attended Harvard University, receiving a B.A. in classics in 1954 and a Ph.D. in Classical Philology in 1960. He has taught in the Classics Department at Harvard University, 1959–62; at Stanford University, 1962–65; and at Yale University since 1965, becoming Professor of Greek and Latin in 1971. He held a Fulbright Fellowship for study in Italy during 1954–55. His publications include *Democritus and the Sources of Greek Anthropology,* 1967, and several articles dealing with aspects of Greek political and sociological theory. He is at present engaged in a comprehensive study of the rhythms of Greek lyric verse.

EDWARD STANKIEWICZ. SLAVIC

Edward Stankiewicz was born 17 November 1920 in Poland. After studies at the Art Institute in Rome and at the University of Rome, he attended the University of Chicago, where he received an M.A. in Linguistics in 1951, and Harvard University, where he studied with Roman Jakobson and received a Ph.D. in Slavic Linguistics in 1954. He has taught at Indiana University, 1954–60, and at the University of Chicago, 1960–71, becoming Professor of Slavic Languages and Literature in 1962. Since 1971, he has been Professor of Slavic Languages at Yale University. His publications include *Selected Bibliography of Slavic Linguistics* (with D. S. Worth), two volumes, 1966; *Declension and Gradation of Russian Substantives,* 1968; and numerous articles on general linguistics and poetics, on Slavic dialectology, typology, and morphology, and on the history of linguistics. He is at present carrying on research in all these subjects.

JOHN LOTZ. URALIC

See above, John Lotz, Elements of Versification.

W. P. LEHMANN. GERMANIC

W. P. Lehmann was born 23 June 1916 in Surprise, Nebraska. He received a B.A. at Northwestern College in 1936, and an M.A. in 1938, and a Ph.D. in 1941 at the University of Wisconsin. He has taught at Washington University, 1946–49, and since 1949 at the University of Texas, Austin, where he is now Ashbel Smith Professor of Linguistics and Germanic Languages. His publications include *Proto-Indo-European Phonology,* 1952; *The Alliteration of Old Saxon Poetry,* 1953; *The Development of Germanic Verse Form,* 1956; *Historical Linguistics: An Introduction,* 1962; and *Descriptive Linguistics: An Introduction,* 1971.

CHARLES W. DUNN. CELTIC

Charles W. Dunn was born in 1915 in Arbuthnott, Scotland. He attended McMaster University, receiving a B.A. in 1938, and Harvard University, receiving an M.A. in 1939 and a Ph.D. in 1948. He has taught at Stephens College, Cornell University, the University of Toronto, and New York University. He is now Margaret Brooks Robinson Professor of Celtic at Harvard University and Master of Quincy House. His publications include *A Chaucer Reader,* 1952; *Highland Settler: A Portrait of the Scottish Gael in Nova Scotia,* 1953; and *The Foundling and the Werwolf: A Literary-Historical Study of Guillaume de Palerne,* 1960. He is at present preparing a *Middle English Reader,* an *Anthology of Scottish Gaelic Poetry,* and a *Literary History of the Twelfth Century.*

A. BARTLETT GIAMATTI. ITALIAN

A. Bartlett Giamatti was born 4 April 1938 in Boston, Massachusetts. He attended Yale University, receiving a B.A. in 1960 and a Ph.D. in 1964. From 1964 to 1966 he taught Italian and Comparative Literature at Princeton University. Since 1966 he has been a member of the English Department at Yale University; and since 1971, Professor of English and Comparative Literature. He is Master of Ezra Stiles College. He held a Fellowship of the John Simon Guggenheim Memorial Foundation in 1969–70. His publications include *The Earthly Paradise and the Renaissance Epic,* 1966, and several essays on Edmund Spenser, Christopher Marlowe, and aspects of Renaissance literature. He is co-editor of *The Songs of Bernart de Ventadorn,* 1962; the W. S. Rose translation of Ariosto's *Orlando Furioso,* 1968; and the Italian poems in Volume 1 of *A Variorum Commentary on the Poems of John Milton,* 1970.

LOWRY NELSON, JR. SPANISH

Lowry Nelson, Jr., was born 1 May 1926 in Provo, Utah, and grew up in Minneapolis, Minnesota. He attended Harvard University, receiving a B.A.

in 1947; and Yale University, receiving a Ph.D. in Comparative Literature in 1951. He has been a member of the Society of Fellows, Harvard University, 1951–54; has taught Romance Languages at Harvard University, 1954–56; English at the University of California, Los Angeles, 1956–64; and Comparative Literature at Yale University since 1964, becoming Professor in 1970. He held a Fellowship of the John Simon Guggenheim Memorial Foundation in 1962–63. His publications include *Baroque Lyric Poetry,* 1961; *The Disciplines of Criticism: Essays in Literary Theory, Interpretation and History* (edited with Peter Demetz and Thomas Greene), 1968; *Cervantes: A Collection of Critical Essays* (edited), 1969; and various essays, encyclopedia articles, and reviews. He is at present collecting some of his essays for a volume to be called *The Rhetoric of Ineffability* and is working on an extended study of the literary tradition of the *Song of Songs.*

JACQUELINE FLESCHER. FRENCH

Jacqueline Flescher was born in 1930 in Brussels, Belgium. She studied at the University of London, receiving a B.A. in French and German in 1951; and at the University of Paris, receiving a Licence in 1956, a Diplome d'Etudes supérieures in 1961, and an Agrégation in English Language and Literature in 1966. She has been Assistant Professor of French at Yale University, 1966-69; and since 1970, Assistant in English at the University of Paris. She is the author of an essay entitled "The Language of Nonsense in *Alice*" appearing in *Yale French Studies,* No. 43, 1969.

PAUL FUSSELL, JR. ENGLISH I. HISTORICAL

Paul Fussell, Jr., was born in 1924 in Pasadena, California. He attended Pomona College and Harvard University, where he received a Ph.D. in 1952. He taught English at Connecticut College from 1951 to 1955. Since 1955, he has been a member of the Department of English at Rutgers University, and since 1964, Professor. He was a Fulbright Lecturer at the University of Heidelberg in 1957–58. His publications include *Theory of Prosody in Eighteenth-Century England,* 1954; *Poetic Meter and Poetic Form,* 1965; *The Rhetorical World of Augustan Humanism,* 1965; *Samuel Johnson and the Life of Writing,* 1971; and numerous articles and reviews in scholarly journals, quarterlies, and journals of opinion. He is currently working on a study of the rhetoric of the first World War and its impact on modern writing and memory.

RAE ANN NAGER. ENGLISH II. BIBLIOGRAPHICAL

Rae Ann Nager was born 16 October 1939 in Cheswick, Pennsylvania. She attended the Catholic University of America, receiving a B.A. and an M.A. in English; and Harvard University, where she is completing a Ph.D. in Comparative Literature. Her M.A. thesis was a study of the prosody of Wallace Stevens; her doctoral dissertation is a study of the relations of John of Salisbury's *Metalogicon* and Geoffrey de Vinsauf's *Poetria Nova* to classical sources. From 1966 to 1970 she was a Teaching Fellow at Harvard University in General Education and Comparative Literature. She held a Harvard Travelling Fellowship in 1970-71. She is currently Curator of the Keats Collection, Houghton Library, Harvard University, and Associate Editor of the *Keats-Shelley Journal.*

MORRIS HALLE and SAMUEL JAY KEYSER. ENGLISH III. THE IAMBIC PENTAMETER

Morris Halle was born 23 July 1923 in Liepaja, Latvia. He has studied at the City College of New York, at the University of Chicago, at Columbia University, and at Harvard University, receiving from the last a Ph.D. in 1955. Since 1951, he has been a member of the faculty of the Massachusetts Institute of Technology. His publications include *Fundamentals of Language* (with Roman Jakobson), 1956; *The Sound Patterns of English* (with Noam Chomsky), 1968; *English Stress: Its Form, Its Growth, and Its Role in Verse* (with Samuel Jay Keyser), 1971; "On Meter and Prosody," in *Progress in Linguistics, A Collection of Papers,* edited by Manfred Bierwisch and Karl Erich Heidolph, 1971; and various articles on Arabic, Slavic, and English prosody. He writes that his "main professional interest has been the study of human language in all of its manifestations from semantics to poetics."

Samuel Jay Keyser was born 7 July 1935 in Philadelphia, Pennsylvania. He studied English literature at George Washington University and later, as a Fulbright Scholar, English and Germanic philology at Merton College, Oxford. He received a Ph.D. in Linguistics at Yale University in 1962. Since 1965 he has been a member of the faculty of Brandeis University. He is the author of *English Stress: Its Form, Its Growth, and Its Role in Verse* (with Morris Halle), 1971. He is editor of *Linguistic Inquiry.* The essay in this volume is a result of long collaboration with Morris Halle on questions of linguistics and literature. Professor Keyser is currently at work on problems relating to Old English phonology and to the syntactic analysis of the poetry of Wallace Stevens.

MONROE C. BEARDSLEY. VERSE AND MUSIC

Monroe C. Beardsley was born in 1915 in Bridgeport, Connecticut. He attended Yale University, receiving a B.A. in 1936 and a Ph.D. in 1939. He has taught at Yale University, Mt. Holyoke College, and Swarthmore College, before coming to Temple University as Professor of Philosophy in 1969. His extensive writings have been principally in the field of aesthetics. They include *Aesthetics: Problems in the Philosophy of Criticism,* 1958; *Aesthetics from Classical Greece to the Present: A Short History,* 1966; and *The Possibility of Criticism,* 1970. He has collaborated with his wife, Elizabeth Lane Beardsley, also Professor of Philosophy at Temple University, on an introduction to philosophy, *Philosophical Thinking,* 1965, and they are joint editors of a continuing series of volumes under the general title *Foundations of Philosophy.* He was Vice-President (1971) of the Eastern Division of the American Philosophical Association and a past President of the American Society for Aesthetics. He is currently at work on a book on the philosophy of history, to be entitled *The Language of History.*

W. K. WIMSATT, the editor of this volume, was born 17 November 1907 in Washington, D.C. He attended Georgetown University, receiving a B.A. *summa cum laude* in 1928, and an M.A. in 1929. He taught English and Latin at the Priory School, Portsmouth, Rhode Island, 1930–35, and returned to graduate studies at the Catholic University of America in 1935, and at Yale University in 1936, receiving a Ph.D. at the latter in 1939. Since 1939 he has been a member of the English Department of Yale University, Professor since 1955, and since 1965 Frederick Clifford Ford Professor of Literature. His publications include two collections of critical essays, *The Verbal Icon,* 1954, and *Hateful Contraries,* 1965; and *Literary Criticism: A Short History* (with Cleanth Brooks), 1957.

ELEMENTS OF VERSIFICATION

By JOHN LOTZ

Versification: Verse and Prose

Versification, the production of verse (< Latin *versum facere* 'to make verse') implies a specific, converted, or, if you wish, perverted use of language.[1] The term verse (< Latin *versus* '(di)verted'), though referring to the graphic representation of verse in lines, expresses this insight, setting verse in opposition to prose (< Latin *(oratio) pro(or)sa* 'straight forward (talk)').

The problem of the boundaries between prose and verse is a delicate one; no sharp defining characteristic feature separates the two modes. We have rather the opposition of a small set of language texts characterized by numerical regularity of speech material within certain syntactic frames as contrasted with texts which lack such a characteristic. The outward boundary of verse is so-called free verse, regarded by many as not a *bona fide* metric phenomenon.[2] Verse and prose are opposed to each other as two types of which one, verse, has definable properties, and the other, prose, is characterized by lack of any such features. The members of an unbalanced opposition, such as that between verse and prose, are called "marked" vs. "unmarked."[3]

The terminology and the concepts in the field of versification are heterogeneous and often confusing, especially as used in different literary traditions. The basic terms most often used in versification are: prosody, meter, verse, and poetry.[4] Prosody (<Greek προσωδία 'that which is added to song') originally referred to features of sound (e.g., pitch, duration, and stress), and Greek scholars of antiquity treated prosody in conjunction with sequential arts other than poetry (e.g., music and dancing). They considered it a discipline separate from grammar. In modern phonetic-linguistic usage prosodic features include pitch, stress, length, and, often, syllabicity. In the usage of metricians, prosody has an even wider coverage. It refers to versification in general, including rhyme, assonance, alliteration, and other characteristics of verse.

Meter (< Greek μέτρον 'measure') in antiquity was a general philosophical concept which later in the study of versification became restricted to the study of numerical regularity in verse. The corresponding Latin term *numerus* 'number' emphasizes this concept of numerical regularity.

In this article we use the term versification, not prosody, to refer to the general study of verse. Prosodic is used in conformance with modern linguistic terminology to refer to pitch, stress, and duration (syllabicity is not included). Verse is defined as a language text viewed in all its linguistic functions and characterized by meter, which is the numerical regulation of certain properties of the linguistic form alone. The literary use of verse is called poetry.

Approaches to the Analysis of Verse

There are various ways in which verse can be approached. It could be approached from the point of view of art in general and especially from the point of view of music.[5] The most elaborate example of this is in Paul Maas's treatment of classical Greek verse, where the constitutive "metron," for instance, in the iambic trimeter is represented in the following way:

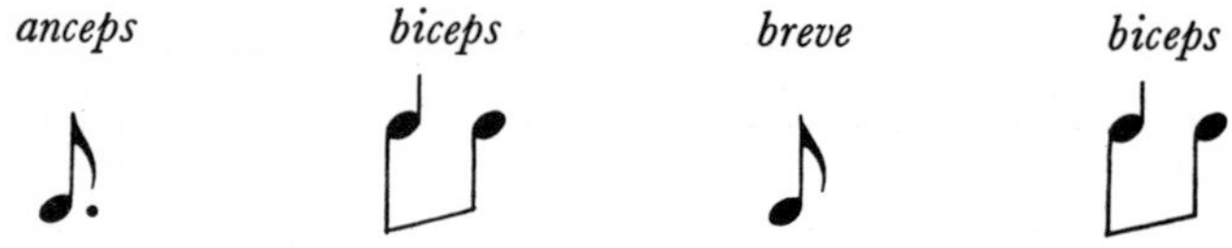

The view that syllabic duration can be matched with the length of notes is based on a partial misconception of the temporal nature of the two phenomena, verse and music. Metric structure does have analogies in its sequential character with music, but in music the notes are completely regulated temporal phenomena, whereas in speech the sounds are evaluated in a looser way. In Greek, for instance, not only the bases consisting of a short vowel, but also those consisting of a short vowel and a single consonant (or a short vowel and a *muta cum liquida*), are classed as short bases; a long base includes an even larger variety of possibilities, ranging from a single long vowel or a short vowel followed by two consonants to a long vowel followed by four consonants. Thus, the temporal variation is much larger than, let us say, between (♪) and (♩). The following phenomena in Greek verse have to be distinguished: (a) the metrical scheme, which requires either a short (∪) or a long (—) base in some well-defined positions and which allows variation of short and long bases in other well-defined positions; (b) a concrete verse (a line), where the choices have been made, and every base is in fact either short or long; and (c) the actual performance, where both short and long bases vary in length. Dionysius of Halicarnassus reports that in the performance of the Homeric epics by the bards the long base was longer than the two short bases in obligatory positions.

Clearly, verse and music share some common characteristic features, which are most obvious in songs, but the two are not identical, either in score or performance. Verse has its own independent organization, which is not the same as the organization of sound in music. Both temporal and dynamic relations in music are much stricter and organized in a different way from those of poetry. Music cannot be the basis for metric analysis.[6]

Another approach to verse is the "objective approach," which takes its point of departure either from the physical recording of the event itself, as Edward Wheeler Scripture did in his treatment of English verse, or from a phonemic description such as that employed by modern American structuralists.[7] The idea that it is possible to reduce these phonetic data to significant units without making any special assumptions about them is an untenable oversimplification of phenomena employed by pure phoneticians and behaviorists. Only by pre-established rules is it possible to produce satisfactory results in metric analysis.

The rules should not be confused with measurements of actual performance. The same Shakespearean line can be performed in a prosaic manner or in a manner that emphasizes the metric structure. The phonemic units cannot be deduced from the sound wave alone. There is a correlation between metric rules and metric performance, but no deductive relationships.[8]

Thus, within the field of metrics we have to distinguish the following: metric performance, which is characterized by the physical concepts of wave shape, frequency, intensity, time, and their psychological correlates, timbre (especially syllabicity), pitch, loudness, and duration; metric score, in which non-measurable relations are established on the basis of linguistic function; metric line-type, into which scores are abstracted (in this case we may have variables in certain positions, besides the fixed values); and finally, metric system, in which all the various aspects of meter are subsumed.

The most common approach to verse is to regard it as part of literature under the sub-heading poetry. This is the usual Western tradition and is in general the orientation of the Modern Language Association of America.

(My own schooling went in the same direction and included Hungarian language *and* literature and German language *and* literature.)[9] This orientation is a specially Western ethnocentric one. In Sinology, the Chinese language is not exclusively associated with Chinese literature but with a number of other disciplines such as history, art, religion, philosophy.

The function of verse is by no means solely a literary-aesthetic one. Meter, the constitutive property of verse, does not serve a single function or purpose but can correspond with a variety of functions. It is a purely formal phenomenon which refers to the language signal alone without reference to the semantic content of that signal.[10] Even in our culture, where the role of meter is predominantly literary-aesthetic, verse is used in advertising jingles. Old Germanic legal texts are couched in verse to prevent alteration. Poetic function is only one, though the most common, function of verse. Poetic function consists in the fact that versification with its paraphernalia of rhyme, assonance, alliteration, and the like is used for literary-aesthetic effect. The classification of verse according to its poetic function is not satisfactory because it does not establish a comprehensive definition of the term. It would, of course, be possible to subsume verse in all its varied uses under a single psychological label, such as attention-getting, but a labeling of the extension of a term does not mean an intensive definition of that term.[11] An added difficulty in approaching verse from the literary point of view is the delimitation of a well-defined universe of discourse and the specification of verse within it.

The correct approach to verse, in my opinion, is the linguistic one, which regards verse as a subset—to be sure a very small subset—of all language phenomena. Since all verse is a product of the use of language, it is entirely within the competence of linguistics.[12] If there were a uniform function behind verse, it would be possible to approach it from the point of view of this specific function and to regard the language aspect as differentiating. Since there is no uniform function, it is impossible to define verse from any of the above points of view. The only feasible basis and workable method for the analysis of verse and meter is linguistics.

In the following we are concerned only with meter, the specific mark of verse.

The Linguistic Base of Metrics

In most languages there are texts in which the phonetic material within certain syntactic frames, such as sentence, phrase, and word, is numerically regulated.[13] Such a text is called verse, and its distinctive characteristic is meter. Metrics is the study of meter. A non-metric text is called prose. Numerical regulation may refer to a variety of phenomena; therefore, verse and prose are distinguished not as two sharply differentiated classes, but rather as two types of texts. (This, however, should not obscure the fact that verse and prose are polar opposites, as mentioned above.)

Meter can mean a strict determination of the occurrence of the syllabics in the poem and, in some cases, also of certain prosodic features. The regulation can be very strict. For instance, the *haiku* in Japanese has exactly seventeen syllables (metrically simple, but culturally intricate):

Shiki (1867–1902)

Tsurigane ni	On the temple bell
tomarite hikaru	has settled, and is glittering,
hotara ka na	a firefly

In comparison to the simple *haiku,* the *sonetti a corona,* invented by the *Academia degl'Intronati* of Siena in the second half of the *cinquecento,* imposes exceedingly strict technical requirements on the poet. This highly stylized and complicated genre is an arrangement of fifteen sonnets in cycles. The rules require that the first fourteen sonnets shall form a coherent, connected, and closed series of variations on the subject, the transitions being effected by the repetition of the last line of each sonnet as the first line of the next, and that the whole chain of thought shall return to its starting point at the end of the fourteenth sonnet; and also that the fifteenth or master sonnet shall constitute a thematic summing-up of the preceding ones, so that both the formal expression and the arrangement are determined by the initial lines of the base sonnets. In the *sonetti a corona* the number of closely regulated syllables is about 2,240 as compared to seventeen in the *haiku.*[14]

But the regulation in verse can also be relaxed in various ways. In some types of Hungarian poetry a metrically relevant phrase can contain either six or five syllabics; and such a variation can be even wider, as in West Siberian folk poetry or in Hebrew Psalms. Or the numerical regulation can refer only to some parts of the text, as when prose and verse are mixed in the same literary work, e.g., in the Chinese *fù* genre. A text can be even more intricately interwoven, as in proto-Indo-European verse, where the beginning of the line was fairly free, but a substantial final portion was regulated. In certain types of classical rhetorical texts, only a small final portion (*clausula*) was determined. (The difference between these two last modes is a question of degree.)

Furthermore, such a numerical regulation may involve a strict determination of syntactic units, with a wide variation in phonetic material. Free verse often tends to move in this direction. In Ghê, an African language, there are texts which are repetitions of units of five or three syntactic phrases bound together by rhyme. Other "rhythmic" texts appear also in the enumeration of sport scores on the radio (team-score-team-score).

All these types of verse deviate from straight prose; the deviation can be put in terms of numerical regularity, or meter, and this regularity is the *differentia specifica* of verse. We could argue about where verse ends and prose begins, or whether or not we should introduce new intermediary types. In the following, however, we shall concentrate only on texts in which the entire phonetic material in its syllabic, and sometimes also in its prosodic, aspect is regulated. Such strictly formalized verse gives a contrasting background to other less regulated phenomena where they do occur. The use of the term "versification" without the notion of a strictly regulated verse is a contradiction in terms.

As a first example let us take the text of a Hungarian folksong:

Hej páva, hej páva,	Hey peacock, hey peacock,
császárné pávája	Peacock of the Empress!
Ha én páva volnék,	If I were a peacock,
jó reggel felkelnék,	I would rise in early morning,
folyóvizre mennék,	I would go to running water,
folyóvizet innám,	I would drink the running water,
szárnyam csattogtatnám,	I would rustle my wings,
tollaim hullatnám.	I would let my feathers fall.
Szép leány felszedné,	A pretty girl would gather them
az ő édesének	would fix them to the hat
a kalapja mellé	of her beloved sweetheart
bokrétába tűzné.	like a pendant plume.

In this text the regularity is very simple: after every six syllables there is a phrase break, and a certain undefined number of such stretches, usually a small number, ends a sentence; the total utterance, the song, consists of an undetermined number of such intervals.

As a second example let us take a scheme from another type of poetry, which I will not reproduce in words, the classical T'ang Dynasty poetry:

. X . O . (R)
. O . X . (R)
. O . X .
. X . O . (R)

[. = any syllable;
X = syllable with distinctive tone, even or non-even;
O = the *other* distinctive tone;
R = rhyme]

The total of twenty syllabics, repeated a number of times in the poem, includes four pentasyllabic phrase groups. In the first such stretch the second position must be filled by a syllable with either an even or a non-even tone, the fourth position must be filled by the opposite distinctive tone; the rest of the syllabics are undetermined. The second and third pentasyllabic stretches mirror this line, so that the second and fourth positions are the opposites of what they are in the first line; the other syllabics are undetermined. The fourth stretch repeats the scheme of the first. Here tonal features are regulated in addition to the number of syllabics.

As a third example let us take the late Sapphic verse (as normalized by Horace) where the versification scheme is as follows: (1) word limit occurs after the eleventh, twenty-second, and thirty-third syllabic pulses; (2) sentence limit after the thirty-eighth syllabic pulse (though occasionally strophic enjambment does occur); (3) syllabics 1, 3, 5, 8, 10, 12, 14, 16, 19, 21, 23, 25, 27, 30, 32, 34, and 37 are either long or diphthongal, or, if short, are followed by at least two consonants; (4) syllabics 2, 6, 7, 9, 13, 17, 18, 20, 24, 28, 29, 31, 35, and 36 are short and not followed by more than one consonant; (5) the poem ends after a certain number of the stretches described in this versification scheme.[15] It may be represented graphically:

— ∪ — X — ∪∪ — ∪ — X
— ∪ — X — ∪∪ — ∪ — X
— ∪ — X — ∪∪ — ∪ — X
— ∪∪ — X

X(anceps) = ∪ or —

Thus Horace, *Ode* I.xxii:

Integer vitae scelerisque purus
non eget Mauris jaculis neque arcu
nec venenatis gravida sagittis,
Fusce, pharetra . . .[16]

As a last example let us take English blank verse, or iambic pentameter, where there is: (1) word limit after every tenth or eleventh syllabic pulse: (2) sentence limit after a certain number of such decasyllabic or hendecasyllabic stretches (number undetermined); (3) syllabics in even numbered positions relatively heavier than syllabics in odd numbered positions as a thoroughgoing tendency (deviation at the beginning of the verse is frequent); (4) text ending after an indeterminate number of the three stretches just described. For instance, Shakespeare: "I come to bury Caesar, not to praise him."

The above examples from several, diverse systems of versification demonstrate the wide variety of possible schemes of phonetic material in syntactic frames. They all represent verse types where the number of syllabics in the verse line are determined (isosyllabic). There are, however, other regular metric types where the syllables may vary, but some feature, other than syllabicity, regulates the verse line. For instance, in the Greek or Latin hexameter the number of syllabics varies from thirteen (twelve in the rarely occurring *versus spondeacus*) to seventeen, but the durational aspect is regulated in that each line contains twenty-four time units (*morae*).

A certain *plasticity* of the phonic material often appears in the fit of the metric scheme—e.g., in the initial sequence x x x x in the English iambic pentameter. The overall scheme, nevertheless, is maintained; the meter is not obscured.

A complete analysis of any system of versification would, of course, include a detailed linguistic description of all the means employed to differentiate language material from regular use of language. The study of the phenomena which differentiate verse from prose constitutes a special case of grammar which might be called poetic grammar. Poetic grammar is a selective and specific aspect of the total grammatical description of a language, just as phonology is a selective evaluation and classification of physical-physiological acoustic phenomena for linguistic purposes. It includes the linguistic analysis of all verse phenomena, such as phonology, morphology, syntax, and vocabulary.

The constitutive aspect of poetic grammar, however, is the specific organization of the phonetic material in certain grammatical frames, namely meter. Other aspects of the poetic grammar may be utilized in a system of versification but do not by themselves create verse. We are concerned here only with those aspects of language that are relevant for metrical purposes. Yet even among those that are relevant we have to distinguish the basic constitutive factors of meter and the additive-variative ones.

Linguistic phenomena are selected according to the principle of metric relevancy, in analogy with the principle of relevancy in phonological and grammatical analysis; for example, syllabic stress is not metrically relevant in Classical Greek, whereas it is metrically relevant in English. Hungarian offers a clearcut example of how phonetic material of the same language can be used in two different metric systems; base length is disregarded in the "national" versification, yet it is the constitutive element in the "quantitative" versification. Thus, metric relevancy implies a selection among the various phonetic phenomena of a language for metric purposes.

The linguistic study of meter has two parts: (a) study of the linguistic constituents and (b) study of the metric superstructure.[17]

Study of the Linguistic Constituents

The linguistic components of meter are divided into two parts in accordance with the structure of natural language: on the one hand, a small number of physiologically produceable, acoustically perceivable, and linguistically relevant sound features (phonological constituents) and, on the other hand, a large number of meaningful signs (syntactic, grammatical or semiotic constituents). Therefore, our study of the linguistic constituents of meter is subdivided into two sections: (1) study of the phonological constituents of meter, and (2) study of the syntactic (also called grammatical or semiotic) constituents of meter.

Phonological Constituents. All strictly regulated metric systems are founded on syllabification, which occurs on the physiological, physical, and psychological levels of speech transmission. It is, however, the occurrence of a syllabic pulse characterized by a syllabic peak rather than the syllable as a sound stretch that is metrically relevant. Syllable implies both culmination and delimitation; this latter is not relevant metrically. Even in the so-called "quantitative" meter, as in Classical Greek, the metrically relevant stretch is not identical with the syllable. It is possible, however, to use "syllable" to mean a portion of sound determined by one syllabic crest, where the boundaries are not necessarily definite. A more or less arbitrary convention for syllable boundaries ("syllabification") comes from hyphenation and the breaking of words at line-ends in script or print.[18]

The simplest metric type is one which utilizes only the number of syllables within the syntagmatic frames. Here the metrically relevant notion is syllabicity, and the metric unit is the syllable. The regulation involves the number of syllables. This type is represented in many types of folk poetry: as, for instance, in the Hungarian folk song quoted above.

A more complex metric system is one in which, besides syllabicity, a prosodic feature is relevant.[19] Here we have to differentiate between various types of syllabic materials, which we may call bases. Thus, in the tonal meter of the T'ang Dynasty, the even tone was opposed to the other tonal classes for metric purposes. In durational, or "quantitative," poetry—as in Classical Greek or in Arabic—the distance from one syllabic onset to the next one was organized into long and short bases. In dynamic types—like English or German—the syllabics are classified into heavy and light bases, with a great degree of freedom in the interpretation for metric purposes.

Syntactic Constituents. The syntactic constituents of meter provide the frame within which the numerical regulation of phonological material can be stated. The meaningful semiotic frames which always function in verse are sentence and word, consisting of various kinds of morpheme groupings marked differently in each language. The smallest syntactic unit, the morpheme, does not figure constitutively in meter, although it may be used to indicate verse structure, as in parallelism. The syntactic units, phrase or clause, cannot be utilized as such for metric purposes, because they may be discontinuous stretches; a metrically relevant unit, obviously, must be a cohesive stretch of the language sequence.

The relationship of word and sentence can be expressed in a diagram indicating all the syntactic relations in a sentence (which for linguistic purposes would have to be specified and labelled). An example where the syntactic relations are fairly simple and lend themselves to a linear, sequential representation can be seen in a Middle High German line from Walter von der Vogelweide's farewell elegy:

A syntactically more complex line, where the syntactic phrases are discontinuous and the relations are intersecting, is represented by the following line from Blake's *Tyger:*

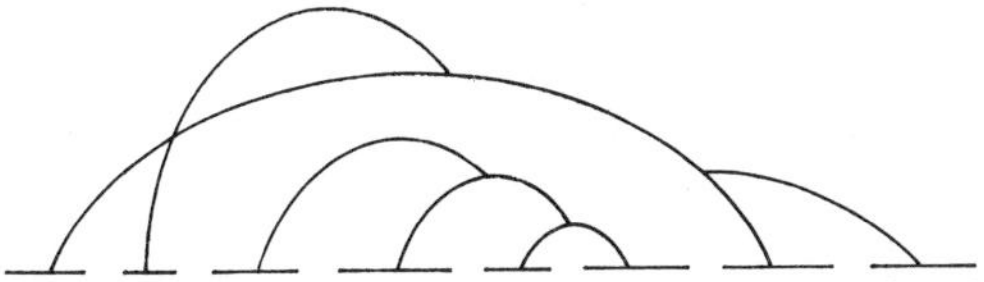

Did He who made the lamb make thee?

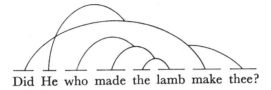

In addition to sentence and word, there is another syntactic sequence which often serves as a basic semiotic frame for meter. This unit is the colon (< κῶλον 'member'), a notion which comes from Greek metricians but which is often unrecognized in modern metric theory. Although cola sometimes correspond with the concept of phrase or clause, they are not syntactic units in the same sense. The colon is a cohesive, sequential stretch of the verse line characterized by syntactic affinity or connectedness utilized for metric purposes. The lower limit of the colon is one word, but this is usually not the case; if it were, the notion of colon would be unnecessary. Besides being characterized by sequential cohesiveness and syntactic affinity, a colon is relative within the sentence-morpheme span. For instance, "big house," "very big," and "very big house" are all cola, though of different degrees. In the Hungarian folk song quoted above, each line constitutes a colon. The verse line of Walter von der Vogelweide is divided into two cola for metric purposes: (1) *O wê war sind verswunden* and (2) *alliu mîniu jâr*. In the Blake example, on the other hand, the division of the line into cola is metrically irrelevant.

In the study of metrics, the colon is a syntactic unit of material utilized for metric purposes and is related to the notion of caesura. In an overwhelming number of Greek hexameters there was a cut in the third metric unit, either following the obligatory *longum* (—) (masculine caesura); or, if the variable position in the third unit consisted of two short bases (∪∪), after the first breve (∪) (feminine caesura). In the French alexandrine there is a syntactic cut in the middle, dividing the line into two comparable syntactic frames; later a tripartite division was made by the Romantics. Colon is an especially important metric concept in folk poetry (see the first Hungarian example above).

Metric usage of cola is also dependent on "syllabic weight." For instance, a two-word attribute noun phrase in Hungarian is evaluated one way if the constituents are monosyllabic and another way if they are tetrasyllabic: for example, *szép nő* 'beautiful woman' is considered as consisting of a single colon, whereas *gyönyörűséges boszorkány* 'ravishing enchantress' is considered as consisting of two.

It should be noted that the concept of colon is not restricted to metrics alone. Though unrecognized as a functional linguistic unit, it is the basis for intonation and stress patterning in general use of language.[20]

Besides the constitutive linguistic components necessary for meter, there may be other phonological and grammatical features which underline and emphasize the metric structure. These, however, do not by themselves create meter, and they may also function independently in prose. Such features include *assonance* and *alliteration*, which can function as indicators of cohesion in the line; *rhyme*, which is usually correlated with inner response in the metric structure;[21] *refrain*, which often indicates a higher order of construction; and *parallelism*, which shows a correspondence in the grammatical structure of responsive lines. These phenomena can even be required constituents in a given metric system, e.g., alliteration in Finnish, rhyme in Classical Chinese, parallelism in Obugric folk poetry.

Metric Superstructure

Metric units are those syntactic frames for which the numerical regulation of the phonological material can be stated. A metric utterance, the poem, can be constructed repetitively of shorter units, called lines, or it can be constructed more freely, astichic verse. Lines may be organized into higher-order constructs such as strophe and cycle, and may have an internal organization into segments characterized by certain types of word boundaries called caesurae. The relation among comparable elements in the metric structure is called response. Where there is only one line in a poem, such as a single hexameter, this response may refer to other examples of metric structure given in the culture. Thus the rhetorical formula "Quis? Quid? Ubi? Quibus auxiliis? Cur? Quomodo? Quando?" echoes similar lines in classic Latin poetry. The components of the linguistic base and the metric superstructure may be summarized:

Linguistic Base	*Metric Superstructure*
a. Phonological:	α. Astichic
Vowel	
Consonant	β. Stichic:
Syllable	Segment
	Line
b. Semiotic:	Strophe
(Morpheme)	Cycle
Word	
Colon	
Sentence	

Utterance = Poem

Metric Typology

In the metric typology that follows we have considered only those aspects of language that are relevant for metrical purposes. The aim is to include in a unified framework the diverse systems of versification known from various cultures. The presentation concentrates on the central core of phenomena and does not follow up the tangents which can lead off at every single aspect of this most deliberately formulated and experimentally varied use of language. We consider a variety of metric systems, each of which presents a complete regulation of a set of texts.

Typologies can be set up in different ways, and they vary accordingly as to their use. The primary characteristic of the typology presented here is that it is deduced from observation of diverse versification systems, but at the same time it takes into account the general nature of speech itself. It has, therefore, a claim for more theoretical validity than a typology which is only a taxonomic classification of observed data.

Speech occurs in two parameters: timbres and prosodic features. Timbres, or sound qualities, are utilized for meter only as to syllabification, which is the obligatory base for all metric systems. Timbres occur in the physical world and can be measured. (They also occur in the psychological world, but there they cannot yet be satisfactorily described.) Prosodic features are chiefly three: duration, pitch (or tone), and stress. Prosodic features are also anchored in physical reality. Psychological perception of these physical parameters is very complex, but a certain correlation exists between duration and time, between pitch (tone) and frequency, and, to a much less clear degree, between stress and intensity. These four features (syllabification and the three prosodic features) give the total framework for a metric typology, and there are high culture examples for meters based on each of the four. It should also be pointed out that, as in all typologies, transitory metric systems and phenomena do occur.

The typology includes pure-syllabic meter: only the number of syllabics within the syntactic frames—word, colon, sentence—is regulated (example: Hungarian folk poetry); and syllabic-prosodic meter: in addition to the number of syllabics certain types of prosodic features must occur. According to the kinds of prosodic features, three subclasses can be distinguished: (1) Durational meter (commonly called "quantitative"): In some positions the length of the syllabics and, in some cases, the complexity of the following consonant cluster are regulated. Example: Classical Greek and Latin verse. (2) Dynamic meter: Besides a certain number of syllabics, heavier and lighter syllabic pulses are required, in certain positions. Example: English and German verse. Durational and dynamic meters show an affinity in that both utilize "weightier" vs. less "weighty" bases. The distinctive mark of these two types of meter may be subsumed under the term "accent." In Old Germanic verse the accented positions were filled by either a long or a stressed syllable, whereas there was considerable freedom in filling out the rest of the verse line. (3) Tonal meter: In certain positions well-defined tonal classes, representing classes of distinctive pitch phonemes of the language, are required. Example: even and non-even tone in Classical Chinese. Recently a theory has been advanced that the regular T'ang dynasty verse was essentially durational (quantitative), not tonal, in nature, the even tone corresponding to a longum (—), the deflected tone to a breve (∪). This view seems implausible, however, for two reasons. The measurement of the duration of various tonal segments does not set the even tone apart, and, in addition, what is known about the development of Chinese dialects does not support such a theory.

It should be noted that the above metric types can coexist in the same language: for example, in Hungarian both the pure-syllabic meter and the durational meter occur.

Besides these "pure" types, intermediate or mixed (as in most typologies) can be found. For example, French meter is basically "pure" syllabic, but the final syllabic in a segment, other than a final *e-muet*, must be stressed; in early Byzantine hexameter, when quantity was disappearing in the spoken language, the prefinal syllabic had to be accented; or, in some Hungarian verse, a choriamb is superposed on a pure syllabic structure. If ictus was used in some Classical Greek or Latin "quantitative" verse—a hotly debated issue—it would provide another example of such a mixture.

This typology (summarized in Figure 1) seems to be the most adequate for metric purposes. It would be possible, of course, to use other aspects of verse for erecting different typologies. For instance, we could set up a typology of syntactic frames utilized in verse. (Greek hexameter was delineated more clearly by words and word groups than Latin hexameter; free verse—when it is still verse—often has a firm syntactic composition; folk poetry often uses cola as units.) Or, we could make a typology of the numerical regulations imposed on the meter (strict, loose, or permitting variations; for examples, see the beginning of this article). These typologies, however, would probably turn out to be less informative and, some of them, trivial.

In syllabic-prosodic meters the notion of the syllable alone will not suffice. A second concept has to be introduced: the organization of the syllabic material according to certain prosodic features, called long and short base for durational meter, heavy and light base for dynamic meter, and even and changing base for tonal meter.

It is interesting to note that the phonological elements are grouped into only two base classes, never into more, although in principle much finer gradations would be possible. For example, in English more than two stress levels could be utilized, but, apart from the tendency in the so-called dipodic meters, there are never more than two classes utilized systematically; in Classical Greek the length of the syllabic and the following consonant clusters would have allowed a large number of classes, but only two types of bases were utilized for metric purposes, the short and the long; in Classical Chinese there were nine (or six) phonemic tones, but for metric purposes there was only one opposition, that between even and non-even tones. Dual opposition may prove to be a metric universal or at least a universal tendency.

In syllabic-prosodic meters the numerical regulation refers not only to the syllabics as such but to the base classes as well; that is, in certain positions only one base class is allowed. Positions must, therefore, be introduced as a second numerical principle, in addition to the number of syllabics, the sole characteristic of pure-syllabic meter. Positions which have to be filled out by a definite base class are called fixed. Other positions, those which allow variations, are called free. No syllabic-prosodic systems exist in which all positions are fixed. Free positions may be filled by either of the two base classes (anceps).[22] Or there may be more complex substitutions. In a hexameter certain positions can be filled either by one long base or by two short bases. In Corinna's anaclasis the scheme allows four choices: (— —), (— ∪), (∪ —) or (∪∪∪). In this case, no position is fixed; groups of syllabics (feet) have internal compensations.

Metric Types:

A. Simple
Metric relevancy: Syllabicity.
Metric unit: Syllable.
Numerical regularity: Number.
(Example: *Hungarian folk poetry*)

B. Complex
Metric relevancy: Syllabicity and Prosodics.
Metric unit: Base.
Numerical regularity: Number and Position.

a. Tonal: frequency-defined
Base classes: 1. Even.
2. Changing.
(Example: *Chinese*)

b. Dynamic: energy-defined
Base classes: 1. Heavy.
2. Light.
(Examples: *English and German*)

c. Durational: time-defined
Base classes: 1. Long.
2. Short.
(Examples: *Classical Greek and Arabic*)

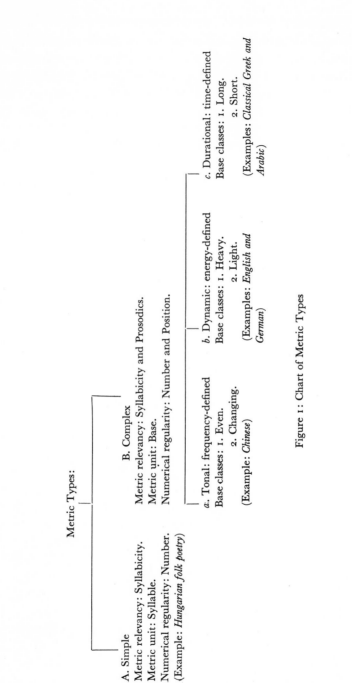

Figure 1: Chart of Metric Types

Metrics as a Discipline

Metrics, a division of linguistics, is in fact a simple discipline for the following reasons: it is fairly well understood, and it is purely formal, since it represents linear and coherent phonetic-syntactic material. Other aspects of language such as stylistics, the study of poetic figures, or rhetoric, all of which involve variation, individuality, and semantics, are obviously much more complicated.

At the same time, it must be pointed out that verse, which is basically a poetic device in language, is also part of a much wider complex of cultural phenomena, even though its characteristic property, meter, is relatively simple linguistically. Verse is complicated because the content is usually very concrete and personal, it often contains archaic elements, and it is constantly in a state of flux because it is not the natural use of language by a speech community but a conscious creative production of individuals.

Metric Coverage in this Volume

This book describes a large, varied number of versification systems. Besides some that are better known to the English reader—the Western systems such as French, Italian, Spanish, English, and Germanic—the less familiar Slavic and Celtic systems are included. The Orient is represented by the systems of Chinese and Japanese. Biblical Hebrew is included, and likewise the classical systems, Latin and Greek. In the Uralic language family, three types are presented: Hungarian, the all-but-lost nomadic Kamassian as an illustration of Siberian folk verse, and Mordvinian from Central European Russia.

Significant omissions are, for example, the Vedic-Indic verse system, the Arabic (which, in conjunction with the spread of Islam, influenced a large number of systems reaching down into Africa and including Swahili), and the Persian. Yet all in all there is perhaps no other book that covers so many verse systems in such an extensive fashion. This book contains much interesting information for both the specialist and the non-specialist. It should improve the systematic and comparative treatment of verse phenomena.

The methods employed vary. They are mostly descriptive. But the essay on French verse is largely historical in orientation, and so is the first of the three on English. That on Germanic includes a historical treatment, and so does that on Japanese. Besides the traditional philological approach, formal logical and generative-transformational approaches are represented. A bibliographical essay is included for English verse. A final essay describes the relationship between verse and another time-sequential art form, music,

NOTES

1. This presentation of versification is a revision of the following three general theoretical papers: "Notes on Structural Analysis in Metrics," *Helicon*, 4 (1943), 119–46; "Metric Typology," in *Style and Language*, ed. Thomas A. Sebeok, pp. 135–48; "Metrics and Linguistics," in *Report on the Tenth Annual Round Table Meeting on Linguistics and Language Studies*, pp. 129–37. For full reference of works cited in notes, see selected bibliography at end.
2. Cf. Chesterton's view of free verse: "Free verse is like free love, a contradiction in terms," or, with reference to relaxation of the French alexandrine, the view of Suberville (quoted in Jacqueline Flescher's article, p. 189): "Cette impuissance ne trahirait-elle pas en définitive un vice d'origine, qui est la confusion des genres, le refus de se soumettre à la nature des choses et aux règles qu'elle impose, d'un mot, l'individualisme anarchique?"
3. The universe of discourse is divided into two parts unequally. Although the notion of markedness is not universally applicable, there is no doubt that the paired terms "marked" and "unmarked" give significant information in many cases. With verse and prose, calling one "marked" and the other "unmarked" indicates an imbalance in the division of the universe of discourse. The division of a language text into verse and prose represents an extreme case where one of the terms (prose) has no defining characteristics. The concept of markedness has been reintroduced recently in modern American linguistics following Trubetzkoy's phonological theory.
4. Often another term, rhythm, occurs in discussing versification. Rhythm, however, is not a specific property of verse; it occurs in prose as well. Moreover, rhythm is a general phenomenon present in any periodically recurring phenomena, for instance, in music, in mathematics, tidal waves, and the recurring seasons. Relevant here is the remark of St. Augustine: "Omne metrum etiam rhythmus, non omnis rhythmus metrum est."
5. The relationship of verse to the spatial (non-sequential) arts, such as painting and drawing, is less immediate. The relationships which occur here are of several kinds. A poem might be represented in a certain shape, as Simias' Egg in Antiquity, or Appollinaire's *calligrammes,* or Christian Morgenstern's poem about the funnels:

DIE TRICHTER

Zwei Trichter wandeln durch die Nacht.
Durch ihres Rumpfs verengten Schacht
fliesst weisses Mondlicht
still und heiter
auf ihren
Waldweg
u. s.
w.

(Note the use of the letter *w* to represent the opening of the funnel.)

A deeper relationship between graphic art and the semantic implications of poetry exists with artists who are both poets and painters such as William Blake, Henri Rousseau, and Paul Klee; see Roman Jakobson, "On the Verbal Art of William Blake and other Poet-Painters," *Linguistic Inquiry*, 1 (January 1970), 3–23. It is also possible to establish a mathematical relationship between poem and drawing, where the isomorphic relations can be mathematically described. Such an attempt was made by me in *The Structure of the* Sonetti a Corona *of Attila József*, Acta Universitatis Stockholmiensis,

6. See W. K. Wimsatt, Jr., and Monroe C. Beardsley, "The Concept of Meter: An Exercise in Abstraction," *PMLA*, 84 (1959), 590: "The measurement of verse is determined by some recurrent linguistic feature, peg, obstacle, jutting stress, or whatever. If we read this recurrence so as to give it equal times, this is something we do to it. Maybe we actually do, and maybe this is a part of our aesthetic satisfaction; still it is not a part of the linguistic fact which the poet has to recognize and on which he has to rely in order to write verses."

7. Edward Wheeler Scripture, *Grundzüge der englischen Verswissenschaft,* also P. Verrier, *Essai sur les principes de la métrique anglaise.* See Seymour Chatman, *A Theory of Meter,* for references to American phonemic approaches to verse.

8. We can, of course, subject both metric numbers and metric performance to statistical analysis, and this kind of analysis is valuable especially for stylistic and historical purposes. But statistical analysis, even of metric numbers, cannot define and determine meter.

9. In American language and literature departments, the specifically linguistic component has often been neglected and linguistics has had to evolve on its own as a powerful, separate discipline.

10. Though meter is a formal notion, it may convey symbolic effect, as onomatopoeia does in speech. Contrast, e.g., the following two examples from Virgil, where meter expresses first equine speed, then slow force: (1) "Quadrupedante putrem sonitū quatit ungula campum" and (2) "Illi inter sese magnā vī bracchia tollunt." Likewise the increase of bisyllabic valleys between the stressed peaks expresses the growing tension and fright of the child in Goethe's *Erlkönig.*

11. "Metrics is less an inherent *feature* of language than a conventional *use* to which language is put. By the same token, meter, in poetry, is a convention rather than an inherent feature." Karl D. Uitti, *Linguistics and Literary Theory,* p. 224.

12. This linguistic approach to metrics is by no means new or original. It has a long tradition going back to the Latin grammarians. In older school books, for instance, metrics always occupied a final part, an appendix, often, to the grammatical description.

13. It is very likely that not all cultures have verse, though I cannot think of any cultures, except dying cultures with only a few survivors, which do not have ritualized texts where some limitation of the language material is used.

14. The exact number of syllables in the *sonetti a corona* is between 2,100 (15 × 14 × 10) if all the lines are decasyllabic and 2,310 (15 × 14 × 11) if all the lines are hendecasyllabic.

15. The rules could be given in a mathematically more elegant form. E.g., Rule (4) would be: Positions 2, 6, 7, 9 (*modulo* 11 n, where n = 0 or 1 or 2) and 35, 36 are *brevia* (◡).

16. Early Sapphic verse was somewhat simpler; the third and fourth lines represented a unit not necessarily divided by a word boundary; the result was a three-line structure.

17. All of the above discussion deals with speech sound. Terminology is often determined, however, by the graphic representation of verse: text, line, stichic and astichic verse, eye-rhyme etc. In discussion of language, there is often confusion between speech and script, sound and letter.

18. The notion of syllable is one of the most obscure issues in linguistics. There is no doubt that there is an underlying pulse phenomenon in all speech more readily perceived than phonemes. The consistent matching of speech pulses with musical notes and the rhythmic chanting of children are evidence for the reality of syllabicity. (This pulse phenomenon, while universal, is in part socially regulated.) The difficulties stem from the fact that on the one hand a great number of correlated phenomena are subsumed under the term syllable and on the other hand, two disparate sets of phenomena, one of culmination and the other of delimitation, are thrown together into one unit. Some structural linguists, such as the Danes Brøndal and Hjelmslev, and, later, American linguists, such as Hockett, Haugen, and Pike have used the term "syllable" either for the place of the phonologically relevant accent,

or as a minimal distributional model. In the first usage, languages like French, which have no distinctive accent, would have no syllables, and, of course, such a theory would be useless for metric purposes. The second interpretation, syllable as a basis for a distributional model, cannot be used as a constitutive feature for metrics either.

I think "syllable" needs an intensive phonetic definition, just as *p* is defined by bilabial closure, plosion, and open glottis. Such a theory was offered by Stetson, who ascribed "syllable" to a single action of the intercostal muscles. His theory is original and of great importance. Yet it does not seem quite convincing to me. Menzerath thought that the rhythm of jaw movements would provide a cue for the syllabic pulse. I do not think that this will be proved correct either, since one can articulate speech with constant mandibular angle, for instance when a pencil is stuck between the teeth.

I have a different idea about the nature of syllabic pulse and its phonetic structuring and linguistic role. In my opinion, syllabification depends on the optimal filtering pulses in the buccal cavity. It represents a speech sound which is a filtered, sustained relative maximum in the speech chain. The pulse begins with the onset of the syllabic peak and continues until the onset of the next syllabic peak and does not depend on syllabic cuts as required in conventional usage. This approach solves the controversy about a case like *split,* which obviously has two energy and loudness peaks in *s* and *i,* but *s* has no filtered formant structure, and the word is monosyllabic. This would also explain why the cluster [str] when it occurs as word initial, e.g., in *στρατός*, has no base-lengthening effect on the following vowel, whereas medially, e.g., in *ἄσρτα*, it does result in a preceding long base (*positione longum*).

19. The term prosodic is replaced in modern American structural linguistic usage by the term suprasegmental. The term implies that speech has, in addition to segmental features, properties which extend beyond a single segment. Use of this term is misleading, in my opinion, because it does not accurately characterize the group of phenomena aimed at, while including other phenomena which one does not want to consider among suprasegmentals. For instance, voicing in English, which is not regarded as a suprasegmental feature, extends inherently beyond one speech sound in all cohesive obstruent clusters. On the other hand, tone, which is regarded as a suprasegmental feature, is not longer than the underlying timbre, e.g., Cantonese *á* (rising tone) vs. *à* (falling tone).

20. The earlier preoccupation of American linguists with phrase-structure grammar was based on a desired identification of linearity and coherency of cola with syntactic structure in general.

21. The idea advanced by some American structuralists that "pure" rhyme should be incorporated as a cornerstone into phonological theory for determining phonemic units is based on an ethnocentric Western view of rhyme. Rhyme is a culture-bound phenomenon. In Germanic languages the ideal rhyme is completely identical phonetic material beginning with the vowel of the last stressed syllable and continuing to the end of the line. (There are, of course, deviations for emotive effect; e.g., Poe's *Ulalume* contains the rhyme: sister, kissed her, vista.) In Arabic, however, only the final consonants are identical; in Spanish assonance only vowel identity is relevant; whereas, in Hungarian the identity of the final vowels is required, and only a similarity in the manner of articulation of consonants, not their total identity, is regarded as desirable (e.g., *hat* and *kap* but not *hat* and *hal*). It should also be noted that the use of rhyme is not restricted to verse alone. For instance, a popular genre in Arabic, the *Makama,* uses rhyme systematically in prose.

22. The term anceps, historically much older, can correspond to the notion of neutralization in modern linguistics. Neutralization means that distinctions normally employed are not made in certain well-defined positions. For instance, in English there are two sets of stops as to their force feature, *fortis* vs. *lenis* (e.g., *pit* vs. *bit*), but the distinction is neutralized after /s/, and only one set of stops occurs (e.g., *spit* but not *sbit*).

SELECTED BIBLIOGRAPHY

Austerlitz, Robert. *Ob-Ugric Metrics. Folklore Fellows Communications* 174. Helsinki, 1958.

Chatman, Seymour. *A Theory of Meter*. The Hague: Mouton, 1965.

De Groot, A. Willem. *Algemene versleer*. The Hague: N. V. Servire, 1946.

Grammont, Maurice. *Le Vers français, ses moyens d'expression, son harmonie*. 4th ed. Paris: Delagrave, 1957.

Heusler, Andreas. *Deutsche Versgeschichte*, I–III. In *Grundriss der deutschen Philologie*. Ed. Hermann Paul. Berlin: Walter de Gruyter, 1925–29.

Jakobson, Roman. "Studies in Comparative Slavic Metrics." *Oxford Slavonic Papers*, 3 (1952), 21–66.

Kenyon Review, 18 (Summer 1956).

Lehmann, Winfred P. *The Development of the Germanic Verse Form*. Austin: Univ. of Texas Press and the Linguistic Society of America, 1956.

Levin, Samuel R. *Linguistic Structures in Poetry*. The Hague: Mouton, 1962.

Liu, James J. Y. *The Art of Chinese Poetry*. Chicago: Univ. of Chicago Press, 1962. Rpt. in paperback by Phoenix Books, 1966.

Lotz, John. "Notes on Structural Analysis in Metrics." *Helicon*, 4 (Budapest, Leipzig, 1943), 119–46.

——— "Metric Typology." In *Style in Language*. Ed. Thomas A. Sebeok (New York, London: M.I.T. Press and John Wiley, 1960), pp. 135–48.

——— "Metrics and Linguistics." In *Report on the Tenth Annual Round Table Meeting on Linguistics and Language Studies*. Ed. Richard S. Harrell, Monograph Series on Language and Linguistics, No. 12 (Georgetown Univ., 1959), pp. 129–37.

——— *The Structure of the* Sonetti a Corona *of Attila József*. Acta Universitatis Stockholmiensis, Studia Hungarica Stockholmiensia, I. Stockholm, 1965.

Maas, Paul. *Griechische Metrik*. Gercke-Norden: Einleitung in die Altertumswissenschaft. Vol. I, Fasc. 7 (photocopy reproduction with additions). Leipzig, Berlin: Teubner, 1929.

Norberg, Dag. *Introduction à l'étude de la versification latine médievale*. Acta Universitatis Stockholmiensis, Studia Latina Stockholmiensia, v. Stockholm: Almqvist & Wiksell, 1958.

Poe, Edgar Allan. "The Philosophy of Composition." In *The Complete Poems and Stories of Edgar Allan Poe With Selections From His Critical Writings*. Ed. A. H. Quinn. New York, 1951. Pp. 978–87. (First Published in *Graham's Magazine*, April 1846.)

Preminger, Alex, Frank J. Warnke, and O. B. Hardison, Jr., eds. *Encyclopedia of Poetry and Poetics*. Princeton: Princeton Univ. Press, 1965. See esp. Craig La Drière, "Prosody."

Scripture, Edward Wheeler. *Grundzüge der englischen Verswissenschaft*. Marburg: N. G. Elwertsche Buchhandlung (G. Braun), 1929.

Sievers, Eduard. *Altgermanische Metrik*. Halle a.S.: Max Niemeyer, 1893.

Snell, Bruno. *Griechische Metrik*. Göttingen: Vandenhoeck & Ruprecht, 1957.

Uitti, Karl D. *Linguistics and Literary Theory*. The Princeton Studies of Humanistic Scholarship in America. Englewood Cliffs, N.J.: Prentice-Hall, 1969.

Wilamowitz-Moellendorff, Ulrich von. *Griechische Verskunst*. Berlin: Weidmannsche Buchhandlung, 1921.

Wimsatt, W. K., Jr., and Monroe C. Beardsley. "The Concept of Meter: An Exercise in Abstraction." *PMLA*, 74 (1959), 585–98.

Wright, William. "Prosody." In *A Grammar of the Arabic Language*. 3rd. ed., Vol. II. Cambridge: Cambridge Univ. Press, 1955. Pp. 350–90.

CLASSICAL CHINESE

By HANS H. FRANKEL

Introductory Remarks

In this essay I intend to bring out the essential features of Chinese prosody as found in five representative poetic genres, without giving all the metric variations found in these genres. I do not take up other equally important genres, nor do I trace the historical development of prosodic features. I exclude twentieth-century poetry in the colloquial language, which has been experimenting with such Western importations as the sonnet and free verse. I make no reference to the Chinese writing system because it is on the whole irrelevant to Chinese prosody: nearly all the prosodic features that occur in the poetry of the literati can also be found in the oral compositions of unlettered farmers. I transcribe the Chinese texts as they are read in standard modern pronunciation (Mandarin), using the Wade-Giles system of romanization.[1] For the four tones of modern Mandarin, I use diacritical marks as follows:

Mark	*Chinese name*	*Translation of name*	*Pitch pattern*
—	*yīn-p'íng shēng*	female level tone	constant on high level
/	*yáng-p'íng shēng*	male level tone	rising from fairly high to high level
⌣	*shǎng shēng*	rising tone	rising from low to high level
\	*ch'ǜ shēng*	going (i.e., falling?) tone	descending from high to low level

We do not know how the tones sounded in times past, but we can be certain that the differences between them were significant phonemically and prosodically. Despite their remarkable stability, the tones have naturally undergone some changes, two of which must be mentioned here. First, literary (classical) Chinese does not make the modern distinction between the "female" and the "male" level tone. Second, in addition to the "level," the "rising," and the "going" tone, literary Chinese has a fourth tone, called *jù(p) shēng* 'entering tone.' This tone goes with words ending in unvoiced plosives (-p, -t, -k). Around A.D. 1200, the final plosives, and with them the entering tone, disappeared in the dialects of North China (including Mandarin), and the former entering-tone syllables were distributed among the other tones. In my transcriptions I indicate the entering tone by enclosing the final plosive in parentheses, and I add a diacritical mark to show the modern tone which replaced the entering tone in each case. It is the entering tone, as we shall see, which is relevant to the metrical analysis.

Prosodic features are naturally bound up with linguistic features. Chinese is a predominantly monosyllabic, tonal language. The basic structural units of Chinese poetry are syllables, lines, couplets, and sometimes stanzas. The meters are syllabic. A line of verse usually coincides with a grammatical sentence. (The same word, *chǜ,* is used for both.) *Enjambement* is comparatively rare. Important prosodic devices are end rhyme, tonal balance, and parallelism.

I will now proceed to the presentation and discussion of five distinct genres with one example apiece. For each poem I will give a romanized text with a word-for-word translation, followed by a freer translation. R indicates end rhyme. When the rhyme changes in the course of a poem, I number the successive rhymes R1, R2, and so on. In the literal translations, I use hyphens to connect two or more words which correspond to a single monosyllable in Chinese.

Shīh chīng (*The Classic of Songs,* anonymous, about tenth to sixth century B.C.)

Example: Poem No. 115 of the *Shīh chīng*

shān yǔ shū R1
mountain has prickly-elms
hsí(p) yǔ yǘ R1
marsh has white-elms
tzǔ yǔ ī sháng
you have clothes garments
fú(t) ì fú(t) lóu R1
not-them don not-them wear

tzŭ yŭ chǖ mă
you have chariots horses
fú(t) ch'íh fú(t) ch'ǖ R1
not-them gallop not-them drive
yüăn ch'í ssŭ ĭ
decay you'll died have
t'ā jén shìh yǘ R1
other people these enjoy

shān yŭ k'ăo R2
mountain has ailanthus
hsí(p) yŭ niŭ R2
marsh has trumpet-creepers
tzŭ yŭ t'íng nèi
you have courtyards halls
fú(t) să fú(t) săo R2
not-them sprinkle not-them sweep
tzŭ yŭ chūng kŭ
you have bells drums
fú(t) kŭ fú(t) k'ăo R2
not-them strike not-them beat
yüăn ch'í ssŭ ĭ
decay you'll died have
t'ā jén shìh păo R2
other people these possess

shān yŭ ch'ī(t) R3
mountain has varnish-trees
hsí(p) yŭ lì(t) R3
marsh has chestnut-trees
tzŭ yŭ chiŭ shíh(k)
you have wine food
hó pū(t) jìh(t) kŭ sè(t) R3
why not daily drum pluck
ch'iĕh ĭ hsĭ lò(k)
as-well to be-happy take-pleasure

22 *ch'iěh ǐ yǔng jìh(t)* R3
as-well to prolong day
yüǎn ch'í ssǔ ǐ
decay you'll died have
24 *t'ā jén jù(p) shìh(t)* R3
other people enter house

On the mountain there are prickly elms,
2 In the marsh there are white elms.
You have clothes and garments,
4 But you don't don them, you don't wear them.
You have chariots and horses,
6 But you don't gallop them, you don't drive them.
When you wither and die
8 Others will enjoy them.

On the mountain there are ailanthus trees,
10 In the marsh there are trumpet creepers.
You have courtyards and halls,
12 But you don't have them sprinkled, you don't have them swept (for use).
You have bells and drums,
14 But you don't have them struck, you don't have them beaten.
When you wither and die
16 Others will possess them.

On the mountain there are varnish trees,
18 In the marsh there are chestnut trees.
You have wine and food,
20 Why don't you drum and pluck (make music, make merry) every day,
Both to enjoy yourself
22 And to prolong the day?
When you wither and die
24 Others will enter your house.

Line length is not quite uniform in the Classic of Songs, but the four-syllable line predominates. The lines are paired syntactically as couplets throughout. Every poem is divided into stanzas (three in this case) of nearly identical metrical structure, with many elements of repetition and variation. Rhyme schemes are varied and fairly intricate at times. There is occasional parallelism, working with a combination of identical and matching words. It operates between paired lines (in this poem, the first couplet of each stanza, and lines 21 and 22), between couplets (in this example, the middle couplets of the first and second stanzas), and between stanzas; the last stanza typically shows a greater amount of variation (a surprise turn), with a final return to the pattern set by the two preceding stanzas.

Kŭ shīh (Old-Style Verse)

Example: "Song of the East and West Gates," by Ts'áo Ts'āo (155–220 A.D.). (The title indicates a traditional song pattern and is not relevant to the form or content of the poem.)

húng yèn ch'ū(t) sài(k) pĕi(k)
wild-swans wild-geese born passes north
2 *năi tsài wú jén hsiāng* R
namely in without men land
chǚ ch'ìh wàn yǘ lǐ
raise wings myriad more miles
4 *hsíng chĭh tzù ch'éng háng* R
travel stop naturally constitute rows
tūng chiéh(t) shíh(k) nán tào
winter season eat south rice
6 *ch'ūn jìh(t) fù(k) pĕi(k) hsiáng* R
spring days back north fly

t'ién chūng yŭ chuăn p'éng
field inside there-is revolving tumbleweed
8 *suí fēng yüăn p'iāo yáng* R
follows wind far drifts raises
ch'áng yǚ kù kēn chüéh(t)
forever with old roots cut-off
10 *wàn suì pū(t) hsiāng tāng* R
myriad years not them meet
nài hó tz'ŭ chēng fū
remedy what this campaigning man
12 *ān té(k) ch'ǜ ssù fāng* R

how can leave four directions
júng mǎ pū(t) chiěh ān
martial horse not releases saddle
14 *k'ǎi chiǎ(p) pū(t) lí p'áng* R
mail armor not leaves side
jǎn jǎn lǎo chiāng chih
slowly slowly old-age about-to arrive
16 *hó shíh fǎn kù hsiāng* R
what time return old home

shén lúng ts'áng shēn yüān
holy dragon hides profound deep-water
18 *měng hǔ pù kāo kāng* R
fierce tiger paces lofty ridge
hú ssǔ kuēi shǒu ch'iū
fox dies goes-back toward cave
20 *kù hsiāng ān k'ǒ wáng* R
old home how can be-forgotten

The wild geese are born north of the passes,
2 In a land without men.
Raising their wings, they fly a myriad miles,
4 Traveling and stopping as a flock.
In winter they eat the rice of the South,
6 In spring they fly back to the North.

In the field there is the tumbleweed,
8 Borne by the wind, it drifts far and high,
Forever cut off from its native roots,
10 Never to meet them again in a myriad years.

What shall he do, this soldier on the march?
12 How can he get away from the earth's four corners?
His war horse is never without a saddle,
14 His armor never leaves his side.
Slowly old age comes upon him,
16 When can he go home?
The holy dragon stays in the water's depth,
18 The fierce tiger paces the lofty ridge.
The fox, about to die, makes for his cave.
20 How can one forget his home?

In Old-Style Verse, the lines are generally of equal length throughout a given poem. The favorite line lengths are five and seven syllables. The lines are nearly always paired syntactically as couplets. Stanzaic divisions, if any, are based on content, not on meter. Rhyme generally occurs at the end of each couplet. Rhyme may be constant (as in this example) or change in the course of the poem. Parallelism, with antithesis and some repetition, occurs irregularly between the two lines of a couplet (in this poem, between lines 5 and 6, 13 and 14, 17 and 18). There is a caesura, made possible by the syntax and required by the verse, in nearly every five-syllable line between the second and third syllables. (In a seven-syllable line, the caesura is between the fourth and fifth syllables.) The three syllables following the caesura are not uniformly structured as far as syntax is concerned: the next-to-the-last syllable may be in closer juncture with the preceding syllable than with the following syllable, or the other way around. This free and unpredictable alternation of two patterns adds a dynamic element to the five-syllable and seven-syllable meters of Old-Style and Regulated Verse (see below).

The distribution of tones plays a definite role not easily defined. For prosodic purposes, the four tones in this and other genres fall into two categories: the level tone is opposed to the other three, which are collectively called *tsè(k) shēng* 'deflected tones.' Old-Style Verse aims at a euphonious and balanced distribution of the two tonal categories. Just what constitutes euphonious distribution in a single line or couplet cannot yet be stated with any degree of objectivity. But in each Old-Style Verse poem as a whole, the number of syllables in the two tonal categories tends to be nearly equal (in the above poem forty-nine level-tone syllables and fifty-one deflected tones), while in writings that pay no attention to tonal balance, only about forty per cent of the syllables are in the level tone. The distribution of the two types of tones in the poem can be seen in the following schema, where O represents a level tone and X a deflected tone:

OXXXX
2 XXOOO
XXXOX
4 OXXOO
OXXOX
6 OXXXO

OOXXO
8 OOXOO
OXXOX
10 XXXOO

XOXOO
12 OXXXO
OXXXO
14 XXXOO
XXXOX
16 OOXXO

OOOOO
18 XXXOO
OXOXO
20 XOOXO

Lǜ shīh (Regulated Verse)

Example: "Passing through Huà-yīn," by Ts'uī Hào (704?–754 A.D.)

t'iáo yáo t'ài huà fǔ hsién chīng R
lofty high T'ài Huà overlooks Hsién capital
2 *t'iēn wài sān fēng hsüèh(k) pū(t) ch'éng* R
heaven beyond three peaks carved not completed
wǔ tì tz'ú ch'ién yǘn yǜ sàn
Martial Emperor temple front clouds about-to disperse
4 *hsiēn jén chǎng shǎng yǔ ch'ū ch'íng* R
immortal person hand above rain first cleared-up
hó shān pěi(k) chèn ch'ín kuān hsiěn
rivers mountains north pillow Ch'ín passes dangerous
6 *ì(k) lù hsī lién hàn chìh p'íng* R
post-stations roads west connect Hàn altars flat
chièh wèn lù p'áng míng lì k'ò(k)
beg ask road side fame wealth travelers
8 *hó jú tz'ǔ ch'ù hsüéh(k) ch'áng shēng* R
what like this place learn long life

High and lofty, Mt. T'ài-huà overlooks the capital Hsién,
2 Its three peaks, reaching beyond heaven, could not be wrought by carving.
In front of the Martial Emperor's temple, the clouds are about to disperse,
4 Above the Immortal's Hand, the rain has just stopped.
Rivers and mountains support in the north the fastnesses of the Ch'ín passes,
6 Post stations and roads link in the west with the plains of the Hàn altars.
May I ask the travelers by the road who seek fame and wealth:
8 What about learning here the art of long life?

In Regulated Verse, the prosodic trends developed in Old-Style Verse hardened into set patterns that may be summed up as follows:

(1) The poem consists of eight lines (four couplets).

(2) The line length is constant throughout the poem, either five or seven syllables.

(3) A single rhyme is used. It is nearly always in the level tone and occurs at the end of the even-numbered lines. In addition, the first line of the poem may end with the same rhyme; it usually does in the seven-syllable form (as in our example) and occasionally in the five-syllable form.

(4) The distribution of level and deflected tones follows a fixed pattern.

(5) The fourth line parallels the third line, and the sixth line parallels the fifth line.

(6) There is a caesura in the five-syllable form between the second and the third syllable of every line. In the seven-syllable form, there is a major caesura between the fourth and fifth syllables, and a minor caesura between the second and third syllables.

Points 4 and 5 require amplification. (4) In taking up distribution of tones, I will simplify the exposition by speaking of the seven-syllable form only, but my remarks will be equally applicable to the five-syllable form, which as far as prosody is concerned differs from the longer form only in that it lacks the first two syllables of every line. That is to say, the seven-syllable schema below can be converted to the five-syllable form by omitting the first two syllables of every line. I base this discussion on the article by Downer and Graham (see Bibliography), where the principles underlying the distribution of tones have been recognized for the first time as resulting from the meshing of two independent systems. One system governs the alternation of tones in the even-numbered syllables of each line. They will be marked A and B, A representing one tonal category—either level or deflected—and B the opposite tonal category. The other system governs the alternation of tones in the fifth and seventh syllables of each line. They will be marked x and y, x representing the tonal category of the rhyme word—usually but not necessarily level—and y the opposite tonal category. The poem as a whole can be divided into two equal halves for the purposes of tonal patterning. In each half (quatrain), the two systems combine as follows:

1	2	3	4	5	6	7
	A		B	x	A	y
	B		A	y	B	x
	B		A	x	B	y
	A		B	y	A	x

The tonal category of the first and third syllables of each line may vary, but these syllables, too, tend to follow a pattern: the first syllable tends to agree in its tonal category with the second, and the third with the fourth. Whenever the first line of the poem shares the rhyme (an optional feature), x and y change places in the first line but not in the fifth. In this case, then, the two halves of the poem are not entirely alike in regard to tonal pattern. In writing a poem in Regulated Verse, the poet may make either A the level tone and B the deflected tone, or he may do it the other way around. He also determines the tonal categories for x and y, but the rhyme (x) is nearly always in the level tone; the alternative of making x deflected and y level is seldom chosen.

This meshing of two independent systems, each of which is symmetrical in a different arrangement, produces an artfully patterned tonal structure characterized by balance and variety. The number of level and deflected tones is approximately equal in every couplet (hence also in the whole poem). In each couplet, most of the syllables of one line are matched by syllables in the opposite tonal category in the corresponding positions of the other line. Each couplet, in turn, has a total tonal pattern that sets it apart from its neighboring couplets (or couplet), just as each line differs in its tonal pattern from the preceding line and the following line.

The distribution of level and deflected tones in the example may again be shown more clearly by using the symbols O for a level tone and X for a deflected tone:

OOXXXOO
2 OXOOXXO
XXOOOXX
4 OOXXXOO
OOXXOOX
6 XXOOXXO
XXXOOXX
8 OOXXXOO

(5) Parallelism, which is required in each of the two middle couplets, means word-for-word matching. Realized with varying degrees of perfection, it is a combination of sameness, likeness, difference, and antithesis, embracing phonological, grammatical, and semantic features. The phonological feature is the contrast of tones just described. Grammatically and semantically, the matching words are supposed to be in the same category: nouns are paired with nouns, verbs with verbs, adjectives with adjectives, colors with colors,

numerals with numerals, place names with place names. And the paired words generally perform the same syntactic functions. The semantic categories may be quite narrow, such as points of the compass (e.g., "north" and "west" in lines 5 and 6 of the example), or names of dynasties (Ch'ín and Hàn in the same couplet), or postpositions marking location ("front" and "above" in lines 3 and 4). Unlike the parallelism in other forms of Chinese poetry, the parallelism of Regulated Verse never repeats the same word in matching positions. (Contrast the repetition of the negative in the "Song of the East and West Gates" above, lines 13 and 14, and the repetition of the genitive particle *chīh* in the "*Fù* on Ascending a Tower" below, lines 5 and 6, and again lines 7 and 8.)

Tz'ú (Lyric Song)

Example: Poem in the tune pattern "The City by the River," by Ch'ín Kuān (1049–1100 A.D.)

hsī ch‘éng yáng liŭ nùng ch'ūn jóu R
west city salix willows play spring pliant
2 *tùng lí yū* R
stir parting sadness
lèi nán shōu R
tears difficult restrain
4 *yú chì tō ch‘íng ts‘éng wèi hsì kuēi chōu* R
still remember much feeling once for tied-up returning boat
pì(k) yĕh chū ch‘iáo tāng jìh(t) shìh
green plain vermilion bridge that day events
6 *jén pū(t) chièn*
person not seen
shuĭ k‘ūng liú R
river vainly flows

8 *sháo huá pū(t) wèi shào nién liú* R
vernal flowering not for young years remains
hèn yū yū R
grief long long
10 *chĭ shíh hsiū* R
what time stop

fēi hsǜ lò(k) huā shíh hòu ī(t) tēng lóu R
flying catkins falling blossoms time period once ascend tower
12 *pièn tsò ch'ūn chiāng tū shìh lèi*
even make spring river all be tears
liú pū(t) chìn
flow not exhaust
14 *hsǚ tō ch'óu* R
very much sorrow

The willows in the West City play in their springtime pliancy,
2 Stirring up the sadness of parting,
Tears are hard to restrain.
4 I still remember their great sympathy, for us they tied up the returning boat,
The green plain, the vermilion bridge, that day's events.
6 The person is not to be seen,
The river flows in vain.

8 Spring's flowering does not linger for the young,
Long, long is my grief,
10 When will it stop?
At the time of flying catkins and falling blossoms, I once ascend the tower.
12 Even if the spring river were all tears,
It could not exhaust in its flow
14 So much sorrow.

The schema below shows the distribution of level tones (O) and deflected tones (X).

OOOXXOO
2 XOO
XOO
4 OXOOOXXOO
XXOOOXX
6 OXX
XOO

8 OOXXXOO
XOO
10 XOO
OXXOOXXOO
12 XXOOOXX
OXX
14 XOO

The *tz'ú* were originally song words written in fixed patterns to go with new or old musical tunes. Even after the melodies were forgotten, *tz'ú* continued to be written, bearing the names and following the patterns of the tunes. Each pattern determines the number of lines, the number of syllables for each line, the sequence of tonal categories in each line, and the positions and tonal category of the end rhyme or rhymes. The lines of a given pattern are usually of uneven length, and each poem tends to be divided into two or more stanzas which may be identical or different in their metric patterns. (In the example the two stanzas are identical except for the tonal categories in two places: lines 1 and 8, syllable 3; and lines 4 and 11, syllable 3.) From about the thirteenth century on, a certain tone rather than a tonal category was required in certain positions in some *tz'ú* patterns.

During the first flourishing of the Lyric Song in the tenth and eleventh centuries, poets felt free to vary the tonal and rhyme patterns of the tunes they were following. But thereafter the patterns became more rigid. The *Ch'ín-tìng tz'ú-p'ŭ* (*Imperial Register of Tz'ú Prosody*), completed in 1715, lists 826 tune patterns, illustrated with 2,306 varying forms. Whether two given patterns should be considered separate tunes or variants of one tune is often an arbitrary decision.

Fù

Example: "*Fù* on Ascending a Tower" (first of three parts), by Wáng Ts'àn (177–217 A.D.)

tēng tzū lóu ĭ ssù wàng hsī
ascend this tower to four look *hsī*
2 *liáo chiă jìh(t) ĭ hsiāo yū* R1
will avail-of day to melt sadness
lăn ssū yǚ chīh sŏ chiŭ hsī
view these eaves ' that-which located *hsī*
4 *shíh(t) hsiĕn ch'ăng érh kuă ch'óu* R1
truly clearly-visible spacious moreover few equals
chiā(p) ch'īng chāng chīh t'ūng p'ŭ hsī
clasps limpid Chāng 's joining confluence *hsī*
6 *ī ch'ǖ(k) chü chīh ch'áng chōu* R1
leans-on winding Chǖ 's long banks
pèi fén yĕn chīh kuăng lù(k) hsī
turns-back-on high level 's wide dry-land *hsī*

8 *lín kāo hsí(p) chīh wò(k) liú* R1
looks-down-on banks marshes ' enriching running-water
pěi(k) mí t'áo mù(k)
north ends T'áo grave
10 *hsī chiēh(p) chāo ch'iū* R1
west joins Chāo tomb
huá shíh(t) pì yěh
flowers fruits cover countryside
12 *shǔ chí(k) yíng ch'óu* R1
grain millet fill fields
suī hsīn méi érh fēi wú t'ǔ hsī
though indeed beautiful yet is-not my land *hsī*
14 *ts'éng hó tsú(k) ǐ shǎo liú* R1
ever how worthy to short-time remain

I ascend this tower to look out in the four directions,
2 I'll avail myself of the day to melt my sadness.
Viewing the area below the tower's eaves,
4 Truly clear and spacious it is, and has few equals.
It clasps the limpid Chāng River's joining confluence,
6 It has at its back the winding Chǖ's long banks.
It turns its back on a broad expanse of high, level ground,
8 It looks down on enriching water courses with banks and marshes.
In the north it ends with T'áo's Grave,
10 In the west it adjoins Chāo's Tomb.
Flowers and fruits cover the countryside,
12 Grain and millet fill the fields.
Though beautiful indeed, it's not my homeland,
14 It would never do to remain here even a short time.

The *fù* is a miscellaneous genre, descriptive or philosophical or both, often quite lengthy and ornate, and frequently intermingled with prose. It became preeminent in the second century B.C., deriving from an earlier type of poetry represented in the anthology *Ch'ǔ tz'ú* (*The Songs of the South*). The *fù* shows much variety and fluctuation in prosody. Characteristic features (which need not always be present) are the monosyllable *hsī* and the use of function words in fixed positions. The monosyllable whose modern reading is *hsī* is a kind of exclamatory interjection and marks a break. In some early poems of the *Ch'ǔ tz'ú*, it occurs within the line to indicate a caesura. Most generally it is found at the end of the odd-numbered lines to signal the end of the first half of the couplet, while the even-numbered lines carry the rhyme, which signals a fuller stop.

The other characteristic feature is the use of a limited number of function words (particles) in a fixed position at or near the center of the line. In the example, the three function words *ǐ*, *chīh*, and *érh* occur as the fourth syllable in lines 1–8 and 13–14. Particles and the like, called *hsü tzù* ("empty words") in Chinese, are avoided in many poetic genres. In some of the early poems of the *Ch'ŭ tz'ú*, those particles which are reserved for the fixed center position also occur outside that position, but in that case they are excluded from the syllable count. They were obviously unstressed.

Lines 9–12 are in a different meter, without *hsī* and without particles, but with the same rhyme. The two remaining parts of the poem, which I have omitted, are in the same meter as lines 1–8 and 13–14, but with a different rhyme for each part.

Concluding Remarks

That Chinese meters should be primarily syllabic is natural in a monosyllabic language. Since syllables are counted, it matters whether the lines of a given prosodic genre are equal or unequal in length. In general, Chinese poetry favors short lines: four, five, and seven syllables are the most common. The five-syllable and seven-syllable lines of Old-Style and Regulated Verse possess dynamic qualities: the caesura which divides them near the center creates two asymmetrical halves, and in the three syllables following the caesura two syntactic patterns alternate freely.

Variety of tones is another dynamic element that relieves the monotony of short lines and lines of equal length. Reducing four tones to two categories —level and deflected—is comparable to the binary opposition of other multiple contrastive features, such as stress and duration, in other languages.[2] The tones in past times probably implied quantitative distinctions as well as differences in pitch.

As for stress patterns, they are unlikely in a short line which is at the same time a complete sentence: every word bears a heavy burden. However, there is evidence for a stress pattern in the *fù* and its predecessors. End rhyme functions simultaneously as a divisive and unifying factor, marking off sections and binding them together, and often welding together the whole poem. Parallelistic structures are a natural development in a monosyllabic, isolating language.

These are some of the linguistic features methodically exploited in Chinese poetry. Future research may reveal that other features known to be present, such as internal rhyme, assonance, and other elements of sound orchestration, or certain grammatical constructions and rhetorical devices, also fall into definite prosodic patterns.

NOTES

1. For a detailed explanation of the Wade-Giles romanization of Mandarin, see, e.g., Shau Wing Chan, *Concise English-Chinese Dictionary,* 2nd ed. (Stanford: Stanford Univ. Press, 1955), pp. xv–xvii.
2. See J. C. La Drière, "Prosody," in *Encyclopedia of Poetry and Poetics,* ed. Alex Preminger et al. (Princeton: Princeton Univ. Press, 1965), p. 677.

SELECTED BIBLIOGRAPHY

Baxter, Glen W. "Metrical Origins of the *Tz'u.*" *Harvard Journal of Asiatic Studies,* 16 (1953), 108–45. Rpt. in *Studies in Chinese Literature.* Ed. John L. Bishop. Cambridge: Harvard Univ. Press, 1965. Pp. 186–224.

Downer, G. B., and A. C. Graham. "Tone Patterns in Chinese Poetry." *Bulletin of the School of Oriental and African Studies,* Univ. of London, 26 (1963), 145–48.

Graham, A. C. "The Prosody of the *sao* Poems in the *Ch'u tz'u.*" *Asia Major,* N.S. 10 (1963), 119–61.

Hawkes, David. *Ch'u Tz'ŭ: The Songs of the South.* Oxford: Clarendon Press, 1959.

Hightower, James Robert. *Topics in Chinese Literature.* Rev. ed. Cambridge: Harvard Univ. Press, 1962.

Liu, James J. Y. *The Art of Chinese Poetry.* Chicago: Univ. of Chicago Press, 1962.

Wáng Chūng-lín. *Chūng-kuó wén-hsüéh chīh shēng-lǜ yén-chiù* [*Studies in the Prosody of Chinese Literature*]. Diss. Taiwan Normal Univ. 2 vols. Taipei: Taiwan Normal Univ., 1963.

Wáng Lì. *Hàn-yǚ shīh-lǜ hsüéh* [*Chinese Prosody*]. 2nd ed. Shanghai: Chiào-yǜ ch'ū-pǎn shè 1962.

JAPANESE

By ROBERT H. BROWER

Traditional Japanese prosody is surely one of the simplest metrical systems to be found in any of the world's major bodies of poetry. The prosody is syllabic, virtually the only recognized metrical principle being the number of syllables or morae per line; and the various forms from earliest times to the appearance of Western-style *vers libre* in the modern age have nearly all been based on some simple pattern of alternating shorter and longer lines. From about the mid-seventh century, the line length came to be fixed at alternations of five and seven syllables. Further, although Japanese classical poetry is characteristically complex and rich in texture, and although numerous rules and conventions were elaborated over the centuries governing subjects, materials, and treatment, the learned poetry has consisted for most of its history of a single persistent and pre-eminent form—the *tanka* or "short poem"—a 31-syllable poem of five lines in the pattern 5–7–5–7–7. Such astonishing simplicity of metrical pattern embodying a richness of figurative language and a great variety of syntactic and rhetorical techniques can be seen to be in large measure a natural consequence of the nature of the poetic medium, the language itself.

Japanese is not closely nor even clearly related to any other language, ancient or modern, but modern linguistic scholars have generally classified it on structural principles among the Altaic or Ural-Altaic languages—a group comprising the Turkic, Mongolian, and Tungus families, and including such individual languages as Korean as well as Japanese. The language is agglutinative and polysyllabic, contrasting markedly in this respect with Chinese, the language and literature from which the Japanese borrowed much of their learned vocabulary and many of their literary conventions and techniques. Of the five principal word classes (nouns, verbs, adjectives, adverbs, and particles), the verbs and adjectives are highly inflected, with numerous categories of mood, aspect, and tense; the nouns and other categories are uninflected. The syntax lacks the great variety of the Latin, say, but is more fluid and flexible than English; in classical prose and in the longer poetic forms, sentences tend to be long and complex, with many constructions, both paratactic and hypotactic.

More important to the development of Japanese prosodic conventions is the phonology of the language, a phonology as simple as the poetic forms themselves. The prosodic unit, the syllable, is one mora in length. In the modern language, a syllable may consist of a short vowel (a, i, u, e, or o), a consonant plus a vowel, a consonant plus y plus a vowel, or a syllabic n or m (phonemically, n). Long vowels (indicated with a macron except for ii) and long consonants (written double) count as two syllables or morae. There are, however, no long consonants in the classical poetry. The phonology as well as the grammatical structure of the language has of course undergone change over the centuries. The records show, for example, that in the eighth century, when the language was first committed to writing, there were still eight distinct vowels, whereas in the ninth century the number was reduced to five. However, for the last twelve or thirteen hundred years, at least, there has been no significant change in the basic pattern of open syllables and of the regular alternation of vowels and consonants. As a consequence, it is possible to read the oldest poetry in the modern pronunciation without changing the scansion or distorting the basic syllabic prosody, which has been a constant in all periods and poetic genres down to modern times.

As far as can be determined, Japanese lexical accent has also shown no alteration of its basic character since early times. Japanese is a "tone language," employing relative levels of pitch to mark lexical accent. Every word has a basic accent pattern, which often undergoes alteration depending on phrase environment. In the modern language, there are two basic classes of words: tonic—words with lexical high pitch on any syllable; and atonic—words without high pitch. Intermediate levels may be distinguished by the ear, but the differences between pitch levels are subtle at best, and there is wide local variation in the pitch patterns of individual words. In general, Japanese may be described as a language of little accent, and in any case lexical accent is irrelevant to prosody, which has never made any use of this particular feature of the language.

The oldest extant Japanese poetic texts are the primitive songs first written down in the chronicles of the early eighth century, the *Kojiki* (*Record of Ancient Matters,* 712) and *Nihongi* (*Chronicles of Japan,* 720); in certain other later continuations and song collections; and in the first great anthology of Japanese song and poetry, the *Man'yōshū* (*Collection for Myriad Ages,* ca. 759). Allowing for duplications, these sources contain in the aggregate some 500 songs of the seventh century and before, varying in length from brief, incantatory fragments to fairly long sequences of as many as seventy lines. Some of the texts may be reasonably accurate versions of songs that had been handed down in the oral tradition for as long as two centuries or more before they were committed to writing; others are clearly revisions of older material or are contemporary or very nearly so with the written records in which they are found. Such later songs show the influence of literary techniques upon a basically oral tradition of bardic song. The songs of the chronicles are found in pseudo-historical contexts where they emanate from the mouths of gods and culture heroes, and the contexts often obscure their age and distort their meaning. These and other factors make it always difficult and often impossible to date individual songs, but in general it may be observed that the older the song the more irregular its prosody, the later the song the more closely it approaches a regular alternation of five- and seven-syllable lines. The length of the most primitive songs and of the individual lines within them was presumably determined in large measure by the traditional tunes to which they were sung. And, no doubt, in singing the prosodic raggedness was smoothed out by elisions, drawn-out sounds, and the various equivalents of our "heys" and "nonnies" that have always remained a conspicuous feature of popular Japanese song and chant. However, there are many exceptions even to the general tendency to alternate shorter and longer lines, and the primitive songs are so irregular that it is impossible to speak of specific poetic forms.

In the seventh century, the emergence of a central government and a certain degree of political unification made it possible for the Japanese aristocracy to set about modernizing the country along the lines of the great center of East Asian civilization, imperial China. The process of borrowing and adapting was carried on avidly and with little intermission throughout the eighth century and most of the ninth. The Chinese classics became the staple of secular education among the upper classes, and Chinese poetry was enthusiastically studied and imitated by the Japanese literati in Chinese compositions of their own. During the seventh century the Japanese also began to adapt the Chinese writing system to their own very different language, developing a system of phonetic writing by using Chinese characters phonetically to represent the Japanese syllables. The system was cumbersome and was later modified and simplified into the abbreviated characters of the modern *hiragana* and *katakana* syllabaries, but it enabled the Japanese for the first time to record their songs and legends, which had hitherto been passed down among the folk or through hereditary corporations of reciters. This early writing system is the basic one used to record the songs in the *Kojiki* and *Nihongi* and the poems of the *Man'yōshū,* and it is from the *Man'yōshū* that it derives its name, *Man'yōgana,* or "*Man'yō* script." Concurrent with the development of a writing system was the creation of a literate vernacular poetry treating sophisticated subjects and employing sophisticated techniques, such as highly complex patterns of contiguous and non-contiguous parallelism, adapted from the Chinese.

The change from primitive song to sophisticated poetry was rapid: one of Japan's greatest poets, Kakinomoto Hitomaro (fl. ca. 680–710), emerges with dramatic suddenness from a misty background of clan reciters and oral tradition. In the new poetry, intended to be read or recited aloud rather than sung, prosodic regularity is an accomplished fact, with the line-length stabilized at five and seven syllables. It is also now possible to speak of specific poetic forms. Already pre-eminent in the seventh century was the *tanka*: of the 4,500-odd poems in the *Man'yōshū* more than 4,100 are in this form. Next in importance was the *chōka* (also called *nagauta*), or "long poem," brilliantly practiced by Hitomaro, somewhat less so in the two generations following him. It consisted of an indefinite number of pairs of five- and seven-syllable lines with an extra seven-syllable line at the end. The *chōka* was not particularly long by Western standards—the longest is one by Hitomaro in 149 lines—and it might be as short as seven lines. During the seventh century it became customary to add one or more short envoys (*hanka* or *kaeshiuta*), identical in form with the *tanka.* The envoy was probably invented by analogy with a similar convention, the *fan-tzu,* or "repeating words," in the Chinese *fù.* The use of the envoy was one of several factors that led to the decline of the *chōka* in the late eighth century and its virtual disappearance from the literary tradition by the end of the ninth: the envoy tended to draw attention away from the *chōka* and to become the lyrical focus of the composition.

There were four other "forms" of early literary poetry, all of which except the *renga,* or "linked poem," had died out by the end of the eighth century. The shortest form was the *katauta* ("half-poem"): three lines in the pattern 5–7–7 (or sometimes 4–7–7) syllables. As its name suggests, it was not felt to be complete, and although it sometimes appears as an independent form, it was most often combined in pairs in dialogue. The *katauta* could thus be regarded as half of a *sedōka,* or "head-repeated poem," a form which owes its name to its repeated pattern in six lines of 5–7–7–5–7–7 syllables. The *sedōka* was most commonly used for dialogue, but some examples consist of a single sentence uttered by a single speaker. It was probably above all a song form—its even number of lines is characteristic of Japanese song of all periods as contrasted with the odd number which became the rule in literate poetry—and it did not long survive the seventh century. The *Bussokuseki no uta,* or "Buddha's Foot-Stone poem"—so called from the stone stele in the shape of the Buddha's footprint on which most of the extant examples of the form are engraved—has six lines in the pattern 5-7-5-7-7-7. It may be considered a variant of the *tanka*: the last line is usually only a slightly altered repetition of the fifth; and the form perhaps derived from the practice of repeating the last line of a *tanka* when it was read or recited aloud. Finally, the *renga,* or "linked poem," was, in the early literary period and until the late twelfth century, simply a *tanka* whose first three lines were composed by one person, the last two by another. It was usually playful and was employed in gallant exchanges or in games of verse-capping. It was, however, the only one of the minor forms of early literary poetry to survive into the classical periods, and it must be recognized as an antecedent of the fully-developed linked verse in fifty or a hundred stanzas which became a major form from the fourteenth century through the eighteenth.

Just how and why Japanese prosody came to be defined in terms of five- and seven-syllable lines is a mystery that has never been satisfactorily explained, although two different explanations are commonly given. The first theory holds that twelve syllables—the number made up by a pair of such lines—is the average length of a breath unit in Japanese, that the five- and seven-syllable units are a natural outgrowth of what can only be called the genius of the language. The second theory is more plausible and historically probable, although the details are obscure: namely, that the Japanese fives and sevens developed by analogy with the common five- and seven-word lines of Chinese poetry. Certainly, the line-length was regularized during the seventh century when the Japanese were undergoing intensive Chinese influence. But one of the most remarkable characteristics of the developing tradition of vernacular poetry in this age of cultural inundation from China remains its very freedom from—one might almost say resistance to—direct Chinese influence. The Japanese poets seemed always conscious of the resources and limitations of their language and of its difference from the Chinese, and from the first they made a clear distinction between Chinese poetry, or *shi* (which they also wrote), and the native poetry, or *waka.* This consciousness led towards the end of the seventh century to the exclusion of all recognizably Chinese loan-words from the vocabulary of serious Japanese poetry. It also seems to have precluded any rash or grotesque attempts to derive tone patterns from the subtle variations of Japanese pitch accent, or to impose rhyme-schemes on the Japanese open syllables, in which only five rhymes are possible. In the ninth century, certain critics did produce sets of rules for the avoidance of "poetic ills" in a desperate attempt to provide for Japanese poetry some equivalent to the complicated taboos of Chinese, but most of the rules were ignored by the poets. Indeed, the only rule that was much regarded was a strict prohibition against end-rhyme in the third and fifth lines of the *tanka*. The Japanese borrowed rhetorical techniques, imagery, subjects, and esthetic ideals from the Chinese, but if they owe their syllabic fives and sevens to the analogy of Chinese poetry, this was about all they could profitably take for their prosody from such a totally different linguistic medium.

The Japanese syllabic meter of course needed to be controlled and varied by rhetorical and other means if it was not to become hopelessly singsong and monotonous, especially in the *chōka*. The best poets of the *chōka* often varied the form by marking divisions within the body of the poem by an extra seven-syllable line, or by inserting a short line of three or four syllables between the usual five- and seven-syllable pairs. Yamanoe Okura (ca. 660–733) was particularly given to this kind of metrical experimentation. However, after his time the *chōka* became metrically fixed and increasingly monotonous. By the thirteenth century the practice of adding or subtracting syllables came to be strictly limited: a line might be lengthened beyond the usual five or seven syllables only in the most exceptional circumstances, and a line almost never had fewer than either five or seven syllables. In the poetry of the age of the *Man'yōshū* there was a good deal more freedom: lines both shorter and longer than the norm are found, although the latter are far more numerous. Only rarely was a line lengthened by more than one syllable, however. Of the 4,100-odd *tanka* in the *Man'yōshū,* over 1,200 have more than thirty-one syllables. Only forty-three poems have fewer syllables than thirty-one; of these, thirty-nine poems have thirty syllables, four have twenty-nine. Of the *tanka* with more than thirty-one syllables, 1,060 poems have thirty-two syllables; 149 have thirty-three syllables, ten have thirty-four syllables. The most common variant, then, is the 32-syllable poem, and within this type the following syllabic patterns are found: 5–7–5–7–8, 442 poems; 6–7–5–7–7, 209 poems; 5–7–6–7–7, 188 poems; 5–7–5–8–7, ninety-seven poems. These are merely statistics and do not as far as is known represent literary fashions or a conscious aesthetic, but it is a fact that the first two patterns, with the extra syllable in either the first or the last line of the poem, remain the dominant irregular types in the *tanka* of later ages as well.

Probably in many cases two syllables in an irregularly long line were elided when the poem was recited or read aloud. Almost all lines containing an extra syllable have at least one syllable besides the first consisting of a single vowel, and this vowel—most commonly the fourth syllable—was presumably elided with the preceding syllable. Such lines as *Asana asana, Omoiide no, Hana no iro wa, Tago no ura ni* would thus be elided as *Asanasana, Omoide no, Hananiro wa,* and *Tagonura ni*. The only vowel not elided was *e,* perhaps because in most phonological environments it was pronounced with a perceptible initial *y*-glide. The most common position for the single elided vowel was the fourth syllable of a five-syllable line and the fifth syllable of a seven-syllable line. No prosodic rule governing elision was ever formulated, but the trend may represent a feeling of what was appropriate to produce a pleasing cadence.

Alliteration, consonance, and assonance are found in the earliest Japanese songs, and were used by poets of all periods to give richness, rhetorical complexity, and interest to their verse. Such techniques never became obligatory in any poetic form, nor were any rules ever formulated governing their use. Nevertheless, it is clear that they were used consciously and often with telling effect in some of the most highly esteemed poems of the tradition, as in this anonymous poem from the first imperial anthology, the *Kokinshū* (905):

Honobono to	Dimly, dimly
Akashi no ura no	In the morning mist that lies
Asagiri ni	Over Akashi Bay,
Shimagakureyuku	My longings follow with the ship
Fune o shi zo omou.	That vanishes behind the distant isle.

The heavy *o* and *a* sounds of the first two lines are varied in the third with the lighter *i* sounds, balanced against the *u* sounds of the fourth, and combined with them in the fifth. It should also be noted that the first and second and fourth and fifth lines rhyme. The rhyme contributes to the pleasing effect in this particular poem, but it would have been too unvaried and monotonous had it been used with any regularity. At any rate, this poem (piously attributed to Hitomaro by later poets although very unlike his characteristic style) was so highly valued that in the middle ages it was forbidden to use the adverbial phrase *honobono to* (dimly, dimly) in poetry because it had come to be regarded as the exclusive property of this particular composition.

The cadence of traditional Japanese poetry may be freely varied with a syntactic pause at the end of any or all of the lines of a poem. Internal caesura is almost never found. Lines of five and of seven syllables came in the course of time to be grouped characteristically in pairs marked by syntactic pause at the end of the second line. In the poetry of the *Man'yōshū*, particularly in the *chōka*, the dominant cadence was 5–7 (called *goshichichō*); towards the middle of the eighth century, the *tanka* and even the *chōka* began to show a tendency to group lines in the opposite fashion, and the 7–5 cadence (*shichigochō*) began to gain ground. The Japanese response to these two types of cadence is a feeling that the 5–7 cadence, with the pause coming at the end of the longer line, is more solemn, more elevated, more suited to the *chōka,* and expressive of the romanticized "spirit of the age" of early poetry. In the 7–5 cadence; the pause at the end of the shorter line creates the effect of evening the length of the lines, and is regarded as lighter, more onward-pressing, and more suited to the *tanka* of the sophisticated classical periods.

Whatever the virtues of the two types of cadence, the 7–5 cadence became dominant in the *chōka* during the period of its decline. The *tanka,* on the other hand, began to show a tendency to fall into two parts, with a syntactic pause at the end of the third line: 5–7–5: 7–7. The division was often marked by a participle at the end of the third line; by reversing the syntax and placing in the last two lines the clause that would normally come first; or by dividing the poem into a generalization in the first three lines followed by a syntactically unrelated symbolic description—often terminating in a noun—in the last two, as in this poem by the priest Saigyō (1118–90):

Kokoro naki	While denying his heart,
Mi ni wa aware wa	Even a priest cannot but know
Shirarekeri	The depths of a sad beauty:
Shigi tatsu sawa no	Snipe that rise to wing away
Aki no yūgure.	From a marsh at autumn twilight.

The classical critics called the two units created by the division of the *tanka* "upper verses" (*kami no ku*) and "lower verses" (*shimo no ku*), and recognized various ways of integrating them by rhetorical and other means, such as using in the lower verses images related to those in the upper ones. Critical disputes arose as to the relative merits of "closely related verses" (*shinku*) and "distantly related verses" (*soku*): the innovating poets of the last great period of classical *tanka* poetry in the fourteenth century tended to favor the latter, the conservatives the former.

The 7–5 cadence did not become fully realized in the *tanka* until the twelfth century. In this period—the age of the eighth imperial anthology, the *Shinkokinshū*—the innovating poets began to fragment the *tanka* into smaller units by often using syntactic pause at the end of the first line and sometimes also at the end of the fourth. The second and third lines usually formed a single syntactic unit, however, and the 7–5 cadence was felt in these lines. The following poem, "On the Spirit of Travel," by Fujiwara Ariie (1155–1216) shows the 7–5 cadence of the second and third lines, but also the extreme fragmentation often found in the *tanka* of the age:

Fushiwabinu	I slept in suffering.
Shino no ozasa no	From the cuttings of the small bamboos
Karimakura	An instant's pillow:
Hakana no tsuyu ya	The transience of dew and tears!
Hitoyo bakari ni.	The anguish of a single night.

The first line is a complete sentence; the second and third are a series of three nouns joined by possessive particles, syntactically unrelated to the following lines; the fourth line ends in an exclamatory particle; and at the end of the fifth is of course the pause that comes with the end of the poem.

Although Ariie's poem is integrated by rhetorical and other means, its extreme fragmentation is a prosodic fact: he has broken up the onward-pressing, fluid Japanese syntax into short syntactic units of strongly end-stopped lines. There are a number of possible explanations for this trend in the poetry of the age. The growing popularity of descriptive poetry led poets to use a larger proportion of nouns and fewer verbs; the search for originality of treatment in a poetry whose diction and subject matter had become largely fixed by tradition encouraged them to experiment with those aspects of their poetry, such as cadence, which were not fixed by rule. It is also possible that Chinese poetry had some influence. Whatever the Chinese response to the cadences of their own verse, to the Japanese it seemed fragmented and choppy—although the great prestige of Chinese culture ensured that such a characteristic would be regarded as a virtue by Japanese poets taught to admire Chinese literature. The syntactic fragmentation of the *tanka* may be in part the result of an effort to produce an equivalent in Japanese poetry to the caesuras and end-stopped lines of the Chinese.

Such extreme fragmentation as we have seen in Ariie's poem was never more than one of a number of possible styles, however, and he and the other poets of his age composed many poems with the smoother cadences of earlier poetry. But the syntactic division of the *tanka* into two parts remained dominant, as did the 7–5 cadence of the second and third lines. The 7–5 cadence was also followed in most forms of popular song, religious hymns, and in the poetic passages of the *nō* drama which came into prominence in the fourteenth century. It was rigorously followed in the *imayō,* a popular song form of the twelfth century consisting of four pairs of seven- and five-syllable lines. Generally speaking, the 7–5 cadence has persisted down to modern times in all forms of popular song, as well as in the verse passages of *nō* and of the *jōruri* puppet drama and the *kabuki* which became popular in the seventeenth century. There are some exceptions: one variety of medieval popular song has four lines of seven syllables each; and the *dodoitsu,* a popular song form that developed in the seventeenth century, also contains four lines in the pattern 7–7–7–5.

The division of the *tanka* into upper and lower verses contributed with other literary developments not related to prosody to the rise of a new form of learned poetry to which we have already referred—the *renga,* or linked verse—which came into prominence in the fourteenth century and was practiced widely until the middle of the nineteenth. As we have seen, originally, a *renga* was merely a *tanka* whose first three lines were composed by one person and last two by another. As such, it had been recognized as a separate "form" and had been included in imperial anthologies. During the thirteenth century, however, the custom grew for poets to gather in twos and threes after formal poetry contests or parties to compose fairly long linked poems (*kusarirenga,* or "chain *renga*"), alternating stanzas of 5–7–5 and 7–7 syllables. Each participant would produce a stanza of his own as a possibility for each link; the best stanza would then be selected by an umpire and added to the lengthening chain. At first there were no fixed rules for length or for the techniques of linking each successive stanza to the preceding. The verses were often humorous, and the practice was looked upon as a game, an accompaniment to drinking and relaxing after the formalities of serious poetic composition. But what began in jest came to be pursued in earnest, and during the fourteenth century two kinds of linked verse came to be distinguished: serious *renga,* which rigorously preserved the decorum, the diction, and the conventions of subject and treatment of the *tanka* tradition; and *haikai,* or "unconventional verses," which retained some of the playfulness of the early informal linked verse and permitted a much freer diction, including colloquialisms and Chinese loan-words, which were taboo in the *tanka* and serious *renga*. Both varieties of linked verse came to be governed by almost incredibly complex rules for the handling of imagery, the appearance in certain stanzas of words associated with the seasons and various human affairs, the relationship, rhetorical and otherwise, of one stanza to the next, and the like. Forms of fixed length also were established for both *haikai* and *renga*. Thirty and fifty stanzas were common lengths, but 100 stanzas became popular in the fourteenth century and continued to be the most common length thereafter until displaced by the thirty-six stanza *Kasen* in the seventeenth century.

Detailed rules were necessary for *renga* composition if it were not to fall into anarchy and the resulting composition be utterly incomprehensible and disorganized. And in devising their rules, the *renga* masters often required or made explicit practices that had been optional or implicit in the *tanka* tradition. Such *renga* rules as that the first stanza must end in a full stop and the third in a participle made requirements of syntactic patterns that had been common but optional in the upper verses of the *tanka.*

From the fifteenth century, *renga* (including *haikai*) became the dominant form of Japanese learned poetry and more popular than the *tanka,* although the latter continued to be composed in great numbers. And once the rules were established, a single poet would often compose a whole *renga* by himself. The *hokku,* or first stanza, was considered the most important, and collections of famous first stanzas of *renga* and *haikai* were made for poets to study and emulate. From this practice and from the habit of composing first stanzas for practice, the *hokku* came to be regarded as a kind of separate form—the briefest form of Japanese poetry—in the pattern 5–7–5 syllables. In the nineteenth century a new name for the form came into common use: *haiku,* a combination of the first character used to write *haikai* and the second of *hokku.* Although most of the famous *haiku* of the great master Bashō (1644–94) were actually first stanzas composed for *haikai* or *renga,* he did compose independent *hokku,* often interspersing them through prose narratives of his travels throughout Japan. From the time of Bashō the *haiku* gained increasing popularity, and in modern times it has been the most popular form of Japanese poetry among the masses.

The meter of the *renga* and *haiku* might be varied in the same manner as in the *tanka.* The poets often used irregular lines containing more, or occasionally fewer, syllables than the normal five or seven. Such an example as the following *hokku* by Bashō in the pattern 8–8–4 is, however, very unusual.

Higekaze o fuite	The wind in his beard,
Boshū tanzuru wa	He who grieves for autumn's death—
Ta ga ko zo.	Whose child is he?

The *haiku* form is so brief that, unlike the *tanka,* it can give little effect of a protracted, melodic flow. At the same time, the cadence was frequently broken and the *haiku* fragmented into two or three separate or even unrelated syntactic units. Frequently, "cutting words" (*kireji*)—exclamatory particles, final indicative verb terminations, and the like—were used to end-stop lines; sometimes the lines were simply juxtaposed with no syntactic relation between them. Bashō's most famous *hokku* is an example:

Furuike ya	The ancient pond:
Kawazu tobikomu	A frog jumps in—
Mizu no oto.	The sound of water.

The poem has a "cutting word"—the exclamatory particle *ya*—at the end of the first line; the second line is a complete, independent sentence; and the third is a syntactic fragment simply juxtaposed to it.

In the late feudal period, from the seventeenth to the middle of the nineteenth century, a revival of interest in the *Man'yōshū* began with the work of the "National Scholars" (*Kokugakusha*), who in addition to performing feats of scholarship composed poems in the "*Man'yō* style," imitating its diction and attempting to restore to the *tanka* the old 5–7 cadence. Their enthusiasm was inherited by the most influential traditional poet of the nineteenth century, Masaoka Shiki (1867–1902), who extravagantly admired the *Man'yōshū* and advocated its styles and rhythms. As a result, a good deal of poetry—including even *chōka*—using the rhythms of the eighth century has been produced by his many followers in modern times.

In addition to the continuation of traditional forms and the imitation of older styles in the modern period, the experience of contact with the West opened up a new poetic world to the Japanese. English, French, and German poems were enthusiastically read, studied, and translated. Soon Japanese poets began to write poems of their own patterned on the longer forms of Western verse. In 1882 the *Shintaishishō,* or "Anthology of Poetry in the New Style," was published. It contained translations from Shakespeare, Tennyson, Longfellow, and Kingsley, as well as original poems by the compilers.

Many poets of the new age have tended to reject, or at least show impatience with, the traditional forms of Japanese poetry, and various reform movements have sprung up, seeking to abolish the fixed prosody of the *tanka* and *haiku* and substitute for it a "free meter" (*jiyūritsu*). The efforts of the reformers have been more productive of theory than of practical results, however, and the basic question of what constitutes a *tanka* or *haiku* in "free meter" has never been satisfactorily answered. The poets who have translated Western poetry and attempted to create new forms for the Japanese have tried everything from the traditional syllabic prosody to free verse. In the 1880's and '90's, the poets of the *Shintaishishō* used the traditional line lengths and the dominant 7–5 cadence both in their translations and in their own poems, although the length of the poem as a whole and the division of it into stanzas was a new departure. Experiments with new line lengths followed—8–7, 8–6, and even such combinations as 3–9 were tried. Run-on lines and internal caesura were also taken over from Western poetry. In general, an attempt was made to use metrical units of varying length but at the same time regular enough to convey an impression of verse rhythm. Two or more of these units were often combined in a line, either with or without syntactic pause between the units. The arrangement often seems artificial and arbitrary, but the printed lines of the new Japanese poetry, at any rate, came to approximate the longer lines of Western verse.

It is French poetry, particularly that of the Symbolists and later groups—surrealists, Dadaists, and the like—that has awakened the most enthusiastic response among the modern Japanese poets. The admiration for French symbolist poetry was doubtless evoked in part because, prosody aside, it is closer in spirit to classical Japanese verse than any other Western poetry. At any rate, in their translations from the French and then in poems of their own, the Japanese experimented with poems in free verse and in prose, and these continue to be written in large numbers today. Alliteration, consonance, assonance, and various kinds of onomatopoeia (in which the Japanese colloquial language abounds) are used with great skill and effect, and help to give structure to some of the more amorphous forms. At the same time, the older syllabic fives and sevens continued to be used by most poets until the 1920's, and they still persist today. Yet of the traditional forms, *renga* and *haikai* are no longer composed except by a handful of scholars, and the *tanka* and *haiku,* though still extremely popular among amateurs and the general public, have not been much practiced by professional poets since the early years of this century. On the whole, the future seems to lie with the longer, freer forms of modern poetry, but it may be said that the Japanese have not yet succeeded in developing a new prosody as satisfactory as their traditional fives and sevens.

SELECTED BIBLIOGRAPHY

Brower, Robert H., and Earl Miner. *Japanese Court Poetry*. Stanford: Stanford Univ. Press, 1961. Treats prosody and other formative principles of Japanese classical poetry in terms of both constant features (Chs. i and ii) and of the development and cumulative tradition of Court poetry between ca. A.D. 550 and 1350, that is, from the age of primitive song through the last of the great classical periods (Chs. iii-vi).

Bownas, Geoffrey and Anthony Thwaite. *The Penguin Book of Japanese Verse*. London and New York: Penguin, 1964. The Introduction provides an easily accessible discussion of prosody and other characteristics of Japanese poetry.

Miller, Roy Andrew. *The Japanese Language*. Chicago: Univ of Chicago Press, 1967. A detailed and authoritative discussion and analysis of all aspects of the Japanese language, both classical and modern.

BIBLICAL HEBREW

By PERRY B. YODER

The Line

Although the corpus of classical Hebrew poetry—comprising at least one third of the Hebrew Bible—spans a period of roughly 800 years, from the twelfth to the fourth century B.C.E., Hebrew poetic form and vocabulary appear to have remained fairly stable.[1] Throughout this time the basic structural unit within the poem was the line, which was usually divided into two parts or cola by a caesura, although it was sometimes divided into three cola by two caesuras. Normally the caesura was marked by both semantic and syntactic juncture, each colon being essentially an independent unit. This customary lack of enjambment is a striking feature of Hebrew poetry. These features of the poetry are illustrated by Hosea xi.8: "How can-I-give-you-up, O-Ephraim || how can-I-hand-you-over, O-Israel."[2] The caesura is clearly marked, the second colon being a repetition both semantically and syntactically of the first.

The caesura, however, does not always fall in the middle of the line, as in this example. More commonly it occurs after the middle, only rarely before. Lamentations iii.11 is an example of such an unbalanced line with the caesura coming after the middle: "He-led-me-off my-way and-tore-me-to-pieces || he-has-made-me desolate." Although the line is unbalanced (three words in the first colon, two in the second), the caesura is no less clearly marked by syntax and semantics than in the balanced line quoted above.

Some lines, however, do not contain such semantic and syntactic breaks, and it may be doubted whether in such cases caesuras do in fact occur; for example, Amos i.3: "Because-they-have-threshed Gilead with-threshing-sledges of-iron." Unlike the English translation, the Hebrew places "Gilead" at the end of the line, preceded by the sign of the accusative. By this formal arrangement, the poet presumably is indicating the unity of the line. A further example is provided by Jeremiah v.17, whose different structural nature is readily apparent when seen in juxtaposition to the segmented line that precedes it in the text:

They-shall-eat-up your-flocks and-your-herds || they-shall-eat-up your-vines and-your-fig-trees. (v.16)

Your-fortified cities in which you trust they-shall-destroy with-the-sword. (v.17)

In the first line (16) the placement of the caesura is clearly marked, while in the second (17) there is neither semantic nor syntactic reduplication to mark the occurrence of a caesura. Furthermore, the placing of the instrument "sword" at the end of the line, while the verb "destroy" in the Hebrew, begins the line, would seem again to indicate the unitary, unsegmented nature of the line.

But such long lines, segmented or unsegmented, were not the only structural units used by the poet in constructing a poem. Units of less than line length, often having the length of a colon or half a line, are also found. Sometimes these short lines are introductory, as the phrase "Thus says the-LORD" often is. A short line may also be used in an exclamatory or rhetorical manner as in Amos ii.11: "Is-it not indeed-so, O-people of-Israel?"[3]

In Hebrew poetry, then, we need to reckon with three different types of line: the segmented, the unsegmented, and the short. The great majority of lines in Hebrew poetry are segmented, either balanced or unbalanced. But what creates the impression that the cola are joined to one another to form segmented lines rather than independent units like the short or the unsegmented line?

Semantic Parallelism

The technique by which the cola are linked together so that they seem to form segments of one line was first clearly delineated by Oxford professor of poetry Robert Lowth in 1753, when he declared parallelism of members to be the basic prosodic feature of Hebrew poetry.[4] Following in Lowth's footsteps, students of Hebrew poetry have distinguished two major types of parallelism: semantic parallelism and formal or structural parallelism. In semantic parallelism the thoughts expressed or the words used in the first colon of the line are echoed either positively or negatively in the second colon of the line. In what is called "structural parallelism" there is a syntactic or metrical similarity between the cola of the line, but no semantic parallel.

Lowth classified the cola of lines with semantic parallelism as either synonymous or antithetic. Synonymous parallelism occurs "when the same sentiment is repeated in different, but equivalent terms" (Lowth, p. 205). As an example, Psalms cxiv.1 is cited: "When-Israel went-forth from-Egypt || the-house of-Jacob from-a-people of-strange-language." If letters were substituted for the members of the first colon, with primes representing parallel members in the second colon, the scansion would be a.b.c.||a′c′. or, since in the second colon each member actually contains two words, it would be more accurate to represent it as a.b.c.||a′2 c′2, the number representing the number of words in each parallel member.

Antithetic parallelism occurs, on the other hand, "when a thing is illustrated by its contrary being opposed to it" (Lowth, p. 210). Antithetic parallelism is characteristic of the book of Proverbs in, for example, x.1: "A-wise son makes-a-glad father || but-a-foolish son is-a-sorrow to-his-mother." The scansion here is a.b.c.d.||a′b′c′d′. An interesting feature of this couplet is that the terms "father" and "mother" complement each other and together form a unit which exhausts the category of parents. The force of each half-line applies to both "father" and "mother." Since the expression "father and mother" occurs frequently in prose (for example, in the Decalogue), we can regard the device used here as the breakup of a fixed pair or stereotyped expression.

A third type of semantic relationship between the cola of a line has been named "emblematic" by Briggs, who added this category to the two of Lowth.[5] As the lines below illustrate, one colon furnishes an emblem or simile for the other colon:

> Like a-gold ring in-a-swine's snout || is-a-beautiful woman without discretion. (Proverbs xi.22)
> (Scansion: a2.b2. || a′2 b′2)
>
> As-a-father pities his-children || so-the-LORD pities those-who-fear-him. (Psalms ciii.13)
> (Scansion: a.b.c.||a′b′c′)

Lines whose cola are bound together by semantic parallelism can be described not only according to the semantic relationship between the members of the cola, but also according to the arrangement of the members. In the line: "Ephraim shall-not be-jealous of-Judah || and-Judah shall-not harass Ephraim" (Isaiah xi.13) (scansion: a.b2.c. || c.b′2.a) the two cola are bound together by synonymous parallelism. But since there is a reversal in the order of the first and last members of the two cola, this line has a chiastic arrangement of members (Briggs, I, xxxvii).

Another formal category of semantic parallelism is repetitive parallelism, in which the second colon repeats a word or words from the first.[6] Usually the repeated material occurs at the beginning of the cola, as in Judges v.12: "Awake, awake, Deborah || awake, awake, utter a-song." If in the scansion we represent a repeated member with the same letter, but without prime, we have a.a.b. || a.a.c. Although the second colon resumes the initial word(s) of the first colon, in most cases it carries the thought beyond the point reached at the end of the first colon; thus:

Awake, awake, Deborah
Awake, awake, utter a-song

This has been termed "stairlike" parallelism, since the second line extends semantically beyond the first, forming a stairlike outline (Briggs, I, xxxvii). Repetitive parallelism often occurs in lines possessing three cola, as in Psalms xciii.3: "The-floods have-lifted-up, O-LORD || the-floods have-lifted-up their-voice || the-floods lift-up their-roaring." The scansion (a.b.c. || a.b.d. || a.b′.d′.) makes clear that the last two cola of the line are parallel to each other. The second colon advances the thought of the line beyond that of the first, but the third does not advance beyond the second.[7]

As we have seen, lines having semantic parallelism show this either completely or incompletely.[8] Incomplete parallelism occurs in two basic variations, with and without compensation. Isaiah i.26 illustrates incomplete parallelism without compensation: "And-I-will-restore your-judges as-at-the-first || and-your-counsellors as-at-the-beginning" (scansion: a.b.c. || b′c′). There is no verb (a′) in the second colon to correspond to the verb (a) in the first. Compensation corrects this imbalance but without completing the parallelism as Amos i.2 demonstrates: "The-LORD roars from-Zion || and-utters his-voice from-Jerusalem" (scansion: a.b.c. || b′ 2 c′). The parallelism is incomplete (there is no parallel for "LORD" in the second colon), but by the expansion of one of its members, the second colon has become as long as the first, thus compensating for its incompleteness. Alternatively, instead of expanding one of the parallel members, the poet may introduce something new into the second colon of the line. In Psalms ciii.15 there is only one parallel member in the second colon binding the two cola together; the rest are new terms: "As-for-man his-days *are like grass* || he-flourishes *like-a-flower of-the-field*" (scansion: a.b.c. || d.c′ 2).

The various types of semantic parallelism discussed thus far occur within the line and are known as internal parallelism in contrast to external parallelism, the semantic parallelism that occurs between lines. Isaiah vi.10 contains two tri-cola displaying both internal and external parallelism.

Make-fat the-heart of-this people ||
and-their-ears heavy ||
and-their-eyes shut.*

Lest they-see with their-eyes ||
and-hear with-their-ears ||
and-understand with-their-hearts and-turn
and-be healed.

Both within and between the tri-cola the synonymous parallelism of "heart," "ears," and "eyes" occurs. In the external parallelism we also have chiasm: "heart" occurs first in the first line, but last in the second, while "eyes" occurs last in the first line, and first in the second.

Fixed Parallel Pairs

A further feature of the semantic parallelism of members is the occurrence of stereotypical parallelistic expressions, first clearly noted and described in conjunction with the study of Ugaritic poetry.[9] Students of Ugaritic discovered many phrases and expressions, especially poetic ones, which were familiar to them from the Hebrew Bible. Especially striking were occurrences of the same words as parallel members in both Hebrew and Ugaritic.[10] These expressions came to be called fixed word pairs or A-B terms. One member occurred in the A or first colon of the line, while the second occurred in the B or second colon. The parallel B member may be the A member repeated rather than a different word, as in the examples of repetitive parallelism given above (Judges v.12 and Psalms xciii.3). Several occurrences of the common fixed pair "mountains||hills" (*harîm*||*g*^{e}*ḇa*^{c}*ôṯ*) will illustrate the phenomenon:

Against all the-high *mountains* ||
and-against all the-lofty *hills*; (Isaiah ii.14)

I-looked-on the-*mountains* and-lo, they-were-quaking ||
and-all the-*hills* moved-to-and-fro. (Jeremiah iv.24)

They-sacrifice on the-tops of-*mountains* ||
and-make-offerings upon the-*hills*. (Hosea iv.13)

The-*mountains* shall-drip sweet-wine ||
and-all the-*hills* shall-flow-with-it. (Amos ix.13)

Altogether this word pair occurs eighteen times in Hebrew poetry and, except for Jeremiah iii.23, always in this order. In fact, "hills" (*g^{e}bāʿôt*) occurs only four times in poetry apart from "mountains" (*hārîm*). The Hebrew poets shared with the Ugaritic poets the practice of utilizing a corpus of fixed parallel expressions, some common to the tradition and some private to the individual poet, to compose lines with parallel cola. By the use of these fixed pairs, the poet was aided in the composition of his lines, for they solved for him two major prosodic requirements of Hebrew poetry: first, the binding together of cola to form lines, and second, the composing of B cola parallel to the A cola. Two cola sharing a fixed pair would be recognized as a unit, and the second colon would be related parallelistically to the first. These word pairs are not merely a "stylistic" feature of the poetry, but a compositional one, underscoring the parallelistic nature of the poetic tradition.[11]

Structural Parallelism

Not all lines with the caesura in Hebrew poetry exhibit semantic parallelism of members. In some there are no fixed pairs, nor are there semantic correspondences between the members of the cola composing the line. Lines of this nature are said, however, to exhibit "structural" parallelism, or, as Lowth phrased it, "synthetic parallelism": lines "in which the sentences answer to each other, not by the iteration of the same image or sentiment, or the opposition of their contraries, but merely by the form of their construction" (Lowth, p. 211). Depending on the relationship in length between the cola, these lines are said to be either "balancing" or "echoing." That is, they show either "complete" or "incomplete" parallelism, respectively.[12] In balancing parallelism there are an equal number of terms in each colon of the line, while in echoing there is one less term in the second than in the first. A normal scansion for these two types would be a.b.c.||d.e.f. and a.b.c.|| d.e. The following examples show the distinction between semantic parallelism and merely structural parallelism.

Weeping may-tarry for-the-night ||
  but-joy with-the-morning.* (Psalms xxx.5)

The-fool says in-his-heart ||
  "There-is-no God." (Psalms xiv.1)

Meter

The lines of Hebrew poetry, as we have just seen, can be described as conforming to one of two patterns, either X/X (balanced) or X/X-1 (unbalanced), X representing the number of terms in the first cola, usually varying from two to four. Since most lines of Hebrew poetry follow one of these two patterns, the poets, presumably, had as one of their objectives to produce lines whose cola conformed to these patterns. This appearance of measuredness strongly supports the contention that meter is a prosodic feature of Hebrew poetry.[13] In fact, some Hebrew poetry has admitted a quite regular metrical scansion.[14]

In previous centuries, under the influence of classical models, metrical theories based on syllable length (quantity) were developed, but in modern times the consensus among those who allow meter in Hebrew poetry is that it is accentual.[15] Opinion differs, however, as to what type of accentual meter is present. Some theorists hold that the word is the basic metrical unit;[16] others count the number of major accents and see the number of unaccented syllables as relatively unimportant.[17] Yet others argue that Hebrew poetry had "feet," and that thus the number of unaccented syllables is important. Within this last group there is a further controversy as to the type of foot, some contending it is a two-syllable foot with alternating accented and unaccented syllables,[18] others, that it is a three-syllable anapestic foot.[19] In contrast, then, to parallelism, the occurrence and basic nature of which are recognized by all, there is little consensus regarding meter. Its very existence is denied;[20] among those who affirm it there is only limited agreement as to its nature; and it is argued that it must have changed in the course of time through changes in the pronunciation of the language.[21]

Much of this debate results from our ignorance of the pronunciation of classical Hebrew and its changes during the period when the poetry was composed. Even if such data could be reconstructed, the manner in which the poetry was read or recited, with elisions, wrenched accents, and the like, would remain unknown. Lowth, who believed that some form of meter did occur in Hebrew, was agnostic with respect to its actual nature. "As to the real quantity, the rhythm, or modulation, these from the present state of the language, seem to be altogether unknown, and even to admit of no investigation by human art or industry." Consequently, he thought that "he who attempts to restore the true and genuine Hebrew versification, erects an edifice without a foundation" (Lowth, pp. 44, 45). To be sure, knowledge of the Hebrew language has advanced beyond that of Lowth's day, but not yet sufficiently to allow a satisfactory solution to the problem of meter in Hebrew poetry.

Four embarrassments seem endemic to the inquiry and indicate that Lowth's agnosticism is still in order. One, which is often quite striking, is the number of emendations necessary to shape recalcitrant texts to a metrical theory. These emendations often include not only changes in pronunciation and syllable count within the word, but also the deletion and addition of words, and the transposition of words, phrases, and lines.[22] A second is the apparent need to disregard parallelism and syntax for the sake of meter. For example, Sievers scans Amos iii.2 as follows:

> You only have I known of all the families of the earth; therefore, I will punish
> You for all your iniquities.[23]

This scansion ignores syntax, creates enjambment between the two lines, which is abnormal in Hebrew poetry, and ignores the natural parallelism of the line. It should scan:

> You only have I known of the families of the earth ||
> therefore I will punish you for all your iniquities.

"Know/punish," in fact, form a fixed parallel pair, occurring again in Job v.24 and xxxv.15.

A third embarrassment is the number of rules necessary to describe the metrics of Hebrew poetry—rules which are sometimes contradictory, or so general as to allow any syllable to receive the stress, the number and placement being determined seemingly by the theory.[24] Occasionally the rules appear to have been generated to bring theory and text together, a metrical counterpart of textual emendation. A fourth embarrassment has been the difficulty of distinguishing between prose and poetry on a metrical basis. Indeed Sievers, having developed his metrical system, proceeded to scan the book of Genesis as verse.[25] Metrical theory, at least in this instance, has not isolated the prosodic feature of Hebrew poetry, the manner in which the poet manipulated his language to create verse rather than prose.

To return to the proportional relationship between cola within the line which has been noted above, it may be presumed, since the balance or unbalance is between cola, that meter ought to be approached from the perspective of the colon. The colon may then be regarded as the metrical unit, rather than some smaller unit like the foot, with parallelism creating a rhythmic accentual balance between the cola of the line. Most lines of Hebrew poetry have their members organized, as we have seen, according to one of two basic rhythmic patterns—either a balancing stress pattern (X/X) or an unbalanced stress pattern in which the second colon is one word short (X/X-1). Which words are to be stressed within the cola, and the number of these stresses, is determined by the parallelism of members within the line.[26]

To what extent these two rhythmic forms were a prosodic requirement is a question. The presence of fixed pairs which have words of unequal length, the longer word being found in the short colon—apparently to make it similar in length to the longer colon—and the phenomenon of incomplete parallelism with compensation would seem to attest such a requirement. An example, used above in another connection, illustrates these features: "The LORD roars from-Zion || and-utters his-voice from-Jerusalem" (Amos i.2) (scansion: a.b.c.||b/2.c/). Since the poet does not repeat the subject, "the-LORD," in the second colon, it will be short, unless he compensates, which he does. First, he uses a compound member as a parallel for a simple member—"utters voice" as a mate for "roar"—second, he uses a longer word in the second colon—"Jerusalem" in contrast to "Zion" in the first. The poet presumably is attempting to stretch the second colon to make it more nearly balance the first, which in fact it does, conforming to an X/X (3/3) rhythmic pattern.

But the evidence is not unambiguous. First, "utters voice" occurs only as a B parallel to "roars," never as its A parallel, regardless of whether the sequence balances the line or not. Jeremiah xxv.30 is an instance where this sequence makes the second colon longer than the first: "The-LORD will-roar from-on-high||and-from-his-holy habitation utter his-voice" (scansion: a.b.c.||c/2 b/2). In this line the abnormal pattern X/X+1 (3/4) could easily have been converted into one of the normal rhythmic patterns, X/X−1, if the poet had reversed the traditional sequence of "roars/utters voice," thereby placing the compound member in the first colon. Evidently the sequence of words within this fixed pair received a higher priority than the balancing of cola within the line.[27]

A similar example is the fixed pair "kindle fire/devour," in which the compound term occurs in the first colon rather than the second.

And-I-will-kindle a-fire in-the-wall of-Damascus ||
and-it-shall-devour the-strongholds of-Ben Hadad. (Jeremiah xlix.27).
(Scansion: a2.b.c.||a/b/c/).

so-I-will-kindle a-fire in-the-wall of-Rabbah ||
and-it-shall-devour her-strongholds. (Amos i.14)
(scansion: a2.b.c.||a/b/)

In the first line, the compound member produces a normal unbalanced X/X—1 (4/3) rhythmic pattern, but in the second, an abnormal X/X—2 (4/2) rhythmic pattern. Here again the sequence of terms appears to override considerations concerning the rhythmic pattern.

Even more instructive are cases in which one of the words in a compound member is dropped when its very presence would yield a normal rhythmic pattern. For example, the fixed pair "shepherds/lords of-the-flock" occurs in a balanced line in Jeremiah xxv.34: "Wail, you-shepherds, and-cry || and-roll-in-ashes you-lords of-the-flock" (scansion: a.b.c.||a/b2/). But in Nahum iii.18 the second colon is short, and the B term instead of being a compound member as above, consists of only a single word: "Your-shepherds are-asleep, O-king of-Assyria||your-lords slumber" (scansion: a.b.c2.||a/b/). If the poet had desired to create one of the normal rhythmic patterns, he could easily, it seems, have added "of-the-flock" after "lords" in the second colon, as the poet in Jeremiah did, producing thereby a normal pattern of X/X—1.

Thus the evidence is inconsistent. It does not seem that composing lines with cola possessing the rhythmic patterns of X/X and X/X—1 was a strong prosodic requirement of Hebrew poetry. The poet was not under constraint to manipulate the parallelistic stereotypes—the fixed pairs—of the Hebrew poetic tradition in order to produce these rhythmic patterns.

A better understanding of the poetic conventions involved in the use of these fixed compositional units is needed. From an understanding of how the Hebrew poets used these fixed pairs it may yet be possible to trace the outlines of the prosodic matrices around which the poet shaped his language in creating verse.[28] Abandoning the guide of parallelism has proved fatal in the past to certain metrical theories; by the same token, ignoring the insight gained through the study of fixed pairs will limit the validity of future theories of Hebrew prosody. For whatever fixed pairs may indicate about meter, it seems certain that they were in part created and preserved to meet the prosodic exigencies involved in creating Hebrew poetry. Thus parallelism, for whose sake the fixed pairs were developed, is a fundamental prosodic feature of Hebrew verse. One of its by-products, it seems at present, was the normal rhythmic pattern X/X and X/X−1, to which the majority of Hebrew poetic lines conform.

NOTES

1. A discussion of the poetic vocabulary is found in Matitiahu Tsevat, *A Study of the Language of the Biblical Psalms* (Nashville: Abingdon Press, 1955).
2. Quotations are from the Revised Standard Version, with minor changes in punctuation and the addition of the caesura bar. The dashes between words denote single words in Hebrew. Due to English word order, in some cases words thus joined may not represent the exact Hebrew units, but the number of units will be the same, which is sufficient for our purposes. In the few cases where changes other than punctuation are made in the translation, an asterisk follows the verse.
3. See Georg Fohrer, "Über den Kurzvers," *Zeitschrift für die Alttestamentliche Wissenschaft,* 66 (1954), 199–236, for a discussion of other uses and types of these unsegmented poetic units.
4. *De Sacra Poesi Hebraeorum,* trans. G. Gregory (London, 1839), Ch. xix, For the work of earlier scholars, see Brooks Waggoner, "Studies in Hebrew Poetry with Special Reference to the Contributions of Robert Lowth" (Diss. Duke, 1951), and Luis Alonso-Schökel, *Estudios de poética hebrea* (Barcelona: Juan Flors, 1963).
5. Charles Briggs, *A Critical and Exegetical Commentary on the Book of Psalms,* I (Edinburgh: T. & T. Clark, 1906), xxxvi.
6. William F. Albright, *Yahweh and the Gods of Canaan* (London: Athlone Press, 1968), Ch. i. A thorough discussion of this type of parallelism is found here along with the implications it has for dating Hebrew poems.
7. Samuel Loewenstam, in "The Expanded Colon in Ugaritic and Biblical Verse," *Journal of Semitic Studies,* 14 (1969), 176–96, analyzes this line type in detail.
8. George B. Gray, *The Forms of Hebrew Poetry* (London: Hodder & Stoughton, 1915), esp. p. 75.
9. Ugaritic, the language of ancient Ugarit, is closely related to Hebrew, and the poetry of Ugaritic, like that of Hebrew, has parallelism of members. For a description of the language and its poetry, see Cyrus Gordon, *Ugaritic Textbook,* Analecta Orientalia 38 (Rome: Pontificum Institutum Biblicum, 1965).
10. This phenomenon was first noted by Ginsberg in Harold L. Ginsberg and Benjamin Maisler, "Semitized Hurrians in Syria and Palestine," *Journal of the Palestine Oriental Society,* 14 (1934), 248, n. 15. In two subsequent articles, "The Victory of the Land-God Over the Sea-God," *JPOS,* 15 (1935), and "The Rebellion and Death of Baᶜlu," *Orientalia,* N.S. 5 (1936), he delineated more precisely the nature of these fixed pairs. U. (M.D.) Cassuto picked up the discussion, listing 22 such pairs in his article, "Biblical Literature and Ugaritic Literature" (Hebrew), in *Tarbiẓ,* 14 (1943). In subsequent articles he and others have

greatly expanded these early lists. The latest and most complete list is to be found in Dahood's Grammar of the Psalter in Psalms iii of the Anchor Bible series (1970).

11. Ginsberg saw this in 1945 when he wrote, "In order to meet the exigencies of such prosody [parallelism of cola], the Canaanite and Hebrew poets have some fixed pairs of synonymous words or phrases for certain concepts which poets have frequent occasion to express (e.g., head, eternity, to fear, to rejoice)." "Ugaritic Studies and the Bible," *The Biblical Archeologist Reader*, II (Garden City, N.Y.: Doubleday, 1964), 48, reprinted from *The Biblical Archeologist*, 8 (1945). That these fixed pairs are the result of a tradition of oral composition has been suggested by Stanley Gevirtz, *Patterns in the Early Poetry of Israel* (Chicago: Univ. of Chicago Press, 1963), pp. 3 ff. and at greater length by William Whallon, first in "Formulaic Poetry in the Old Testament," *Comparative Literature*, 15 (1963), 1–14, and more recently in *Formula, Character and Context* (Washington, D.C.: Center for Hellenic Studies, 1969). A comprehensive treatment of this topic appears in Perry Yoder, "Fixed Word Pairs and the Composition of Hebrew Poetry," Diss. Univ. of Pennsylvania 1970.

12. Gray, *Forms of Hebrew Poetry*, p. 75.

13. Lowth had noted also the regularity of line length in the alphabetic poem (where each successive line or set of lines begins with the next letter of the alphabet) as evidence of meter in Hebrew poetry (p. 40). A further clue cited by Lowth, that of "poetic forms"—linguistic forms occurring only in poetry—was demonstrated by Eduard König to be false. These forms destroy metrical uniformity as often as they aid it. See Eduard König, *Stilistik, Rhetorik, Poetik in Bezug auf die biblische Literatur* (Leipzig: Dieterich, 1900), pp. 332 ff. David Freedman has since argued the significance of at least archaic forms in Hebrew poetry, in "Archaic Forms in Early Hebrew Poetry," *ZAW*, 72 (1960), 101–07.

14. William H. Cobb, *A Criticism of Systems of Hebrew Metre* (Oxford: Oxford Univ. Press, 1905), p. 16.

15. For the history of systems of meter, see the works cited in n. 4 and the articles of Israel Baroway, "The Bible as Poetry in English Renaissance: An Introduction," *JEGP*, 32 (1933), 447–80; "The Hebrew Hexameter: A Study in Renaissance Sources and Interpretation," *ELH*, 2 (1935), 66–91; "The Lyre of David: A Further Study in Renaissance Interpretation of Biblical Form," *ELH*, 8 (1941), 119–43; and "The Accentual Theory of Hebrew Prosody: A Further Study in Renaissance Interpretation of Biblical Form," *ELH*, 17 (1950), 115–35.

16. In this and the following notes, for reasons of space, only certain representatives of the various positions will be cited, along with selected items of bibliography. Hans Kosmala argues for the word as the basic metrical unit; see "Form and Structure in Ancient Hebrew Poetry," *Vetus Testamentum*, 14 (1964), 423–45; continued in *VT*, 16 (1966), 152–80. Elcanon Isaacs also regards the word as the basic metrical unit, but in a quantitative rather than an accentual system of meter; see "The Metrical Basis of Hebrew Poetry," *American Journal of Semitic Languages and Literatures*, 35 (1918), 20–54.

17. Luis Alonso-Schökel, *Estudios de poética hebrea*, groups unaccented syllables around an ictus.

18. Sigmund Mowinckel, *The Psalms in Israel's Worship*, trans. D. Ap-Thomas, II (Oxford: Blackwell, 1962), 159–75, and n. 38, 261–66.

19. Eduard Sievers, *Metrische Studien*, I, Abhandlungen der philologisch-historischen Klasse der königl. sächsischen Gesellschaft der Wissenschaften, XXI (Leipzig, 1903).

20. Douglas Young, "Ugaritic Prosody," *Journal of Near Eastern Studies*, 9 (1950), 124–33.

21. Stanislav Segert, "Problems of Hebrew Prosody," *Supplement to Vetus Testamentum*, 7 (1960), 283–91.

22. Even the conservative treatment of Habakkuk iii by William F. Albright involves over 20 emendations of the text in 18 verses, 5 of these being the insertion of words or phrases not found in the text.

23. Eduard Sievers and Hermann Guthe, *Amos Metrisch Bearbeitet*, Abhandlungen der

philologisch-historischen Klasse der königl. sächsischen Gesellschaft der Wissenschaften, XXIII, No. 3 (Leipzig: Teubner, 1907).

24. Sievers recognized feet of from one to five syllables, allowing thereby almost any combination of words to be scanned in a regular fashion. See *Metrische Studien*, I, Ch. ii, pp. 98 ff., and Ch. vi, pp. 142 ff. Mowinckel allows the *sh*ᵉ*wa* to receive the accent, which in conjunction with other rules allows virtually any syllable to receive ictus. See "Zum Problem der hebräischen Metrik," *Festschrift Alfred Bertholet* (1950), pp. 379–94.

25. As well as I and II Samuel; see *Metrische Studien*, II and III.

26. Benjamin Hrushovski, "On Free Rhythms in Modern Poetry," *Style in Language*, ed. Thomas A. Sebeok (Cambridge, Mass.: Harvard Univ. Press, 1960), pp. 173–90, defines free rhythms as those which "1) have no consistent metrical scheme, that is, in tonic syllabic poetry have a freedom from prevalent, predetermined arrangement of stressed and unstressed syllables; but 2) do have a poetic language organized so as to create impressions and fulfill functions of poetic rhythm" (p. 183). This, as Hrushovski sees, appears to be the situation in classical Hebrew poetry. This view has close affinities to that which holds the word to be the metrical foot in Hebrew; see n. 16.

27. In the example just given, and in the following examples, we are concerned with the balance of terms which, while relevant to metrical theories like those of Kosmala and Alonso-Schökel, may be irrelevant for the accentual-foot theories. For these, presumably, the syllables would need to be counted. Briefly, however, the same types of examples as given for word imbalance can also be given for syllable imbalance. In the next paragraph Jeremiah xlix.27 is an example of both, and a comparison of Psalm lxix.24 and Isaiah x. 5 with regard to *zăᶜăm* (*harôn*) *'ăp* gives a parallel to Nahum iii.18.

28. Similarly, Joachim Begrich, after having surveyed metrical theory and practice between Sievers and 1932, and having concluded that all that had been shown was that a metrical reading was possible but that neither meter nor its type was certain, believed that further certainty could only be found if the influences which the rhythm exercises on the shape of a text are determined. "Zur hebräischen Metrik," *Theologische Rundschau*, 4 (1932), 82.

I would like to thank Dr. Moshe Greenberg for reading this paper and contributing many valuable suggestions.

SELECTED BIBLIOGRAPHY

Albright, William F. *Yahweh and the Gods of Canaan*. London: Athlone Press, 1968.

Alonso-Schökel, Luis. *Estudios de poética hebrea*. Barcelona: Juan Flores, 1963.

Begrich, Joachim. "Zur hebräischen Metrik." *Theologische Rundschau*, 4 (1932), 67–89.

Briggs, Charles. *A Critical and Exegetical Commentary on the Book of Psalms*. Vol. I. Edinburgh: T. & T. Clark, 1906.

Budde, Karl. "Das hebräische Klagelied." *Zeitschrift für die Alttestamentliche Wissenschaft*, 2 (1882), 1–52.

Cobb, William H. *A Criticism of Systems of Hebrew Metre*. Oxford: Oxford Univ. Press, 1905.

Gordon, Cyrus. *Ugaritic Textbook*. Analecta Orientalia 38. Rome: Pontificum Institutum Biblicum, 1965.

Gottwald, Norman K. "Poetry, Hebrew." *The Interpreter's Dictionary of the Bible*. New York, 1963. III, 829–38.

Gray, George. *The Form of Hebrew Poetry*. London: Hodder & Stoughton, 1915.

König, Edward. *Stilistik, Rhetorik, Poetik in Bezug auf die biblische Literatur*. Leipzig: Dieterich, 1900.

Kosmala, Hans. "Form and Structure in Ancient Hebrew Poetry." *Vetus Testamentum*, 14 (1964), 423–45.

Lowth, Robert. *Lectures on the Sacred Poetry of the Hebrews.* 4th ed. English trans. London: Thomas Tegg, 1839.

Mowinckel, Sigmund. *The Psalms in Israel's Worship.* Trans. D. Ap-Thomas. Vol. II. Oxford: Blackwell, 1962.

Robinson, Theodore H. *The Poetry of the Old Testament.* London: Duckworth, 1947.

Segert, Stanislav. "Problems of Hebrew Prosody." *Supplement to Vetus Testamentum,* 7 (1960), 283–91.

Sievers, Eduard. *Metrische Studien,* I. Abhandlungen der philologisch-historischen Klasse der königl. sächsischen Gesellschaft der Wissenschaften, XXI (Leipzig, 1903).

———and Herman Guthe. *Amos Metrisch Bearbeitet.* Leipzig: Teubner, 1907.

Tsevat, Matitiahu. *A Study of the Language of the Biblical Psalms.* Nashville, Tenn.: Abingdon Press, 1955.

Whallon, William. *Formula, Character, and Context.* Washington, D.C.: Center for Hellenic Studies, 1969.

Yellin, David. "The System of Biblical Lyric Style." (In Hebrew.) *Selected Writings,* II (Jerusalem, 1939), 1–149.

CLASSICAL GREEK AND LATIN

By A. THOMAS COLE

General Principles

Any piece of Greek or Latin was heard as a succession of syllables, and among these syllables those which ended in a short vowel ("short" syllables in the traditional terminology) were felt to require less time for their pronunciation than those syllables which ended in a diphthong, long vowel, or consonant ("long" syllables).[1] These two phenomena, the divisibility of speech into syllables and the natural distinction between long and short syllables, are fundamental to the rhythmic patterns of ancient poetry.[2] They determine these patterns in three different ways: (1) Identical sequences of syllables, i.e., those which contain the same number of longs and shorts arranged in the same way, may be felt as equivalent parts in a pattern. (2) A comparable formal equivalence may be established between sequences which require an equal amount of time for their delivery, even if the sequences are not identical. The equivalence of this type most frequently encountered (and the one that probably reflects normal pronunciation most closely) is that between two consecutive short syllables and a single long. This equivalence is called "resolution" (symbolized thus: $\overline{\cup\cup}$) when there is a reason to believe that the single long is the more regular or usual of the variants, and "contraction" ($\overline{\cup\cup}$) when the reverse is true. (3) A formal equivalence may be established between two syllables or two syllable sequences that contain the same number of syllables. When this equivalence exists, any syllable, whether long or short, can be designated by the single symbol "o," and any sequence of syllables by the symbols "o o" (for a disyllabic sequence), "o o o" (trisyllabic), etc.

These equivalences involve the working of three different rhythmic principles which can be called, respectively, the principle of identity, the principle of quantitative equality, and the principle of syllabic equality. In all the rhythmic patterns found in ancient poetry it is possible to see the working of at least two of these principles. More often than not, all three are involved, as in the following example (the opening of Aeschylus' *Prometheus Bound*):

U — U — — — U — U — U —
chtho/nos/ me/n es/ tê/lou/ro/n hê/ko/men/ pe/don/,
U — U — U U U U — U — U —
Sky/thê/n e/s oi/mo/n, a/bro/to/n ei/s e/rê/mi/ân/.

Our journey's end is come, land's distant last expanse,
the steppes of Scythia, an untrodden wilderness.
(Syllable boundary is indicated by /, long vowels by a circumflex accent.)

The pattern of longs and short of the first line is repeated in the second with two variations. In the first line /*tê*/ (—) corresponds to /*mo*/ (U) in the second, and /*lou*/ (—) in the first to /*n a*/*bro*/ (U U) in the second. Neither variation disturbs the over-all equivalence of the lines, however, since there is syllabic equivalence between /*tê*/ (—) and /*mo*/ (U) and quantitative equivalence between /*lou*/ (—) and /*n a*/*bro*/ (U U). The same syllabic and quantitative equivalences make the identical tetrasyllabic sequences that open and close each line equivalent to the sequences in the middle, so that both lines can be marked off into three equal units or measures ("metra"):

U — U — | — — U — | U — U —
chthonos men es | *têlouron hê* | *komen pedon,*
U — U — | U U U U — | U — U —
Skythên es oi | *mon, abroton eis* | *erêmiân.*
(Metron boundary is indicated by vertical bars.)

The entire spoken dialogue of the play, like that of most Greek drama, consists of a series of such equivalent metra grouped in threes. The various forms which the metra may take are given by the general scheme o$\underset{-}{\text{UU}}$ U$\underset{-}{\text{U}}$U, where o indicates the presence of a syllable which can be, by syllabic equivalence, either long or short; and $\underset{-}{\text{UU}}$ a long syllable which is resolvable, by quantitative equivalence, into two shorts.

We may ignore for the present other forms of equivalence that are limited in their use to a specific literary genre, e.g., comedy.[3] Something further should be said, however, about the role played by quantitative equality in creating the verse structure. It is obvious that any two series that show an identical sequence of longs and shorts will also be quantitatively equivalent; and, according to one school of Hellenistic and post-Hellenistic theorists, those who were called *rhythmikoi* or *mousikoi,* the latter equivalence was the more fundamental one. For the *rhythmikoi,* the two lines of Aeschylus just examined are ultimately analyzable, not as a series of metra of the form o ⏕ ⏑ ⏕, but as a series of equal time units (rather like the bars of modern Western music) of six *sêmoi* each (the *sêmos,* equivalent in length to one short syllable, being the basic counting unit or beat). The bar in its normal form is counted as follows: ⏑ — ⏑ — (1, 2,3, 4, 5,6). The long which may stand in equivalence to the first short of each metron is for the *rhythmikoi* an "irrational" syllable, longer than one *sêmos* and shorter than two by an indeterminate amount, and presumably to be accommodated to the regular beat by some kind of *rubato.* In addition to the 6/8 time which this analysis suggests, the *rhythmikoi* recognized other varieties, corresponding roughly to 2/4, 3/8, and 5/8 times. They also allowed, besides the usual diseme long (equivalent to two shorts), triseme and tetraseme longs (designated by the symbols ⏗ and ⏘), and permitted quantitative equivalence between differently arranged sequences of shorts and diseme longs whose total time value (measured in *sêmoi*) was the same (e.g., — ⏑ ⏑ — ⏑ — ⏑ — (1,2, 3, 4, 5,6, 7, 8,9, 10, 11,12) and ⏑ — — ⏑ — ⏑ ⏑ — (1, 2,3, 4,5, 6, 7,8, 9, 10, 11,12), both dodecaseme sequences).

As their other name (*mousikoi*) indicates, the *rhythmikoi* were concerned with the rhythms of lyric poetry (i.e., sung poetry with musical accompaniment), and the few fragments of such poetry that survive from the period in which the *rhythmikoi* were writing give some support to their theory of verse as a series of isochronic bars.[4] Conversely, the poetry composed for reading or recitation that dates from the same period tends to bear out the views of the other main group of Hellenistic and post-Hellenistic theorists, the *metrikoi* or *grammatikoi.*[5] The *metrikoi* do not recognize the existence of composition by bars or of triseme and tetraseme long syllables.

Contemporary students of ancient Greek poetry are, by and large, *metrikoi* rather than *rhythmikoi,* and with some reason. The theories of the *metrikoi,* though they arose at an even later period than did those of the *rhythmikoi,* apply fairly well to the recited poetry of all periods: both the Greek recited poetry of pre-Hellenistic times and the Greek and Roman recited poetry of the Hellenistic and post-Hellenistic times. Their theories are not completely satisfactory when applied to pre-Hellenistic sung verse, but neither are those of their rivals.[6] The principles on which this verse was composed are too imperfectly known to allow us to accept or reject any one theory of its composition, and the discussion of the subject is best kept separate from the fairly orthodox "metrical" analysis to which recited verse lends itself.

Recited Verse (*Archaic and Classical Periods*)[7]

Four basic metra are used in early recited verse: the dactyl (— $\overline{\cup\cup}$); the anapest ($\overline{\cup\cup}$ $\underline{\cup\cup}$ $\overline{\cup\cup}$ $\underline{\cup\cup}$); the iamb ($\circ\underline{\cup\cup}\cup\underline{\cup\cup}$); the trochee ($\underline{\cup\cup}\cup\underline{\cup\cup}\circ$). (The words iamb, trochee, and anapest as originally used refer to the last three sequences. It was only at a later, probably Hellenistic, date that each of these three sequences came to be considered, not as an indivisible whole, but as a combination of two shorter units called feet—whence the modern meanings for iamb [$\cup$ —], trochee [— $\cup$], and anapest [$\cup\cup$ –].)

Each line, or *stichos,* of recited verse is composed of two, three, four, or six repetitions of one of the above metra. Dactylic lines are regularly hexameters; trochaic lines are regularly tetrameters; anapestic lines, tetrameters or (occasionally) dimeters; iambic lines, trimeters or tetrameters. Anapests and, more rarely, iambs and trochees may also be repeated in "systems" of varying lengths. Poems are composed of one or more systems or of a number of repetitions of the same dimeter, trimeter, tetrameter, or hexameter. In the latter case they are said to be "stichic" in form. Each line or system ends in a full stop followed by a pause (indicated thus: $_{//}$).[8] The last trochee or anapest in a line or system is regularly abbreviated into a characteristic closing or "catalectic" form, the trochee into $\underline{\cup\cup}$ $\cup$ — and the anapest into $\overline{\cup\cup}$ — —. A line may never end in two shorts which could be avoided by contraction or which are the result of resolution. Otherwise, both resolution and contraction are rare in the general vicinity of line end, presumably because poets wanted a cadence in which the line's basic rhythmic pattern was restated as unambiguously as possible.

Anapests are in origin a marching meter, first attested in Spartan soldiers' songs and much used in drama, where anapestic systems regularly accompany the exits and entrances of the chorus. Dactylic hexameter is the meter of epics, oracles, and didactic poems. Iambic trimeter and trochaic tetrameter appear first in occasional poems of various sorts, then in the dialogue portions of drama, where the trimeter ultimately prevails over the tetrameter. The word "trochaic" means "running" or "spinning"; and we may infer from the decreasing importance of the tetrameter that dramatic dialogue was coming to be characterized by a varied pace suited to the character of the action rather than by a stylized rapidity of movement. But with this exception the use of certain meters for certain genres seems to have been a matter of tradition rather than intrinsic suitability.

Each line in stichic verse shows not only an absolutely regular succession of metra but a fairly regular disposition of words within the line. Anapestic metra are usually separated from each other by word end, probably to demarcate more clearly the equal units of a verse that had to keep marching feet in time with each other. Dactylic, iambic, and trochaic lines show a more variable internal pattern, whose purpose seems to be to maintain the unity of the line as the main structural element in the poem. There is usually a central caesura that divides the line into two nearly equal parts or "cola." Such cola (set off from each other in rhythmical notation by the symbol /) are never exactly equal, however, nor in general are any successively repeated word groups that are shorter than the line itself. The line is thus made distinctly identifiable. The sequence $\overline{\cup\cup}$ — — followed by word end is felt as a kind of marker of line close in dactylic verse and is accordingly avoided earlier in the line; and there are similar, though less easily explicable, restrictions on the appearance of the sequence ∪ — — followed by word end in iambic and trochaic verse.[9]

In the hexameter these rules are observed less strictly in Homer and Hesiod than in later writers, but even in Homer lines like

— ∪ ∪ | — — | — ∪ ∪ | — — / | — ∪ ∪ | — — //
oulomenên, hê myri' Achaiois alge' ethêken

Withering rage that sent the Achaeans / woes by the thousand
(*Iliad* i.2)

with its suggestion of a premature close after *Achaiois,* or

— ∪ / ∪ | — ∪ / ∪ | — ∪ / ∪ | — ∪ / ∪ | — ∪ ∪ | — — //
polla d'ananta katanta paranta te dochmia t'êlthon

Much upwards / and downwards / and crosswise / and slantwise they went
(*Iliad* xxiii.116)

with its jogging repetition of the unit ∪ — ∪ are rare, and possibly used for special effect. The iambic trimeters of dramatic and particularly comic dialogue are much less rigid with regard to such rules than the non-dramatic trimeter. As a result, the comic trimeter, especially that of New Comedy, is the most conversational of all Greek verses.[10] Its flexibility is increased by the fact that it, like the trochaic tetrameter of comedy and unlike all other Greek verse forms, allows the equivalence of single and double shorts. This equivalence may occur as many as five times in one line, according to the pattern: $\genfrac{}{}{0pt}{}{\cup\cup}{\circ}$ — $\genfrac{}{}{0pt}{}{\cup\cup}{\cup}$ — | $\genfrac{}{}{0pt}{}{\cup\cup}{\circ}$ — $\genfrac{}{}{0pt}{}{\cup\cup}{\cup}$ — | $\genfrac{}{}{0pt}{}{\cup\cup}{\circ}$ — ∪ — //.

Along with these stichic forms one should mention another type of composition, probably derived from them, in which a dactylic or iambic line, or one of the cola into which it regularly subdivides, alternates with another dactylic or iambic line, colon, or pair of cola.[11] The commonest of such forms (usually called "epodic") alternates the hexameter with a line created by a repetition of the common hexameter colon — $\overline{\text{UU}}$ — $\overline{\text{UU}}$ —:

— $\overline{\text{UU}}$ | — $\overline{\text{UU}}$ |— $\overline{\text{UU}}$ | — $\overline{\text{UU}}$ |— UU | — —//
— $\overline{\text{UU}}$ — $\overline{\text{UU}}$ —/ — UU — UU —//

This two-line sequence is called the elegiac couplet or distich, and it can be repeated to form whole poems. The alternating elements in epodic verse may be the two cola of a single line as well as the two lines of a distich. Such bipartite lines can also be repeated to form entire poems.

The first great user, if not necessarily the originator, of epodic composition was Archilochus (early seventh century, B.C.), and it is a fair guess that he found the juxtaposition of diverse and at times contrasting elements, such as dactylic and iambic cola, an apt vehicle for his favorite themes of satire and parody.

U — U U — U U — —/ — U — U — — //
Erasmonidê Charilâe, chrêma toi geloion

Charilaos, seed of Erasmon, here's a funny one

begins one of his poems, and the meter (the common hexameter closing colon U — UU — UU — — followed by the iambic or trochaic — U — U — —) mirrors the contents: a lofty-sounding epic patronymic serving as an introduction to what must have been an everyday anecdote. Archilochus' Latin emulator Horace was to use the same manner of composition for similar effects:

— —| — —| — /UU |- — | —U U | — —
Êheu, trānslâtôs aliô maerêbis amôrês, (hexameter)
UU U—| — —U —
$\overline{\text{ast}}$ ego vicissim rīsĕrô. (iambic dimeter)

Alack—you shall mourn for love transferred to another;
and then it'll be my turn to laugh.

(*Epodes* xv.23–24)

A somewhat more violent departure from a normal metrical pattern is used for more scurrilous purposes by Hipponax (ca. 600 B.C.), who gave vogue to a trimeter that proceeds in regular iambic fashion until its penultimate syllable, which is long rather than short: o $\underline{\cup\cup}$ ∪ $\underline{\cup\cup}$ | o $\underline{\cup\cup}$ ∪ $\underline{\cup\cup}$ | ∪ $\underline{\cup\cup}$ — —//. To the Greeks the line seemed to stumble just before reaching its close and was accordingly called the limper (*skazôn*) or crippled iamb (*choliamb*).

Lyric Verse[12]

The most common recited meters were all in use by the end of the seventh century B.C., and there was little innovation in this area until Hellenistic times. The principal developments during the intervening three hundred years were all in lyric verse, whether solo (monodic) or choral. Choral lyric is first attested at Sparta (Alcman), then in Magna Graecia (Stesichorus, Ibycus), and finally in Athens and the adjoining areas of the Greek world (Pindar, Simonides, Bacchylides, the choral portions of Attic drama). The principal composers of monody are first the Lesbian poets Alcaeus and Sappho (ca. 600 B.C.), then the Ionian Anacreon (late sixth century), and the Attic dramatists, particularly Euripides.

Like recited verse, the earliest lyric verse is composed of a number of repetitions of the same sequence, each repeated or "responding" sequence ending in a full stop followed by pause. But these responding sequences, called strophes, are often not evenly divisible into a number of short metra,[13] and they are much longer than the lines of recited verse. The latter rarely exceed twenty syllables, whereas the strophes of early lyric may be as much as twice as long and tend to become longer as the genre develops. Subdivisions, called periods, each ending in a full stop followed by pause, begin to appear within the strophe. Such subdivisions may be so long that they come to be considered stanzas in themselves; and when, as often, they occur in a triadic AAB pattern, they are called strophe, antistrophe, and epode. Strophe and antistrophe rather than the triad of which they form a part may then be felt as the basic responding elements in the poem, in which case the triad is not repeated. The result is a poem with an AAB structure in which the B section has no responding equivalent. Such astrophic sections eventually came to constitute whole poems by themselves, a mode of composition especially popular in the monodies of Euripides and the so-called "new" dithyramb, both characteristic products of the latest phase in the development of Greek lyric (late fifth and early fourth centuries B.C.).

Concurrently with this tendency toward progressively fewer repetitions of longer patterns one can trace a tendency for the internal pattern of strophe and stanza to become more diversified. In early solo and choral lyric these patterns are usually a fairly homogeneous mixture of two units which repeat or alternate with one another. In the strophes of the Lesbian poets, for example, these units are o — u — and (o) o —uu — u— (i.e., o — uu — u — or oo — uu — u —), the latter replaced occasionally by an expanded version of itself: (o)o — uu (— uu (— uu)) — uu — u — or (o)o — uu — (— uu —) — uu — u —. The whole sequence may be plus or minus a syllable at the start or finish of the strophe.[14] Regularly recurring word end and, occasionally, pause, may give a kind of stichic structure to all or part of the whole sequence, but the resulting lines as found in ancient and modern editions of the poems are only semi-independent units within a larger continuum. Such are the four "lines" into which the two most famous strophes used by the Lesbian poets fall (regularly recurring word end is designated by /):

o–u–|o–uu–u–|/o–u–|o–uu–u–/|o–u–|o–u–|o/–uu–uu–u–|o//

(Alcaic strophe)

–u–|o–uu–u–|o/–u–|o–uu–u–|o/–u–|o–uu–u–|o/–uu–o//

(Sapphic strophe)

Another type of composition, much used by Pindar and Bacchylides and known as "dactylo-epitritic," employs the units — u — and — uu — uu —, usually separated by a single syllable that may be either long or short; another, the units — uu — (a choriamb) and oo — o, usually marked off by recurring word end into octosyllabic units or cola of the form o o — o — uu— that are called choriambic dimeters; a fourth variety, first found in Anacreon and much used in drama, the units u — and o o in strict alternation (the latter with the restriction that both syllables may not be short):

o o u — o o u — o o u —

Word end usually recurs either before or in the middle of every other o o, producing sequences such as the following:

u —] o o u — o o u — [o o
u — u — — u u —
erôs, anîkâte machân,

Love, never yet worsted in battle

(*Antigone* l.781)

or

o] o ∪ — o o ∪ — o [o
∪ ∪ — ∪ — ∪ — —
pher' hydôr, pher' oinon, ô pai,

Bring me water, bring me wine, boy.
(Anacreon, fragment 51 in D. L. Page's edition of the Greek lyric poets)

This colon, a favorite of the poet, became known in later times as the Anacreontic. These cola are usually called dimeters, as if composed of two metra of the form o o ∪ — (iambic or choriambic, depending on the quantities of the first two syllables) or o ∪ — o (ionic). Ionic as used in tragedy is an Oriental rhythm, largely confined to passages delivered by Orientals or intended to portray those qualities which the Greeks associated with the Orient: sensuality, effeminacy, and excitability.

In contrast to such modes of composition, the more characteristic form of dramatic lyric presents a series of distinct patterns, often fairly simple and in many instances identical with sequences found in recited verse, but so dissimilar to one another that their juxtaposition produces an effect of contrast and transition. The same effect is observed in the successions of stanzas preferred in the longer dramatic lyrics: not the recurring AAB AAB AAB that is typical of early choral lyric but a progression: AA BB CC and so on.[15] Such rhythmic transitions often accompany a change in the subject or mood of the poem, but, except in the case of the ionic rhythms just mentioned and dochmiacs (see below, pp. 75–76), a given rhythm does not seem to carry mood associations in itself. The association is one which is established in the context of a given ode or play and need not occur outside this context.[16] Passages sung by a character in a state of excitement or confusion, or passages giving a rapid description of a complicated and varied episode naturally contain more rhythmic transitions, and it is passages of this sort that predominate in Greek lyric in its final stage of development. At this stage the distinct rhythmic patterns are brief and numerous and may succeed each other in almost any way the poet's fancy dictates.

One can also trace in lyric verse as it develops the growing importance of the principle of quantitative equality (see above, pp. 67–68), which is absent from Lesbian lyric and, probably, from all Greek lyric in its earliest stage of development; though part of recited verse from the very beginning.[17] The principle comes to be accepted in the lyric tradition only gradually.

Resolution and contraction appear occasionally in Anacreon and the early choral poets, but become frequent for the first time in drama. Also characteristic of drama is another type of "quantitative" composition, in which normal iambic or trochaic metra appear in series along with metra in which one or two syllables have been suppressed. Such "syncopated" iambic metra show the patterns — ∪ —, ∪ — — and — — (i.e., ∧ — ∪ —, ∪ — ∧ — and ∧ — ∧ —). Their trochaic counterparts are — ∪ —, — — ∪ and — — (i.e., — ∪ — ∧, — ∧ — ∪ and — ∧ — ∧). These metra were probably made quantitatively equivalent to normal ones through the use of triseme longs. Thus the syncopated sequence — ∪ — would be delivered as —ˡ ∪ — in iambic verse and as — ∪ —ˡ in trochaic verse. Quantitative equivalence of this sort, together with exceptional freedom in resolution, made it possible to encompass through the use of variations on a single metron a wide variety of effects. Compare the solemn invocation of the chorus' prayer to Zeus in the *Agamemnon*:

—ˡ —ˡ | — ∪ — ∪ | — ∪ —ˡ | — ∪ — ∪ | — ∪ —/
Zeus, hostis pot' estin, ei tod' autôi philon keklêmenôi,

—ˡ —ˡ | —ˡ | |
Zeus, who|ever He may | be, if He | please to be so | called by us,
(ll. 160–61)

with the excited coloratura of Euripides' Helen as she recalls the misfortunes of her family:

—ˡ — ∪ | — ∪ —ˡ	—ˡ —ˡ
Lêdâ d'en anchonais	Leda, my | mother, hanged:|
∪∪ ∪ ∪∪ ∪ | —ˡ —ˡ |	—ˡ —ˡ
thanaton elaben aischŷ-	under the burden of | my shame |
— ∪ — — | — ∪ —//	
nâs emâs hyp' algeôn.	plunged in grief she | took her life.//
∪ ∪ ∪ ∪ ∪ ∪ | ∪∪ ∪ —ˡ	—ˡ
ho d'emos en hali polyplanês	And in the sea where he | suffered his long |
∪ ∪ ∪ ∪ ∪ ∪ | — ∪ —//	
posis olomenos oichetai.	wandr'ings my husband is | dead and gone.//
— ∪ — ∪ | — ∪ — ∪ |	
Kastoros te syngonou te	Castor and his | twin, my brothers,|

∪∪ ∪ ∪∪ ∪ | — ∪ ∪∪ ∪ |	
didymogenes agalma patridos	pride of their fatherland, | both are gone from the
∪ ∪ ∪ ∪ ∪ ∪ |— ∪ ∪ ∪ ∪	
aphanes aphanes|*hippokrota le-*	gone from the earth and the | plains that clatter to
— ∪ ∪∪ ∪ | — ∪ ∪∪ ∪ |	
loipe dapeda, gymnasia te	horses hooves and the | playing fields by the |
∪∪ ∪ — ∪ |—ı —ı|	—! —ı
donakoentos Eurô-	side of the reed-lined | Euro-
—∪ —∪|— ∪—//	
tâ, neânian ponon.	tas where youthful | athletes toil.//

(ll. 200–11)

Quantitative equivalence is equally important in another rhythm characteristic of tragedy, the dochmiac, a short sequence, often repeated in series as if it were a metron of recited verse, but showing such variety of forms (only partially covered by the general scheme o ∪∪ ∪∪ o ∪∪) that it is difficult to see how they could have been felt as equivalents in delivery except as units of equal over-all duration. The rhythm is regularly used for moments of great emotional intensity, and passages in which the excited dochmiacs of a distraught protagonist alternate with the calming iambic trimeters of the chorus are practically a set piece in tragedy. This type of composition, along with the tendency of dochmiacs to appear in conjunction with iambs, suggests that the dochmiac is a kind of irregular or syncopated iambic sequence, perhaps quantitatively equivalent to half an iambic trimeter (o ∪∪ ∪ ∪∪ o ∪∪).

Quantitative equivalence was probably an important ingredient of the new style of the late fifth century. The patterns of contrasting character whose free combination characterizes that style tend to be octosyllables equivalent in time duration to twelve *sêmoi*. A succession of such units can thus be analyzed as a succession of dodecaseme bars allowing of a variety of internal patterns.[18] Few traces of this style remain from after the middle of the fourth century, but it is possible that the songs of Plautine comedy (ca. 200 B.C.) represent a late, Latin modification of it. The most frequent metra in these songs are the bacchiac (∪ — —) and the cretic (— ∪ —). Both sequences are usually syncopated iambs or trochees when they occur in Greek drama (i.e., ∪ — —ı , —ı ∪ — and — ∪ —ı), but in Plautus the equivalence forms allowed are at times so numerous that the effect in delivery may have been that of a series of hexaseme bars of the form ∪̄ ∪∪ ∪∪ or ∪∪ ∪̄ ∪∪.[19]

In the course of development taken by the Greek lyric one can see the working of a number of different factors. With an increasing body of examples and precedents to draw on, poets naturally tended to favor more complex forms. Dramatic realism dictated the abandonment of regular composition by strophes in favor of a less regulated succession of various rhythmic sequences—a change which probably has something to do with the increasing naturalism that can be seen in the plastic and graphic arts during the period 600–350 B.C. And poetic rhythm developed in response to changing methods of composition and performance. The principal recited forms originated, in all probability, at a time when all poems were improvised by illiterate bards and memorized and passed on by many who were not professional poets. Under such circumstances a fairly simple rhythmical pattern was almost essential. By contrast, the more complex of even the earliest lyrics seem to be the work of literate poet-composers; and their performance, involving as it did a melodic and instrumental accompaniment which would work in conjunction with the words to create the rhythm, could be entrusted only to amateur musicians with some training. The same musicians would have to go through a period of rehearsals before they could render the complexities of a choral ode, which was, in addition, danced as well as sung and played. Finally, the elaborateness of the lyric in its latest stage of development was only possible because in the late fifth century it was becoming the custom to entrust performances to virtuoso specialists.

By the fourth century, both the performance and the musical setting which a Greek lyric received had probably attained such a level of sophistication that they, and not the poetic text, were what an audience went to hear. This is doubtless why such a small quantity of lyric poetry survives from the fourth and later centuries, and why the little that survives is, with the possible exception of the Roman material mentioned earlier, of little or no literary merit. Though the tradition of poetry as part of a larger musical performance continued and even provides the background against which the theories of the *rhythmikoi* are to be understood (pp. 67–68), first-rate poets did not care to enter into the junior partnership with composer and performer that the writing of lyric verse had come to involve.

Recited Verse (Hellenistic and Roman)[20]

The principal recited meters of the Archaic and Classical periods continued to be used after the fourth century, but the Hellenistic poets were literary eclectics who sought to broaden the repertory of recited verse by borrowing from the other tradition. The result, both in these writers and in their better-known Roman imitators (Catullus, Horace, Seneca, Petronius, Statius, and Martial), is a type of composition which adapts a number of originally lyric patterns to recitational use by giving them a stichic structure. The adaptation takes various forms. The fourth-century poet Asclepiades, for example, took the sequence oo — uu — — uu — u — that forms part of a number of early Lesbian strophes and repeated it stichically to form whole poems—hence the name (Asclepiad) by which the sequence is now known. Two other Lesbian sequences got their names in a similar fashion: the Glyconic (oo — uu — u —) and the Phalaecean (oo — uu — u — u — o), the latter best known as the favorite lyric meter of Catullus:

— — — uu — u — u— —
vīvâmus, mea Lesbi(a)[21] *atqu(e) amêmus*
My Lesbia, let us live and love.
(v.1)

Catullus' *Attis* is the principal source of our knowledge of the Galliambic, one of the principal Hellenistic adaptations of ionic sequences to stichic use:

uu — u — u — —/ uu — u uu u —
super alta vectus Attis, celerî rate maria
From across the sea came Attis, sailing swiftly over the deep.
(lxiii.1)

The pattern is ou — oou — oou — oou —, with numerous possible resolutions and contractions. Another well-known Hellenistic line uses the same ionic pattern, but shortened by two syllables at the start and lengthened by a syllable at the end: — oo u — oo u — oo u — o. The verse, called after its inventor the Sotadean, was felt as composed of four metra of the form —oou, the last of which is catalectic.

Some of the simpler lyric strophes were taken over in their entirety by Hellenistic and Roman poets, but when this occurs the strophe is usually demarcated into a series of independent lines with a clearly defined relationship to each other. Thus the alternation and repetition of the units o — u — and o — uu — u — which creates the Alcaic stanza (p. 73) becomes in Horace something rather different:

o — u — —/ — uu — u —//
o — u — —/ — uu — u —//

o — u — — — u — o //
— uu — uu — u — o //

The long fifth syllable followed by word end in each of the first two lines serves to divide them into two clearly distinct parts of contrasting metrical character. The third line expands the first of these and accentuates its relatively heavy movement by the central sequence — — —, usually contained within a single word. The fourth line is an expanded and quickened version of the second part. Rather than a continuous flow the stanza gives the effect of a succession of contrasting movements: moderato, adagio, presto:

— — u — — / — uu — u — // *iust(um) et tenâcem prôpositî virum*	If just and firmly / purposed he be, a man //
— — u — — / — uu — u — // *non cîvi(um) ardor prâva iubentium,*	confronts the people / bent on unjust demands, //
— — u — — — u — — // *non voltus instantis tyranni*	the despot's dark, grim, threat'ning glance, //
— u u — uu — u — — // *mente quatit solidâ nequ(e) Auster*	with resolve never shaken, nor fears the south wind //
— — u — — / — u u — u — // *dux inquiêtî turbidus Hadriae,*	that stirs unquiet, / churning the Adriatic. //
— — u — — / — uu — u — // *nec fulminantis magna manus Iovis.*	nor thunder-hurling / Jupiter's mighty hand. //
— — u — — — u — — // *sî fractus inlâbâtur orbis* //	Though heaven crack, sway, then give way, //
— uu — uu — u — — // *impavidum ferient ruînae.*	he will stand unafraid as it crashes round him. //

(*Odes* III.iii.1–8)

Such recited stanzas are usually adaptations of a whole strophe from early lyric, though the choruses in Seneca's tragedies are at times more independent: a series of lyric lines rounded off by a closing sequence of slightly different character or, rarely, a free combination of cola taken from such lyric lines.[22]

It is in its use of originally lyric meters that Latin poetic practice is most closely modeled on Greek. Recited meters, though largely borrowed from Greek, show a more independent treatment, perhaps because they were delivered in a less artificial manner and needed more modification to accommodate them to the nature of the Latin language as normally spoken. The proportion of long to short syllables was much higher in spoken Latin than in Greek; words were probably separated from each other more distinctly in the delivery of a Latin sentence than in the delivery of a Greek one; and the Latin word bore a stress accent determined by the so-called penult law. The influence of all three linguistic phenomena is evident in the way Greek iambic and trochaic sequences are used in early drama. Line 828 of Plautus' *Captivi:*

∪ ∪ ∪ – ∪|– – – – – – – – – –|–∪–//
quo homine adaequê nêmô vîvit fortunâtiôr

than whom there's none the likes of him, not a man alive more fortunate

is a typical Latin trochaic "tetrameter." The metron is no longer the Greek trochee ($\overset{\cup\cup}{-}$ ∪ $\overset{\cup\cup}{-}$ o) but the sequence $\overset{\cup\cup}{-}$ $\overset{\cup\cup}{o}$ $\overset{\cup\cup}{-}$ $\overset{\cup\cup}{o}$ or, rather, half this sequence, the single trochaic foot $\overset{\cup\cup}{-}$ $\overset{\cup\cup}{o}$. The entire line is felt to be a succession of seven of these feet (the last showing the form $\overset{\cup\cup}{-}$ ∪), followed by a long syllable, and is accordingly called a trochaic septenarius.[23] The replacing of $\overset{\cup\cup}{-}$ ∪ $\overset{\cup\cup}{-}$ o by $\overset{\cup\cup}{-}$ $\overset{\cup\cup}{o}$ | $\overset{\cup\cup}{-}$ $\overset{\cup\cup}{o}$ (and in iambic verse of o $\overset{\cup\cup}{-}$ ∪ $\overset{\cup\cup}{-}$ by $\overset{\cup\cup}{o}$– | $\overset{\cup\cup}{o}$–) was probably necessitated by the preponderance of long syllables in Latin. The nondescript sequences of the type — — — — which can result from this change tend to show an accentual pattern, as if the regular alternation of stressed and unstressed syllables ($\overset{/}{—}$ and — or ∪) was helping to make up for the lack of long and short alternation.[24] This accentual alternation characterizes the example just quoted:

∪|$\overset{/}{—}$ —|$\overset{/}{—}$ —|$\overset{/}{—}$ —|— —|$\overset{/}{—}$∪|—
. . . *adaequê nêmô vîvit fortûnâtiôr*

The line also departs from Greek practice in that there is a hiatus between *homine* and *adaeque,* and the final *-e* of *homine* counts as a long syllable. Both of these licenses are characteristic of line end and suggest that there was some sort of pause after *homine*. Such pauses at word end are characteristic of the recited verse of early drama, appearing regularly at the central caesurae of septenarii and octonarii and sporadically elsewhere. Presumably this departure from Greek practice was possible because single words or word groups in Latin were distinct units which could be separated in delivery by some sort of pause without producing the impression of disjointedness or unnaturalness.

The characteristics of the recited verse of early Latin drama which separate it from its Greek models are even more evident in the two Roman verse forms that are most likely to be the products of an indigenous poetic tradition: the Saturnian and the popular version of the trochaic septenarius, sometimes called the *versus quadratus*. The former is almost certainly a native Roman form, for it was already well established as the verse for hymns, prayers, commemorations, and dedications when the period of extensive Greek literary influence at Rome was just beginning (last half of the third century B.C.). The nature of the Saturnian is imperfectly understood,[25] but one of its most regular features is a quadripartite division into roughly equal word groups, usually of 4, 3, 3, and 3 syllables:

o o o o / o o o / o o o / o o o //
Virum mihî Camêna, insece versûtum.

Of that man, Muse, / sing to me, / the man of / many turns.
(*Odyssey* i.1; trans. Livius Andronicus)

Here the word or word group is sufficiently independent to provide one of the main structural elements in the line. It is also very prominent in the *versus quadratus*, which seems to have been the popular meter par excellence at Rome throughout antiquity, persisting very much unchanged from such early proverbs as:

— ∪ | — — | / — — | ∪∪ — / | — — | ∪∪ — | / — ∪ | — //
rex erit quî rectê faciet; quî nôn faciet nôn erit

Rule belongs to / those who're righteous; / those unrighteous / will not rule

through the insulting soldiers' songs and political lampoons of the first century B.C.:

— — | — — |/ — — | — — |/ — — | — — |/ — ∪ | —//
postquam Crassus carbô factus, Carbô crassus factus est

Crassus' fat is/ in the fire; now/ fiery Carbo's/ getting fat

to the late antique:

— ∪ | — — |/ — ∪ — —|/ — ∪ | — — |/ — ∪ | —//
crâs amet quî numqu(am) amâvit, quîqu(e) amâvit crâs amet

Love ye tomorrow,/ lovers new; /old loves,/ tomorrow love anew

and early medieval:

— ∪ | — ∪|/ — ∪ | — —|/ — ∪ | — — | — ∪ | —//
pange, lingua, glôriôsî proelium certâminis.

Celebrate, my tongue,/the battle/won in contest/glorious.

The word groups usually coincide with one pair of trochaic feet, but because of the infrequency of resolution they are also related to each other as approximately equal syllable sequences, usually forming a 4, 4, 4, 3 pattern. The tendency for word accent to coincide with the first syllable of each foot can be even more pronounced here than in the dramatic septenarius:

/ / / / / / /
— — | — — | — — | — — | — — | — — | — ∪ | —
postquam Crassus carbo factus, Carbo crassus factus est.[26]

Also characteristic of the Saturnian and *versus quadratus* is the frequent use of alliteration, assonance, and rhyme, often serving along with syntactic parallelism to underline the division into half and quarter lines. Such devices are probably not, as some scholars have believed, an essential part of the structure of the verses involved, but they appear in all early Latin and, together with the metrical characteristics under discussion, constitute a kind of stylistic and metrical substratum in Roman poetry. This substratum becomes less and less evident as sophisticated Roman poets become more skillful in reproducing Greek models, but even the most sophisticated Roman poetry never emancipates itself fully from all of these tendencies. Early alliteration, assonance, and rhyme develop into a complex system of sound echoes which provide a kind of continuous ornamentation to distinguish verse from prose, the grand from the plain style, and, in general, Latin verse from Greek. In Greek such *Klangmittel* are used more sparingly and, usually, to underline the formal or rhetorical structure of a poem—as an element of poetic composition and design rather than, as in Latin, poetic coloring.[27]

Concern for patterns of stressed and unstressed syllables continues to characterize the most frequently used of all recitative meters, the hexameter, even at the most refined stage of its development. The inner word groupings preferred by the Greek hexameter seem designed to avoid the cadential sequence — $\overline{\cup\cup}$ — — followed by word end at any point before the end of the line, and, in general, to avoid demarcating identical syllable sequences with word end (p. 69). The Latin hexameter is equally sensitive in these two respects, but is also so constructed that it shows a cadence of stressed and unstressed as well as of long and short syllables. The sequence

/   /
— $\overline{\cup\cup}$ — — marks the end of most lines, and the only other place where two feet with initial stress appear is the start of the line, where the danger of creating a false close is minimal.[28] This principle is first rigorously applied in the hexameters of Catullus, less rigorously by Virgil, who pays attention to the special effects to be obtained by violating it.[29] When Dido adjures the departing Aeneas:

— —| $\acute{—}$ ∪∪ | $\acute{—}$ ∪, ∪ | — — | — ∪ ∪ — —
per cônûbia nostra, per inceptôs hymenaeôs.

In the name of our marriage, the nuptial rites that we began
(*Aeneid* iv.316)

the unusualness of the meter expresses not only the speaker's confusion but a kind of judgment on her: the reference to Dido's relationship with Aeneas as *conubium* is as premature as the cadential sequence *cônûbia nostra* (— $\acute{—}$∪∪ $\acute{—}$∪) in the second and third feet of the line. The rigorous application of such canons of composition in Ovid and later writers of epic (the hexameters used in Latin satire had always been and remained much freer in this respect) produces a smooth monotony that is increased by the rarity of elision, the tendency to make sense units coincide with lines, and a lessened concern with the effects to be gained by varying the frequency and location of contraction from line to line.[30] A similar development in the direction of a polished monotony can be traced in the Latin elegiac couplet, the recited meter which, together with the hexameter, accounts for over ninety per cent of the non-dramatic Latin poetry that survives from ancient times.

The hexameter, elegiac couplet, and iambic trimeter, along with a few of the recited forms borrowed from early lyric, are the main meters used in late antiquity by both Greek and Latin poets, who thus gave final shape to an artificial tradition of poetic composition that has persisted unmodified down to the present day. The best of the Greek and Latin verse written in Europe since the Renaissance is superior in quality to most of that composed in late antiquity, and all such verse was probably produced in much the same way—by careful reading and imitation of earlier writers in an effort to reproduce metrical forms and a poetic style which no longer had any basis in the living language. We do not know exactly when the distinction between stressed and unstressed syllables in Greek and Latin became more important than that between long and short—only that the change had taken place by late antiquity and has left its traces even in the artificial genre which poetry written in classical meters had by then become.[31] In general, however, these meters were too closely linked to earlier tradition to become the vehicle for exploring the new rhythmic possibilities of the two languages.[32]

NOTES

1. A single consonant (or a single consonant followed by *h*) between vowels counts as part of the syllable that follows. Most groups of two or more consonants are divided between the preceding and the following syllables. The group mute consonant plus liquid, however, may either be divided or go entirely with the syllable that follows. Hence the traditional rule that syllables are long "by position" if they contain a short vowel followed by two consonants other than mute plus liquid and "common"—i.e., capable of being scanned as either long or short—if followed by mute plus liquid.

2. This distinction is often assumed to be identical with or related to a different distinction, which is fundamental to many other systems of versification, that between what are in some fashion more and less "prominent" syllables (ó and o). There is some evidence to support this assumption so far as Latin verse is concerned (see below, pp. 78 and 80, and nn. 24 and 26), but none whatsoever in Greek.

3. See below, p. 70.

4. See the discussion of the rhythmical notation of these fragments in E. Pöhlmann, *Griechische Musikfragmente* (Nürnberg: Hans Carl, 1960), pp. 40–48.

5. Recitation in antiquity took various forms, ranging from a purely spoken declamation to something like accompanied recitative; but all the pieces of poetry written for such non-lyric modes of delivery have important rhythmical characteristics in common.

6. A number of nineteenth-century scholars, guided by the theories of the *rhythmikoi* and supposed analogies with modern Western music, attempted to analyze all of early Greek

lyric in terms of regular bar divisions. Their views are now almost universally rejected, though they provide the basis for the sections on meter in a number of frequently consulted reference works, e.g., the standard Greek and Latin grammars (Gildersleeve and Lodge, Allen and Greenough, Goodwin and Gulick), Norwood's *Greek Tragedy* (rpt. New York: Hill & Wang, n.d.) and *Greek Comedy* (rpt. New York: Hill and Wang, 1963), and even Jebb's commentaries on the plays of Sophocles.

7. The classic treatment of the most important of these meters is in P. Maas, *Greek Metre* (English trans. H. Lloyd-Jones,Oxford: Clarendon, 1962), pp. 59–71.

8. The existence of a full stop and pause at line end is an inference from two facts: (1) hiatus is allowed without restriction at this position (evidently because three was a break in the delivery, so that the two vowels were not felt as being contiguous); and (2) the last syllable in a line may be short even when the metrical scheme of the verse calls for a long syllable (presumably because such a short syllable, taken in conjunction with the pause which occurred at the end of a line, could be quantitatively equivalent to a long).

9. The "inner" or "verbal" metric of the dactylic hexameter and the main iambic and trochaic verses has been much studied in modern times. For balanced discussions of the achievements of this type of investigation, along with a valuable critique of some of its assumptions and results, see L. P. E. Parker, "Porson's Law Extended," *Classical Quarterly*, N.S. 16 (1966), 1–26; and G. S. Kirk, "The Structure of the Homeric Hexameter," *Yale Classical Studies*, 20 (1966), 76–104.

10. Aristotle's often-cited remarks (*Poetics* 4, *Rhetoric* 3.1 and 8) about the naturally iambic character of spoken Greek may stem less from linguistic observation than from familiarity with this particular verse form.

11. See the excellent discussion in B. Snell, *Griechische Metrik*, 3rd ed. (Göttingen: Vandenhoeck and Ruprecht, 1962), pp. 31–34.

12. The most important single treatment of Greek lyric verse (in the context of a discussion of Greek verse as a whole) is that of U. v. Wilamowitz-Moellendorff, *Griechische Verskunst* (Berlin: Weidmannsche Buchhandlung, 1921). The work is carelessly composed, however, and makes considerable use of a highly questionable theory of the historical origin of certain rhythmical forms. Sounder methodologically, but much sketchier, are the sections on lyric in Maas, *Greek Metre*, pp. 38–51, Snell, *Griechische Metrik*, pp. 13–44, and W. J. W. Koster, *Traité de métrique grecque* 4th ed. (Leyden: A. W. Sijthoff, 1966). For drama the standard works are A. M. Dale, *The Lyric Metres of Greek Drama*, 2nd ed. (Cambridge: Cambridge Univ. Press, 1968), and J. W. White, *The Verse of Greek Comedy* (London: Macmillan, 1912). D. S. Raven, *Greek Lyric Metre*, 2nd ed. (London: Faber & Faber, 1969), gives a useful introduction.

13. The principal exceptions are poems composed in one or more anapestic, trochaic, or iambic systems. The "ametric" character of much of lyric verse accounts for the term "rhythms" (*rhythmoi*) sometimes encountered in ancient writers as a general designation for lyric verse—by contrast to the "meters" (*metra*) of recited verse. See G. F. Else, *Aristotle's Poetics: The Argument* (Cambridge: Harvard Univ. Press, 1957), pp. 56–57 and 64–65.

14. This analysis is a modified version of that found in A. M. Dale, "The Metrical Units of Greek Lyric Verse," *Classical Quarterly*, N.S. 1 (1951), 124–28 (rpt. in Dale, *Collected Papers*, Cambridge: Cambridge Univ. Press, 1969, pp. 89–94) and taken over by D. L. Page in his *Sappho and Alcaeus* (Oxford: Clarendon, 1955), p. 321.

15. In the more elaborate dramatic odes the "circular" and "progressive" methods of arrangement may be combined, as in the great *kommos* of the *Choephoroe* (ll. 315–422), where the stanzas show the pattern ABA x CBC y DED x FEF.

16. See, in general, A. M. Dale, *Collected Papers*, pp. 248–58. Rhythmical relationships may exist between the various odes of a tragedy, comparable perhaps to the key relationships

between the musical numbers of an opera; see the discussions of the *Medea* and *Andromache* of Euripides in D. L. Page's edition of the former (Oxford: Clarendon, 1936, pp. 188–89) and E. Fraenkel, "Lyrische Daktylen," *Rheinisches Museum*, N.F. 72 (1917), 333, 337–40 (reprinted in *Kleine Beiträge zur klassischen Philologie*, Rome: Edizioni di Storia e Letteratura, 1964, pp. 214, 217–21).

17. An inference from similarities which link the isosyllabic verse of the Lesbian poets to the isosyllabic verse of the Vedas and seem to establish for this mode of composition, in both Greek and Sanskrit, a pedigree that extends back into Indo-European times. See A. Meillet, *Les Origines indo-européennes des mètres grecques* (Paris: Presses Univs. de France, 1923).

18. All of the quantitative equivalences under discussion here would probably require, in order to be felt as such by an audience, a much more artificial delivery of the poetic text than would be necessary to make two identical sequences of longs and shorts seem rhythmically equivalent. The growing importance of quantitative equivalence may therefore have been at the heart of a revolution in poetic style about which several fifth- and fourth-century Greek writers complain. The effect of the revolution, according to these writers, was to make the words of a poetic text follow the music rather than—as had been the custom in earlier times—the music the words. (It is possible, however, that the vague critical language which the writers use refers to something altogether different.)

19. On the possible relationship between Plautine lyric and Greek models see F. Leo, *Die plautinische Cantica und die hellenistische Lyrik* (Berlin: Weidmannsche Buchhandlung 1897).

20. There is no general discussion of Roman versification comparable in fullness or sophistication to the best available for Greek. An up-to-date handbook is D. S. Raven, *Latin Metre* (London: Faber & Faber, 1965). Fine points of prosody and verbal metric are treated in detail in L. Müller, *De Re Metrica*, 2nd ed. (St. Petersburg and Leipzig: C. Ricker, 1894); the elegiac couplet in M. Platnauer, *Latin Elegiac Verse* (Cambridge: Cambridge Univ. Press, 1951); Plautine meter in C. Questa, *Introduzione alla metrica di Plauto* (Bologna: Patron, 1967); and Horatian meters in R. Heinze, "Die lyrischen Verse des Horaz," reprinted in his *Vom Geist des Römertums*, 3rd ed. (Darmstadt: Wissenschaftliche Gesellschaft, 1960), pp. 227–94.

21. Final vowels which, in accordance with the usual Latin practice, are to be elided or somehow merged in pronunciation with a following initial vowel are printed within parentheses.

22. The best brief discussion of Seneca's meters is in H. J. Mette's bibliographical survey, "Die romische Tragödie," *Lustrum*, 9 (1964), 162–65.

23. Similarly, a Greek tetrameter whose final metron shows a normal rather than a catalectic form becomes an octonarius in Latin and the iambic trimeter a senarius. These designations continued to be used, even though Latin iambic and trochaic verse by the first century B.C. had rejected the sequences $\overset{\cup\cup}{\circ}\;\overset{\cup\cup}{-} \mid \overset{\cup\cup}{\circ}\;\overset{\cup\cup}{-}$ and $\overset{\cup\cup}{-}\;\overset{\cup\cup}{\circ} \mid \overset{\cup\cup}{-}\;\overset{\cup\cup}{\circ}$ of early drama in favor of patterns more closely modeled on the Greek ($\overset{\cup\cup}{-}\;\cup\;\overset{\cup\cup}{-}\;\circ$, $\circ\;\overset{\cup\cup}{-}\;\cup\;\overset{\cup\cup}{-}$, and $\overset{\cup\cup}{\circ}\;-\;\overset{\cup\cup}{\cup}\;-$).

24. Such accentual patterns can also be explained in terms of a theory, once widely held for Greek as well as Latin verse, according to which the first long in any dactylic or trochaic foot, and the final long in any iambic or anapestic foot, received a stress accent. According to this theory, Latin poets constructed their verses in such a way that this metrical accent or "ictus" usually fell on the same syllable as did the normal word accent. The notion of ictus is, however, generally abandoned now so far as Greek verse is concerned; and such accentual regularity as there is in Latin can now be explained more economically than by positing the coexistence within a single verse of three different patterns (those involving ictus, word accent, and syllable quantity). It should be added that the very idea of the

presence of stress accent as an ingredient in the construction of Latin verse is no more than a hypothesis accepted fairly consistently by German and English classicists, but denied with equal consistency by their French and Italian colleagues.

25. See the excellent survey of the Saturnian "question" in M. Barchiesi, *Nevio epico* (Padua: Cedam, 1962), pp. 310–27. The best single analysis of the verse is that of F. Leo, *Der saturnische Vers* (Berlin: Weidmannsche Buchhandlung, 1905).

26. The pattern of such septenarii is, in effect, ó o ó o ó o ó o ó o ó o ó o o (see above, n. 2).

27. The sound patterns of Greek and Latin poetry are considered at length in two recent studies: L. P. Wilkinson, *Golden Latin Artistry* (Cambridge: Cambridge Univ. Press, 1963), and W. B. Stanford, *The Sound of Greek* (Berkeley: Univ. of Calfornia Press, 1967).

28. Initial stress is excluded from the third foot of the line by the most common of the regular hexameter caesuras: — ŪU — ŪU —/ŪU — ŪU — ŪU — —. The main alternate scheme to this one: — ŪU — /ŪU — ŪU — /ŪU — ŪU — —// excludes initial stress from the second and fourth feet.

29. Virgil is also reluctant to allow the fourth foot to begin with an accented syllable:

/   /
— — —   — U U — —

hence *arma virumque cano Troi* | *ae quî* ¦ *prîmus ăb* | *ôrîs* rather than the normal word order *qui* |

/
— — — U U — —

Troiae | *prîmus ab* |*ôrîs* that an earlier poet would probably have used.

30. On the last of these tendencies, see G. E. Duckworth, *Vergil and Classical Hexameter Poetry* (Ann Arbor: Univ. of Michigan Press, 1969).

31. See Maas (above, n. 7), pp. 15–16, and W. Beare, *Latin Verse and European Song* (London: Methuen, 1957).

32. In the Latin West there is a kind of continuity between the trochaic sequences of the *versus quadratus* and the heptasyllables and octosyllables with a tendency toward accentual trochaic cadence that provides one of the foundations of popular medieval verse, whether in Latin or the vernacular. But in the Greek East there is no such continuity at all: the principal popular meter of Byzantine times, the fifteen-syllable *stichos politikos,* stands in no demonstrable relation to any Classical form.

SELECTED BIBLIOGRAPHY

Braun, L. *Die Cantica des Plautus.* Göttingen: Vandenhoeck & Ruprecht, 1970.

Dale, A. M. *Collected Papers.* Cambridge: Cambridge Univ. Press, 1969.

——— *The Lyric Metres of Greek Drama.* 2nd ed. Cambridge: Cambridge Univ. Press, 1968.

Heinse, R. "Die lyrischen Verse des Horaz." *Vom Geist des Römertums.* 3rd ed. Stuttgart: Teubner, 1960. Pp. 227–94.

Kirk, G. S. "The Structure of the Homeric Hexameter." *Yale Classical Studies,* 20 (1966), 76–104.

Koster, W. J. W. *Traité de métrique grecque.* 4th ed. Leiden: Sitjthoff, 1966.

Leo, F. *Die plautinischen Cantica und die hellenistische Lyrik.* Berlin: Weidmannsche, 1897.

——— *Der saturnische Vers.* Berlin: Weidmannsche, 1905.

Maas, P. *Greek Metre.* English trans. Oxford: Clarendon Press, 1962.

Meillet, A. *Les Origines indo-européenes des mètres grecques.* Paris: Presses Univs. de France, 1923.

Müller, L. *De Re Metrica.* 2nd ed. St. Petersburg and Leipzig: Ricker, 1894.

Parker, L. P. E. "Porson's Law Extended." *Classical Quarterly,* N.S. 16 (1966), 1–26.

Platnauer, M. *Latin Elegiac Verse*. Cambridge: Cambridge Univ. Press, 1951.
Pöhlmann, E. *Griechische Musikfragmente*. Nürnberg: H. Carl, 1960.
Questa, C. *Introduzione alla metrica di Plauto*. Bologna: Patron, 1967.
Raven, D. S. *Latin Metre*. London: Faber, 1965.
——— *Greek Lyric Metre*. 2nd ed. London: Faber, 1968.
Snell, B. *Griechische Metrik*. 3rd ed. Göttingen: Vandenhoeck & Ruprecht, 1962.
White, J. W. *The Verse of Greek Comedy*. London: Macmillan, 1912.
Wilamowitz-Moellendorff, U. von. *Griechische Verskunst*. Berlin: Weidmannsche, 1921.
Wilkinson, L. P. *Golden Latin Artistry*. Cambridge: Cambridge Univ. Press, 1963.

SLAVIC

By EDWARD STANKIEWICZ

The study of Slavic versification has as its aim the description of the oral (popular) and written (learned) prosodic systems of the Slavic languages in their synchronic and historical aspects. As a comparative study, it aims, further, at the reconstruction of the Common Slavic prosodic system before the breakdown of Slavic unity, around the tenth century A.D., and at an elucidation of the phenomena of convergence and of cross-cultural, Slavic and non-Slavic, influences that effected the development of the individual Slavic systems of versification. The influence of foreign systems was necessarily circumscribed by the prosodic possibilities of the particular language which adopted the foreign model. In recognizing this fact, modern study of versification does not limit itself to an enumeration of ideal metrical schemes. Instead, it views verse as a complex structure within which the metrical constants are modified by the rhythmic tendencies, and in which the types and functions of its elements are hierarchically organized, although they remain in a state of dynamic tension, which provides the condition for further internal transformation.

Attempts to reconstruct Common Slavic prosody are based on the observation of those prosodic features which recur in the oral traditions of various Slavic countries. Common Slavic had, most likely, two types of verse: a spoken asyllabic verse, based on syntactic parallelism of the lines, and a recitative or sung syllabic verse, based on a fixed number of syllables per line, which coincided with a complete syntactic unit. Specimens of the first type are found in Slavic folklore in the form of wedding speeches and sayings, in the imparisyllabic lines of older Western (fourteenth-century Czech epic) poetry and Russian (seventeenth-century) poetry. Descendants of Common Slavic parisyllabic lines may be the laments and epic songs which appear today among the Balkan Slavs and in Northern Russia. The laments (*tùžbalice, plači*) consisted of short or long lines which were divided into two or three uniform cola. The epic songs (the *junački deseterac* and, perhaps, the

Russian *bylina*) were decasyllabic; each line was divided into two asymmetrical cola (four plus six) with a syntactic break and a quantitative clausula approaching a constant at the end. Another variety of Common Slavic epic songs were octosyllabic lines with a trochaic cadence. The Russian *bylina* with its three stresses per line, two-syllable anacrusis, and dactylic clausula has obviously relinquished the syllabic principle in favor of an accentually organized line. The oldest (sixteenth-century) recordings of South Slavic folk poetry reveal also the existence of long-line (fifteen-to-sixteen-syllable) epic songs (the South Slavic *burgarštica*), whereas one of the most popular forms of East Slavic lyric poetry (the Ukrainian *kolomyjka*) consists of fourteen-syllable lines which are subdivided into three cola (four plus four plus six).

The dissolution of the Common Slavic linguistic unity, especially the loss of the weak *jers* (reduced high vowels), entailed a rearrangement of the accentual features and a new syllabic structure of the Slavic word. The syllabic principle which is preserved in Slavic oral and written poetry could have been the result of a readjustment of the verse to the new linguistic conditions through shortening or expansion of lines, or by means of musical modulation (e.g., *homonia* in Southern and Eastern Slavic church songs); it could have been the result of structural convergence, or of an independent development, or, finally, of foreign influence (especially that of medieval Latin poetry).

The oldest learned Slavic poetry, that of Old Church Slavonic of the Moravian and Bulgarian period, was based on parisyllabism without rhyme, and owed some of its supplementary prosodic features to the Greek-Byzantine poetry.

The new political, religious, and linguistic developments which took place around the tenth century A.D. created the conditions for independent Slavic poetic traditions and prosodic systems. The formation of Slavic states and their subsequent destinies, and the adoption of Christianity and the schism, affected the growth and functions of poetry in the various Slavic countries in different ways. The longest uninterrupted tradition of learned poetry existed among the Western Slavs; Great Russian poetry developed only from the late seventeenth century, and the Balkan Slavs witnessed a short period of flowering of learned poetry during the Renaissance on the Dalmatian coast; elsewhere, the rise of learned poetry was a product of nineteenth-century nationalism. Among the orthodox Slavs it was accompanied by a rejection of the tradition of Church poetry, which had led for centuries a marginal and petrified existence.

As a consequence of the breakdown of Common Slavic a new word-prosody developed in the various Slavic languages, which can be formulated as follows: Czech and Slovak, Serbo-Croatian and Slovenian preserved phonemic quantity. In Czech and Slovak, stress has the function of delimiting word-boundaries, being fixed on the initial syllable of a word. In Serbo-Croatian and Slovenian, stress is concomitant with the rising pitch which is phonemically distinctive but metrically irrelevant, whereas the falling pitch delimits the word-boundary, falling on the first syllable of a word (in Serbo-Croatian) or on the final syllable (in Slovenian). In the Eastern Slavic languages and in Bulgarian, stress has a distinctive function, while in Polish it is bound to the penultimate syllable of a word.

Although some Slavic systems of versification have been only incompletely or superficially described, the relationship between the word-prosody outlined above and the prosodic systems is otherwise quite clear. The prosodic principle underlying Eastern Slavic and Bulgarian oral poetry has been accentual (i.e., an equal number or regular distribution of stresses per line), whereas the principle underlying oral poetry of the Western and Southern Slavs has been syllabic with the difference that quantity has been employed metrically in the South, and rhyme in the West. The metrical systems of the corresponding learned kinds of poetry which have shown the greatest vitality and longevity have likewise been founded on these principles, although they were frequently modified or in competition with other systems.

Syllabism has remained until now the basis of Polish versification. In the fourteenth and fifteenth centuries, parisyllabism of the lines was merely a tendency, which was particularly pronounced in the works influenced by medieval poetry. The greatest innovator of Polish syllabic verse was the Renaissance poet Jan Kochanowski. He canonized the principle of strict parisyllabism, eliminated the syntactic unity of the lines as a constant, and stabilized the place of the caesura in lines longer than the octosyllabic. He also introduced a deeper one and one-half rhyme (with a penultimate stress and consonance of the preceding consonant), which was not strictly adhered to by his seventeenth- and eighteenth-century followers. These innovations lent Polish verse new flexibility: they allowed the use of lines and hemistichs of various lengths and released syntactic phrasing for stylistic effects. The consistent adherence to the syllabic principle allowed the utilization of longer lines, especially of eleven (five plus six) and thirteen (seven plus six) syllables, in which the best Polish lyric and epic poetry has been written. The shorter octosyllabic line has generally been used in learned poetry without a caesura. In popular verse, this line is divided into hemistichs (five plus three or four plus four), which entails a break-down of the line into word groups with an equal number of stresses and a strong trochaic tendency. The rhythmical measures of the folk song entered at first into Polish Romantic poetry as a form of popular stylization. The impulse for syllabic-accentual prosody was, however, given mainly by the imitation of classical, quantitative meters and by foreign (Russian) models. Syllabic-accentual meters were used by the Romantics in smaller lyric poems and in sections of dramatic works. The great Romantics, who introduced masculine rhyme and iambic and anapestic feet (Mickiewicz, Słowacki), used these meters with moderation. Syllabic-accentual verse became the norm with the Positivist poets (Konopnicka, Asnyk), who practiced it with severe rigor. Modern poets admit frequent deviations from the metrical scheme, which relaxes the constraints upon the rhythmic vocabulary and syntactic phrasing. The imitation of classical meters, especially the hexameter, was actually responsible for the introduction of purely accentual meters, based on an equal number of stresses in each line. In our times, these meters, as well as free verse, compete successfully with the traditional syllabic verse.

In Czech, where the opposition between short and long vowels impeded the formation of parisyllabic long lines, the octosyllabic line formed the backbone of both lyric and epic Old Czech poetry, with a pronounced trochaic tendency in the former, and syntactic parallelism approaching a constant in the latter. Dramatic works, on the other hand, were based on asyllabism. Syllabic-accentual meters, with a trochaic and iambic cadence, became popular during the Hussite movement with the spread of religious songs. But as a consequence of the frequent discrepancy between music and meter, and the general decline of secular poetry, the fifteenth and sixteenth centuries saw a return to parisyllabism, a development which coincided with the flourishing of Polish syllabic versification and which was partly influenced by it. In this system, quantity served as an element of rhythmic variation. However, in the poems and songs of the Czech humanists who imitated classical meters (e.g., Komenský), it was elevated to a metrical constant. At the end of the eighteenth century, syllabic-accentual meters, based on the congruence of foot- and word-boundaries, triumph in Czech poetry. The poets of the Puchmajer school adhere strictly to the metrical scheme. Later, this rigor is considerably attenuated through the use of quantity, of polysyllabic words, and of heterosyllabic, mainly dactylo-trochaic feet. The Romantics (Mácha) make skillful use of iambic feet, which go contrary to the dactylo-trochaic cadence of the Czech language. Toward the end of the nineteenth century, the metrical scheme is again rigorously implemented (by the *Lumírovci*), but finally gives place to the modified syllabic-accentual meters and to the *vers libre* of the Symbolists (Březina).

In its early, Štur period, Slovak poetry drew its inspiration from the local folk poetry, which is syllabic. In the last quarter of the nineteenth century, the Slovak poets (Hviezdoslav, Vajanský) abandoned syllabism for the syllabic-accentual meters of Czech origin, which were strictly adhered to toward the end of that century. Subsequently the syllabic-accentual frame became more flexible, to mark the transition to free rhythms.

Serbo-Croatian popular verse shows striking similarities to the Czech and Slovak, with the difference that quantity is sometimes endowed with a metrical function (e.g., the quantitative clausula of the *deseterac*). Dalmatian poetry of the Renaissance owed its verse forms to popular and Western inspiration. The influence of Italian poetry has here been responsible for the introduction of end rhyme (accompanied often by internal rhyme), which replaced syntactic phrasing as a constant. Besides the epic asymmetric (four plus six) and the lyric symmetric (five plus five) decasyllable, the most widespread syllabic meters are eight- and twelve-syllable lines (four plus four and six plus six) with a trochaic cadence. These popular meters penetrated into learned poetry during the Renaissance, but gained a new vogue (especially the eight- and ten-syllable lines) in the first half of the nineteenth century. Modern poetry employs also eleven-, twelve-, and thirteen-syllable lines. Syllabic-accentual meters appeared under foreign (German and Russian) influence during the nineteenth century. (Radičević, Zmaj, Kostić; Vraz, Preradović, Šenoa, F. Marković). The division into feet is, as in Czech, dependent upon the arrangement of word-boundaries. Quantity serves mainly as an element of variation, although in some positions it may substitute for stress (especially in rhymes). Trochaic and iambic pentameters, with a masculine or feminine rhyme, are favorite lines; they are divided into hemistichs which admit heterogeneous feet (trochaic-iambic or trochaic with a dactylic close). The inter-war period witnessed the appearance of free verse.

The meters of modern Slovenian poetry, which developed in the nineteenth century, are syllabic-accentual. The role of quantity as a rhythmic factor is more restricted than in Serbo-Croatian, whereas the role of stress (particularly at the close) is more pronounced. In the poetry of Prešeren, the greatest Slovenian Romantic poet, who used primarily the iambic pentameter, the metrical scheme is still rigorously observed. Modern versification (Aškerc, Župančič) has moved in the direction of relaxing the metrical requirements through the omission of stress on non-final heavy syllables; it has also adopted triple meters and free verse.

Syllabic-accentual meters became the basis of Russian prosody in the 1740's under German influence, following a period of syllabic verse which had reached Russia from Poland, via the Ukraine in the seventeenth century (Simeon Polockij, Istomin, Kantemir). Duple meters,[1] especially the iambic and trochaic tetrameter and the iambic hexameter, dominate the eighteenth-century poetry of Lomonosov, Tredjakovskij, and Sumarokov. At the beginning of the nineteenth century Žukovskij and Puškin popularized the use of the iambic pentameter as well. The duple meters are implemented through a compulsory stress on the last downbeat of the line with the possibility of omitting the stress on the other downbeats, especially the even ones, counting back from the last heavy syllable. The regressive undulatory curve thus obtained is the chief feature of the Russian duple meters, in contradistinction to the duple meters of the Slavic languages which lack phonemic stress, in which the stressed downbeats form a progressive curve. In Russian prosody, furthermore, the arrangement of word-boundaries is free to serve as an element of variation. When triple meters prevailed in the second half of the nineteenth century (in the poetry of Nekrasov, Fet, A. Tolstoj), the tendency to stress the heavy syllables became a constant, and the omission of stress on the light syllables a tendency. The excess of consonants finally gave way to a verse with a variable number of unstressed syllables (usually one or two) between the downbeats (the so-called *dol'niki*); this prevails in the twentieth-century poetry of the Symbolists and Acmeists (Brjusov, Blok, Axmatova, and others), to be, in turn, superseded by an accentual verse with a free number of unstressed syllables between the downbeats (Majakovskij). Free verse, introduced by Blok and Kuzmin, never gained as strong a hold upon Russian poetry as it did upon other Slavic literatures.

The development of Ukrainian and Bulgarian versification resembles closely that of Russian. Duple meters appear in the Ukraine at the end of the eighteenth century after two centuries of the almost exclusive prevalence of syllabic verse. Eight- and twelve-syllable trochaic lines which show the influence of folk poetry occur in the first half of the nineteenth century almost as often as the iambic meters which dominate the verse of the first modern Ukrainian poets. In the hands of the greatest national poet, Ševčenko, these meters are skillfully combined with the verse forms of the folk song (*koljadka, kolomyjka,* and others) which reveal a strong tendency toward a syntactic division of the line into cola or hemistichs. Ševčenko also uses enjambment and imprecise rhymes. Triple meters (especially the anapestic) compete successfully in the second half of the nineteenth century with the duple meters, to be superseded in the twentieth century by the *dol'niki,* pure accentual verse and *vers libre* (Tyčyna, Sosjura). Western Ukrainian poetry has never relinquished the use of syllabic verse.

Modern Bulgarian poetry has from its beginning in the nineteenth century experienced the strong influence of Russian versification. After a period of oscillation between the syntactically organized lines of folk poetry and the duple, especially iambic, meters which were inspired by Russian models (Botev, Vazov), triple meters and lines comprising heterogeneous feet gain predominance in the poetry of the symbolists (Slavejkov, Javorov). Syllabic-accentual meters, as well as the *dol'niki,* are also more widely used in this century than pure accentual verse and *vers libre,* which were experimented with in the pre-war period (E. Bagrjana).

The following excerpts (fourteen lines each) and diagrams illustrate the distribution of stresses: (1) in the Russian iambic tetrameter of the eighteenth and nineteenth centuries [transliterated], (2) in the Czech trochaic tetrameter of the nineteenth century, and (3) in Serbo-Croatian epic songs (the *deseterac*).

Evgenij Onegin
by Alexander Pushkin

"Moj djádja sámyx čéstnyx právil,
Kogdá ne v šútku zanemóg
On uvažát' sebjá zastávil,
I lúčše výdumat' ne móg;
Egó primér drugím naúka:
No, bóže mój, kakája skúka
S bol'ným sidét' i dén' i nóč'
Ne otxodjá ni šágu próč'!
Kakóe nízkoe kovárstvo
Polužīvógo zabavlját',
Emú podúški popravlját',
Pečál'no podnosít' lekárstvo,
vzdyxát' i dúmat' pro sebjá:
Kogdá že čórt voz'mët tebjá!"

"Now that he is in grave condition,
My uncle, decorous old prune,
Has earned himself my recognition;
What could be more opportune?
May his idea inspire others;
But what a bore, I ask you, brothers,
To tend a patient night and day
And venture not a step away:
Is there hypocrisy more glaring
Than to amuse one all but dead,
Shake up the pillow for his head,
Dose him with melancholy bearing,
And think behind a stifled cough,
'When will the Devil haul you off?' "

(Trans. Walter Arndt)

Vrba	Willow
	By K. J. Erben
Rāno sèdā ke snīdanī,	In the morning at breakfast
tāže se svē mladē panī:	he asks his young wife:
"Panī moje, panī milā,	"My mistress, dear mistress,
vždycky upřīmnā jsi byla	you've always been frank with me,
vždycky upřīmnā jsi byla	You've always been frank with me
jednoho's mi nesvěřila.	but one thing you've kept from me.
Dvě lēta jsme spolu nynī—	Two years we have now lived together—
jedno nepokoj mi činī.	but one thing disquiets me.
Panī moje, milā panī,	My mistress, dear mistress,
jakē je to tvoje spanī?	what is it with your sleep?
večer lehneš zdrāva, svěžī,	You lie down in the evening healthy and fresh,
v noci tělo mrtvo ležī.	but at night your body turns dead.
Ani ruchu, ani sluchu,	Not a stir, nor sign of life,
ani zdanī o tvēm duchu.	not an inkling of a soul.

(The macron above a vowel indicates length.)

Zidanje Skadra	The Building of Skadar
Grȃd grȃdila trȋ bràta ródjenā,	Three blood-brothers were building a city,
Dò trī bràta, trȋ Mrnjāvčevića:	Three brothers, the three Mrnjavčevići:
Jédno bjèše Vukášine krȃlju,	The first was king Vukašin,
Drùgō bjèše Ùglješa vòjvoda,	The second was duke Uglješa,
Trèćē bjèše Mr̀njāvčević Gjòko.	The third was Gojko Mrnjavčević.
Grȃd grȃdili Skàdar na Bójani,	They were building the city Skadar on the Bojana river,
Grȃd grȃdili trȋ gòdine dánā,	They were building a city for three years,
Trȋ gòdine sà trista mȃjstōrā;	For three years with three hundred master-builders;
Ne mógoše témelj pódignuti,	They could not lay down the foundation,

A kámoli sagrȁditi grȁda:	Let alone raise a city:
Štò mȁjstori zà dān ga ságrādē,	What the master-builders built during the day,
Tȍ svè vīla zà nōć obáljuje.	The vila destroyed during the night.
Kad nástala gòdina čétvr̄tā,	When the fourth year came
Táda vȉčē sa planínē vīla.	The vila cried out from the mountain.

(The macron indicates length; \ = a falling tone, / = a rising tone.)

Rhythmic Patterns
of Russian Iambic Tetrameters

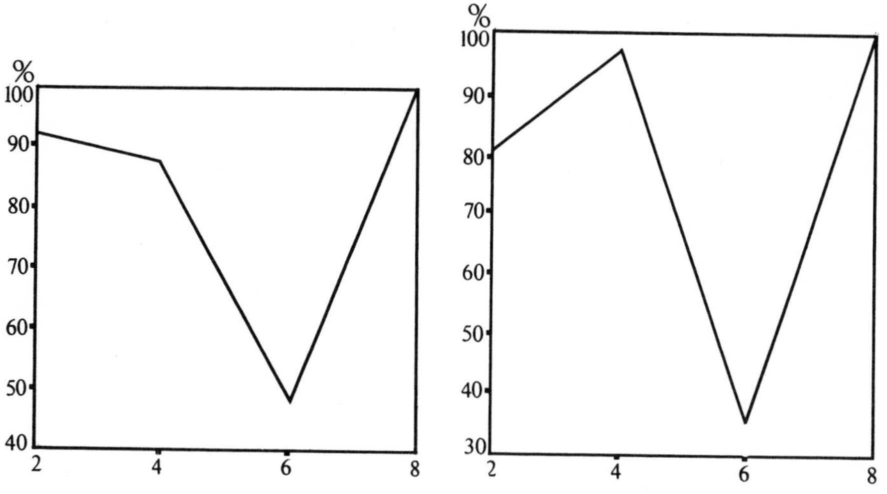

18th Century

19th Century

(From K. Taranovski's *Ruski dvodelni ritmovi*, pp. 76, 83)

Erben's *Vrba*

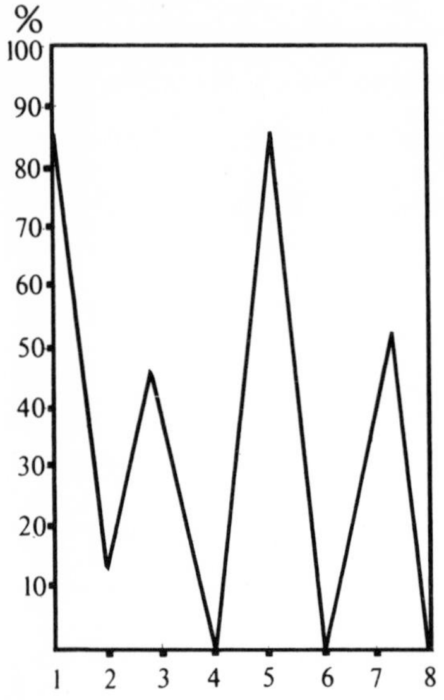

Zidanje Skadra

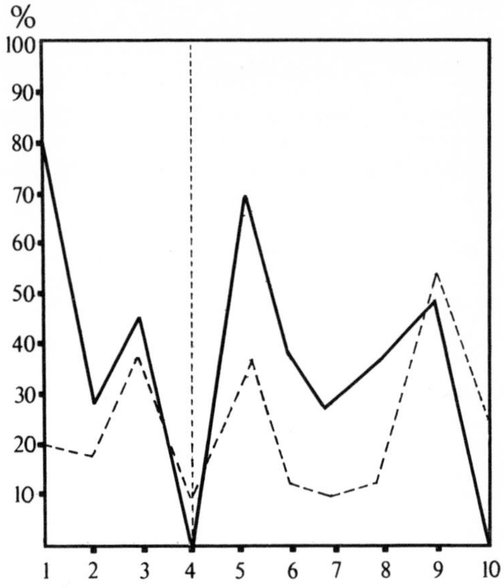

(The broken line indicates the distribution of long vowels)

(From J. Hrabák, *Úvod do teorie verše*, p. 62)

NOTE

1. The terms "duple" and "triple" are an editorial choice. The author prefers "binary" and "ternary."

SELECTED BIBLIOGRAPHY

Bakoš, B. *Vývin slovenského verša od školy Štúrove.* 1949.

Červenka, M. *Český volný verš devadesatých let.* (Rozpravy Československé akademie věd, 73, 13). Prague, 1963.

Furmanik, S. *Podstawy wersyfikacji polskiej.* Warsaw-Cracow, 1947.

Giergielewicz, M. *Introduction to Polish Versification.* Philadelphia, 1970.
Horálek, K. *Zarys dziejów czeskiego wiersza.* Wroclaw, 1957.
Hrabák, J. *Studie o českém verši.* Prague, 1959.
Isačenko, A. V. *Slovenski verz.* Ljubljana, 1939.
Jakobson, Roman. "The Kernel of Comparative Slavic Literature." *Harvard Slavic Studies.* 1 (1953), 1–71.
———"Studies in Comparative Slavic Metrics." *Oxford Slavonic Papers,* 3 (1952), 21–66.
———"Verš staročeský." *Československá Vlastivěda,* 3 (1934), 429–59.
Janakiev, M. *B"lgarsko stixoznanie.* Sofija, 1960.
Kopczsyńska, Z., and M. R. Mayenowa, eds. *Sylabizm. III.* Wrocław, 1956.
——— ——— *Sylabotonizm. IV.* Wroclaw, 1957.
Korš, F. *Vvedenie v nauku o slavjanskom stixosloženii.* St. Petersburg, 1907.
Košutić, R. *O tonskoj metrici u novoj srpskoj poezji.* Belgrade.
Matić, S. "Principi umetničke versifikacije srpske." *Godišnica N. Čupića,* 1930–32.
Mukařovský, J. "Český verš. Obecné zásady a vyvoj novočeského verše." *Československá Vlastivěda,* 3 (1934), 376–429.
Taranovski, K. "Principi srpskohrvatske versifikacije." *Prilozi za književnost,* 20 (1954).
Tomaševskij, B. V. *Russkoe stixosloženie.* Petrograd, 1923.
Unbegaun, B. O. *Russian Versification.* Oxford, 1956.
Žirmunskij, V. M. *Vvedenie v metriku. Teorija stixa.* Leningrad, 1925. (Trans. and ed. Edward Stankiewicz and W. N. Vickery, *Introduction to Metrics,* The Hague, 1966.)

URALIC

By JOHN LOTZ

Introduction

This essay on Uralic versification treats three languages: Hungarian, Kamassian, and Mordvinian. The part on Hungarian, done in a concise form, originally appeared in Swedish in an anthology of translated Hungarian poetry. Hungarian is particularly interesting for general metrics because identical language material serves as the basis for two metric systems: (1) pure syllabic ("national"); and (2) durational (or "quantitative"). In the quantitative type the rules of classical metrics are followed, thus conveying an impression for the modern metrician of the sounds of classical Greek and Latin. It is interesting to note that the verse patterns which have been used extensively in the poetry of the West European languages during the last two centuries show a synesthetic transfer when used in Hungarian; stressed syllables are represented by long bases and unstressed ones by short. The account of the Hungarian "national" versification system given here differs from the usual one in that we regard this system as purely syllabic, whereas Hungarian metricians have traditionally regarded stress (which is always on the first vowel of a word) as a constitutive component. There has been much interest in and excellent scholarship on Hungarian metrics. Unfortunately, most of the work is inaccessible to the general reader because it is written in Hungarian. A brief account in English of Hungarian versification is given by Petr Rákos (see bibliography, p. 121).

Kamassian, a Uralic language on the verge of extinction, is representative of Siberian folk poetry, in spite of the fragmentary form in which it has survived. The section on Kamassian also illustrates a heuristic method by which metric order can be introduced into a set of linguistic field work notes. A more extensive corpus of Vogul and Ostyak materials has been presented in an exemplary fashion by Robert Austerlitz (see n. 8, p. 120.) The Vogul and the Ostyak peoples are the closest kin of the Hungarians living in West Siberia.

The third example, Mordvinian, a Uralic language spoken in Central European Russia, is presented as an exercise in applying methods of mathematical and logical analysis in metrics.

Other important Uralic versification systems not treated here are: Finnish and Estonian (note that the metric form of Longfellow's *Hiawatha* is an imitation of the Finnish folk epos *Kalevala*), Zyrien (spoken in the northeastern-most corner of Europe, and into which Schiller had been translated by the mid-nineteenth century by the older Lytkin), and Cheremis.

The metric systems of the Uralic languages have, of course, been influenced by other poetic traditions, for example, Turkish, Slavic, and Iranian.

I. HUNGARIAN

Like linguistic rhythm in general, Hungarian verse is based on the phonic material of the language, especially on its syllabics, which in Hungarian are always vowels.[1] These can be short or long in all positions. Stress always falls on the first vowel of the word. On this phonic foundation are based two mutually independent metrical systems (apart from free verse): the "national" or syllabic type, in which only the number of vowels is relevant; and the quantitative type, in which the length of the vowels, and to a certain extent the consonants, determine the meter.

(*a*) The syllabic type is the older and more traditional type. In it the meter depends on the regular repetition or variation of the number of vowels, correlated with syntactic boundaries, and often held together by simple rhymes. Stress, which in Hungarian metrical literature is considered decisive for this rhythmic type, is in reality of secondary importance. Though this type is called "national" in Hungary, it coincides with the general metrics of the Danubian area, which thus forms a rhythmico-geographical unit. An example of this type of meter is Balassa's *A költő búcsúja hazájától* (*The Bard's Farewell to his Homeland*), where the first four lines, each with twelve syllabics and a caesura in the middle, constitute a stanza held together by assonances:

Ó én édes hazám,	*te jó Magyarország,*	6	6	a
Ki keresztyénségnek	*viseled paizsát,*	6	6	a

Viselsz pogány vérrel	*festett éles szablyát,*	6	6	a
Vitézlő oskola,	*immár Isten hozzád!*	6	6	a

O my sweet homeland, thou beautiful Hungary,
Who bearest the shield of Christianity,
Thou wieldest the sharp saber, dripping with pagan blood,
Thou school of warriors, now I bid thee farewell.

(sixteenth century)

(In stanzas of four or eight lines in rhyming couplets, this meter was called the Hungarian alexandrine, and became the typical Hungarian epic meter.)

The ballad *Megöltek egy legényt* (*A Youth Was Slain*) shows a certain variation in the number of syllabics. The first stanza consists of four lines containing respectively 6–6–8–6 syllabics, with the second and fourth lines rhyming:

Megöltek egy legényt
Hatvan forintjáért,
Bevetették a Tiszába
Piros pej lováért.

A youth was slain
For his sixty florins,
He was thrown into the river
For his bay horse.

(folk ballad)

(b) The quantitative type uses bases which are long or short according to the metrical principles of the classical languages: a long base consists of a long vowel, or of a short vowel with at least two consonants following before the next vowel; a short base consists of a short vowel with not more than one consonant following it.[2] The bases are combined into lines, and these sometimes into stanzas. Thus the classical meters used in the unrhymed Hungarian Graeco-Roman poetry are governed by exactly the same rules as in the classical languages. The following example of a distich is from Vörösmarty's *Mint a földmüvelő* (*As the Plowman*):

Mint a földmüvelő jól munkált földbe magot vet
S várja virúlását Istene s munka után . . .

— — — ⏑ ⏑ — — — — — ⏑ ⏑ — ⏓[3]
— ⏑ ⏑ — — ⏓ x — ⏑ ⏑ — ⏑ ⏑ ⏓

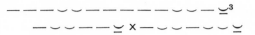

As the plowman sows the seed in well-tilled soil
And awaits its growth from God and after his labor . . .
(nineteenth century)

The first stanza of Berzsenyi's *Fohászkodás* (*Prayer*) is an example of an Alcaic stanza:

Isten! kit a bölcs lángesze fel nem ér,
Csak titkon érző lelke ohajtva sejt:
Léted világít mint az égő
Nap, de szemünk bele nem tekinthet.

— — ⏑ — — — ⏑ ⏑ — ⏑ —
— — ⏑ — — — ⏑ ⏑ — ⏑ —
— — ⏑ — — — ⏑ — —
— ⏑ ⏑ — ⏑ ⏑ — ⏑ — ⏓

God, whom the scholar's genius does not reach,
Only his longing soul can feel in secret:
Thy existence shines like the burning
Sun, into which our eyes cannot look.
(nineteenth century)

Translations of the usual, generally rhyming, West European meters into Hungarian also make use of such long and short bases. Stressed positions are always replaced by long bases and unstressed positions, generally, by short bases, although long bases appear occasionally (i.e., unstressed positions are anceps). For instance,

I come to bury Caesar, not to praise him.
x x́ x x́ x x́ x x́ x x́ x

is translated into Hungarian as:

Temetni jöttem Caesart, nem dicsérni.
⏑ — ⏑ — — — — — ⏑ — ⏑

In a translation into a Germanic language, such as Swedish or English, therefore, faithfulness to the form of these Hungarian poems requires that the rhythmic alternation be rendered by replacing the long bases of the Hungarian original with accentually heavy syllabics and the short bases with accentually light syllabics.

An example of a trochaic meter is afforded by the first stanza of Arany's *Bor vitéz* (*Bor the Knight*):

Ködbe vész a nap sugára, a
Vak homály ül bércen, völgyön. b
Bor vitéz kap jó lovára: a
"*Isten hozzád, édes hölgyem!*" b

— ◡ — ◡ — ◡ — ◡

The rays of the sun are lost in the mist,
Blind darkness sits on hill and dale.
Bor the Knight leaps to the saddle,
"Fare thee well, sweet lady mine!"

(nineteenth century)

An anapestic meter is illustrated in the first half of the first stanza of Petőfi's *Szeptember végén* (*The End of September*):

Még nyílnak a völgyben a kerti virágok, a
    Még zöldel a nyárfa az ablak előtt, b
De látod amottan a téli világot? a
    Már hó takará el a bérci tetőt . . . b

— — ◡ ◡ — ◡ ◡ — ◡ ◡ — ◡
    — — ◡ ◡ — ◡ ◡ — ◡ ◡ —

The garden flowers are still blooming in the valley,
    The poplar is still green before the window,
But do you see over there the wintry world?
    Already snow has covered over the summit of the mountain.

(nineteenth century)

Between these two metrical systems there is a certain stylistic and historical difference in status. Nineteenth-century taste, finding the mechanical caesuras and simple syntactical divisions of the traditional type too simple, chose for its "higher" poetry the quantitative meters. But the tendency to develop the native style persisted, especially in Arany, and recently there has been a noticeable trend toward more extensive use of this form. Ady's poetry after 1900 marks a new era in this development; he returned to the older style with its syllable-counting rhythm, and he even mixed lines of this type with quantitative lines.

Rhyme has been usual in Hungarian poetry since the Middle Ages—the oldest Hungarian verse is unrhymed—but the principles are different from those of Germanic verse. Since Hungarian has very few pure rhymes, Hungarian poets have recourse to sometimes quite daring assonances, insisting only on identity of the vowel, and disregarding word boundaries and stress. The most highly prized rhymes are those which include several syllabics, and which employ words belonging to different syntactical classes, such as *szeretnek* 'they love' and *eretnek* 'heretic.' Alliteration occurs, but is not frequent in modern poetry.

Free verse strives to avoid all tradition in matters of both meter and rhyme. Hungarian poems in free verse are constructed on the same principles as everywhere else in Europe.

II. KAMASSIAN

·From the historical point of view, folk poetry is the foundation of all literary poetry and is still the poetic expression for many people of the world.[4] Kamassian verse is an example of the extremely rich Siberian folk poetry and is illustrative of folk poetry as opposed to literary poetry, which—justifiably—occupies a large part of this volume.

The Kamassians were the last remnant of the once widespread Sayan-Samoyed peoples, who represented the greatest forward thrust into Central Asia by any Uralic-speaking group. Other Sayan-Samoyeds, the Koibal, the Mator, the Karagass, the Soyot, and the Taigi-Samoyeds, have been Turkicized—and to a lesser extent Mongolized—during the course of the last three centuries. At the end of the nineteenth century, the Kamassian language was used in only one village and even there it was on the verge of absorption into the Siberian-Turkic Kach dialect; later both languages of this village were absorbed into Russian because of intermarriage with new settlers (since males were predominant among Siberian natives, they often married Russian women). For the past hundred years, the remaining speakers of Kamassian have lived at the foot of the Sayan mountains, in and around

Abalakova, south of Krasnoyarsk on the Chinese border. A century ago there were still about 150 speakers of the language, but it was used less and less, and when Kai Donner did his field work in the village in 1914 he reported that there were only eight elderly speakers who still used the language actively—the youngest was forty-five years old—and even they were bi- or trilingual. Tugarinov, who visited Abalakova in 1925, states that some knowledge of Kamassian (which was called "taiga-language" by the villagers, as opposed to Kach-Tatar, the "steppe-language") had survived the first World War, but everybody spoke Russian, and he thought that in all probability the language was extinct.[5]

Originally the Kamassians had been nomads, wandering with their reindeer, and were known as skillful hunters. They spent the summer in the cooler regions of the Sayan mountains (called the "white" mountains because of their snow-capped summits), and in the winter they went down to the fertile foothills of the Sayan (called the "black" mountains because of the dark forests and the black soil). In former times they had lived during the summer in conical huts built of birch poles covered with boiled birchbark cloth sewed with braided horse-tail hairs. In the winter they moved to more stable dwellings. Their winter location later became the place of the permanent settlement. Even when they had become sedentary, their houses were covered with birchbark. During the course of the last century, more and more of them abandoned their traditional way of life. Finally, at the end of the century, a plague killed most of their reindeer, and the families that still led a nomadic life turned their few surviving reindeer loose on the steppe. From then on, all the Kamassians were settled and absorbed into a new economy; but for decades after, they still reminisced about the good old days of nomadic life with their reindeer.

Kamassian is the only one of the Sayan-Samoyed languages about which we have information more detailed than meager word-lists; this is due to the work of two Finns: Alexander Castrén and Kai Donner. Castrén spent a few weeks in Abalakova during the fall of 1847 and collected vocabulary and a grammatical sketch. His Kamassian material is less detailed than the rest of his Samoyed collections because of the shortness of his stay in the village and because of his increasingly bad health. A larger amount of Kamassian material was collected by his countryman, Kai Donner. After a brief visit in the summer of 1912, Donner returned to Abalakova toward the end of June 1914—by chance, for his original plan had been to investigate the Tawgi, the most northeasterly Samoyeds on the Tamyr peninsula, but this plan was thwarted because the boat left before he arrived. During the summer he checked Castrén's material and collected new data. There is a good deal of information about his life in the Samoyed village in three sources: in his diary (which he kept in Swedish and which was published in English for the Human Relations Area Files in 1954: *Among the Samoyed in Siberia*); in a travel book written immediately after his return to Finland (the Foreword is dated 1915); and in his doctoral dissertation.

It is our aim to analyze a Kamassian song-text by linguistic methods and demonstrate how metric order can be discovered in it. Such internal structural analysis is necessary for a thorough understanding of the verse itself and its place in any areal, genetic, or typological scheme. It is always possible, of course, that in cases where only a fragmentary corpus is known, the results obtained will be insufficient, and a correct interpretation will await the discovery of other sources.

There is only one Sayan-Samoyed song extant: a Kamassian lament for their lost nomadic life and the disintegration of their tribe; it was sung on 7 August 1914 by Avdakeya Andžigatova, the main informant of Kai Donner, who recorded it.[6] The song is a touching expression of the longing still felt by the older generation for their life in the nomadic desert, a life they had only recently abandoned. Donner states that this was perhaps the only example of genuine poetry he had been able to find among the Samoyeds. After recording the song, he played it back on the phonograph one evening. The Samoyeds reacted with sadness and tears, and one boy believed he recognized in the phonograph the voice of his dead mother. The song gave Donner the impetus to collect additional folklore material: riddles, tales, and prayers.[7] These are the sole textual remains of the Sayan-Samoyeds, and they are considerably influenced by Turkic.

The hand-written text reproduced here is a facsimile of Kai Donner's fair copy of the song transcribed in 1930 from his field notes. As Joki, the editor of Donner's Kamassian collection, indicates in his notes to the printed text, Donner made a few changes in his original field notes, and still other changes appear in the printed version. In the following analysis we will try to restore the original song-text as far as this is possible from existing evidence. Donner's transcription is in the impressionistic style of the Finnish linguistic tradition and has never been interpreted systematically. In the present analysis a phonemicization is attempted, based on the entire Kamassian material of both Castrén and Donner. Certain details of the phonemic system will always remain obscure, because the pronunciation was mixed with Turkic and also contained some Russian features. But we attempt here to establish the uncontaminated Kamassian sound system.

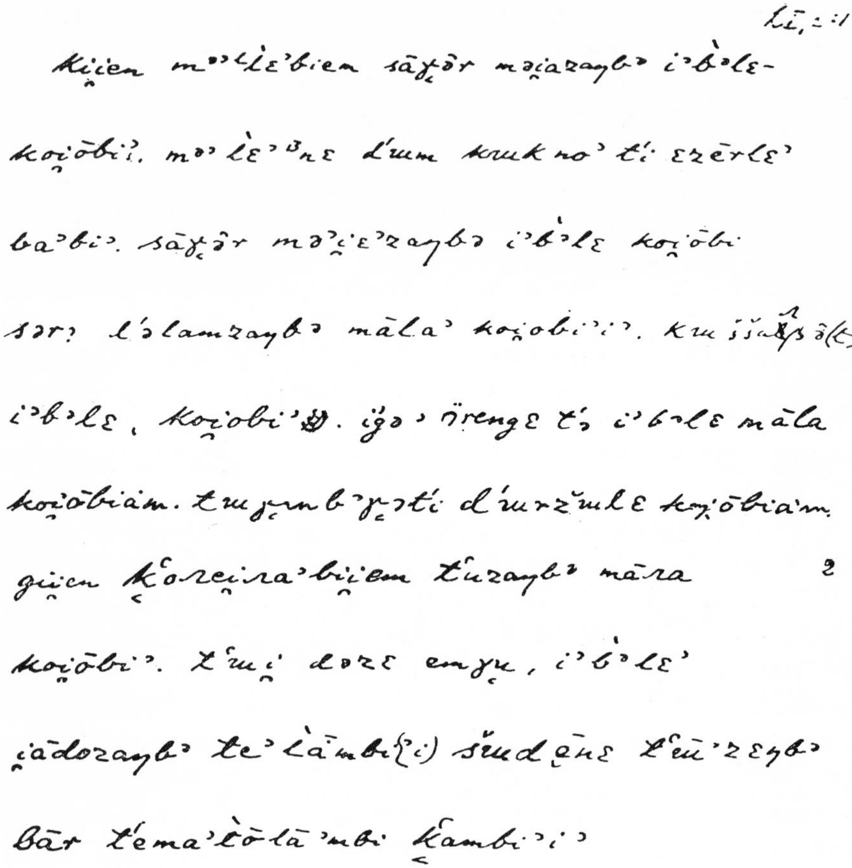

The following is a word by word interpretation of the text, using a phonemicized transcription, taken from Emil Setälä's system (1903), commonly adapted for Finnougric languages.

1. *kijen* 'where' (locative); *məʔlɛpijem* 'I was wandering'; *sākər* 'black'; *məjasaŋpə* 'my mountains';[1] *iʔpəlɛ* 'lying'; *kojōpi* 'it was left behind.'[2]
2. *məlɛpinɛ* 'gone, going';[3] *t'ym* 'my land'; *kyk* 'golden, green, blue'; *noʔt'ə* 'of my grass';[4] *ösērlɛ* 'growing';[5] *paʔpi* (continuative) (literally) 'it threw.'
3. *sākər məjasaŋpə iʔpəlɛ kojōpi.*
4. *səri* 'white'; *t'əlamasaŋpə* my mountain-tops';[6] *māla* 'remaining'; *kojópijəʔ* 'they remained.'[7]
5. *kyš alwət'ə* 'of our strength';[8] *iʔpəlɛ kojōpi.*
6. *ikəʔ* 'much, big, numerous'; *örenkət'ə* of my people'; *iʔpəlɛ māla kojōpijam* 'I am left, behind.'
7. *tykanpəkət'ə* 'of my relatives';[9] *t'yršylɛ* 'straying'; *kojōpijam.*
8. *kijen; kolajlapijem* 'I was fishing'; *tᶜusaŋpə* 'my lakes'; *māla kojōpi.*
9. *tyj* 'now'; *təsɛŋpə* 'these, those';[10] *em* 'I do not';[11] *ku* 'see.'[12]
10. *iʔpəlɛ*; *jātosaŋpə* 'my hut poles'; *teʔlāmpijəʔ* 'they rotted.'
11. *šytēne* 'the sinewed';[13] *tᶜysɛŋpə* 'my birchbark cloths'; *pār* 'all, entirely'; *t'emat ʔtōlāmpi* 'it shrivelled'; *kampijəʔ* 'they went, they are gone.'

1. Kai Donner and Joki regard the final *-pə* as an emphatic particle, and one could accept this interpretation; it should be noted, however, that this suffix can also be regarded as an alternant of the singular first person possessive, and since the pre-final phrase in some instances belongs to this category, we interpret *-pə* as 'my'; in the other interpretation *-pə* would function as a metric filling particle (expletive).
2. The singular predicate can be used optionally after a plural subject.
3. *-i* is inserted between *-p* and *-n* because the form is a participle of the perfect base ending in *-pi*; the transcription obviously represents a rapid form.
4. Donner and Joki regard *-t'ə* as an independent word 'girdle' and the construction as a compound 'grass girdle'; however, it is more likely that *-t'ə* is the ablative singular first person possessive form suffixed to *noʔ* 'grass', since this form obviously occurs two, or possibly three, times again.
5. The initial *ö-* is the form occurring in the field notes instead of the *-e* in the facsimile; there is no convincing reason for the replacement since Kai Donner himself remarks that the rounded vowels were used by the family of the informant.
6. *təlam* 'mountain-top in the Sayan'; for *-pə* see above.
7. Plural for metrical reasons.
8. *kyš* 'strength' and *al* 'substance'; in Kai Donner's fair copy a final- *t'ə* is in parentheses; in all probability it is the ablative of the singular first person possessive; cf. the corresponding forms in the next two sentences.
9. *-pə* is a metric filling particle.
10. *-pə* occurs in the field notes, but not in the facsimile; metric reasons warrant its occurrence.
11. Negative verb.
12. Verbal base.
13. Bound with sinews.

Kai Donner gave a free version of the poem in Swedish in his travel book. His fair copy of 1930 has a Finnish translation (with one explanatory addition in Swedish), but with certain omissions. Joki gives a German translation. The following English translation is based on the above interpretation and emendations.

1 My black mountains where I used to wander have been left behind;
2 My land where I wandered grew my golden grass!
3 My black mountains have been left behind;
4 My white summits have been left behind;
5 [All] of our strength has been left behind;
6 Of my large clan I alone am left behind;
7 Of my family I, straying alone, am left behind;
8 My lakes where I used to fish have been left behind;
9 Now I do not see them!
10 My hut-poles are rotten,
11 My sewn birchbark cloths are all shrivelled; they are gone.

The composition and formal structure of the song-text are very regular in spite of the lament form, which allows great freedom and variation in the use of language.

The text consists of a longer reminiscing part and a final couplet. The reminiscing part contains two themes: the first and more elaborate one is about the land of nomadic wandering, the golden grass-growing steppe, the black mountains with the dark forests, and the white summits of the Sayan which the people had left—the abandonment of places being associated with the decreasing strength of the tribe; the second theme is shorter, and is about the lost fishing lakes; this first part ends with the despairing "Now I do not see them!" The final couplet describes the decay of the old nomadic hut, the symbol of the nomad's life.

The song contains a neatly interwoven pattern of "objective" and "subjective" motifs which are indicated linguistically; the objective, about nature and the hut, are expressed with third person predicates, and the subjective, about the extinction of the people, with singular first person predicates. The text of this song consists of eleven sentences, each ending in a verbal predicative phrase. The short ninth sentence, the last sentence of the reminiscing part, ends in the negative expression *em ku* 'I do not see';

the others have positive predicates. The first seven sentences of the first part end in a finite verb; the second of these, containing the single association of the black mountains with the golden grass of the steppe, differs from the others, all of which contain the root *koj-* 'to leave behind.' (In general, many words are repeated in this song.) As indicated above, in subjective sentences the verbal forms are in the singular first person; in the others they are in the impersonal third person (either singular or plural, possibly for metric reasons). In the final couplet the verbal ending is a contracted continuative form—probably containing a bound alternant form of *kampi* 'it went' as an auxiliary. The full form *kampijəʔ* 'they went' concludes the song. The verbal predicative phrase, ending each sentence of the song, is preceded by either one or two syntactic phrases (two in the first, second, and seventh sentences, and one in the others, except in the short ninth sentence, where the predicative phrase is preceded by two pronominal particles). These phrases express the subject, the object, or the partitive adverbial determination of the verbal predicate. In the final sentence, an isolated word *pār* 'all, entirely' occurs before the verbal phrase. The phrases are of varying length, usually more than one word.

Thus each sentence consists of two or three syntactic phrase units (except the ninth sentence, which will be regarded as one phrase). These phrases may be analyzed into further constituents, words and morphemes. Linguistic organization alone, however, would not lend a metric character to the text, though it could give it a regularity not present in ordinary prose. There are two further devices present in the text for the purpose of versification: the parallel formal and semantic organization of the sentences, and the numerical regularity of syllabics in the phrases.

Parallelism is a common phenomenon in Uralic and Altaic folk-poetry.[8] It consists of a repetition of certain language data. The simplest type is complete repetition, but parallelism usually implies variation of either one or more elements, usually root morphemes, in the syntactic structure. As indicated above in the description of the predicative phrase, parallelism is present in that syntactic group, except in the ninth sentence, which has a deviating negative predicate. Each predicative phrase consists of a participle and a finite verb. In the first part, except in the second sentence (which also differs semantically), the participles are either *iʔpəlɛ* 'lying' or *māla* 'remaining.' In the sixth sentence, both occur together as a case of augmentative repetition. (This seems to be a Russian feature.)

In the seventh sentence, which is subjective, a different word occurs: *t'yršylɛ* 'straying,' in place of the preceding participial repetition. In the final couplet the matching consists of continuative derivations; the augmentation in the final sentence is similar to the repetition of the participles in the sixth sentence. But the parallelism goes beyond the matching of the predicative phrases. The structure of the first sentence is both matched and varied against that of the eighth: a clause consisting of the adverbial pronoun *kijen* 'where' (locative) and a verb in the first person singular perfect (*mə ʔlɛpijem* 'I went' vs. *kolajlapijem* 'I fished') is followed by a subject phrase in the plural third person possessive (*məjasaŋpə* 'my mountains' vs. *tᶜusaŋpə* 'my lakes'). (An attributive adjective corresponding to *sākər* 'black' is missing in the eighth sentence.) Each sentence is concluded by the predicative phrase as described above. The third sentence is a repetition of the second and third phrases of the first sentence, and the fourth sentence matches it: we have antonymous attributes (*sākər* 'black' vs. *səri* 'white'), synonymous subject-nouns in the plural first person possessive (*məjasaŋpə* 'my mountains' vs. *t'əlamsaŋpə* 'my summits'), and a synonymous pair of participles (*i ʔpəlɛ* 'lying' vs. *māla* 'remaining'). Each sentence is concluded by the finite verb. (The difference in number probably occurs for metric reasons.) The final phrase of the fifth sentence is constructed partially parallel to this couplet, but the first phrase seems to go with the following subjective parallels. The sixth and seventh sentences continue the subjective trend with another parallel couplet: we have synonymous nouns in the ablative singular first person possessive (*örenkət'ə* 'of my kin' vs. *tykanpəkət'ə* 'of my family') (there is no attributive adjective in the seventh sentence, but it may have been present originally), matching participles which are semisynonymous (the double *i ʔpəlɛ māla* 'staying, remaining' vs. *t'yršylɛ* 'straying') and identical verbs in the singular first person, of the root *koj-* 'to leave behind.' The final couplet again contains a parallelism: a subject-phrase consisting of an attributive participle (*i ʔpəlɛ* 'lying' vs. *šytēne* 'sewn'—semantically not matching) is followed by the subject nouns in the plural nominative (*jātosaŋpə* 'my poles' vs. *tᶜyseŋpə* 'my birchbark cloths') and concluded by a verbal phrase consisting of a participle in the continuative form, *te ʔlāmpijə ʔ* 'they were rotten' vs. the double *t'ema ʔtōlāmpi* 'they shrivelled' and *kampijə ʔ* 'they went.' The last sentence also contains a non-matching isolated element, *pār* 'all, entirely.' Linguistic analysis thus reveals a structuring of the material not only in its macrostructure, but in its microstructure as well.

Parallelism also occurs in the riddles collected by Kai Donner, which also show how a slight variation of the number of syllables can be due to the occurrence of different words in corresponding positions, for example, Nos. 3, 10, and 19:

wošte šē t'ykyn,	Her body in the other world,
kukojtə tə t'ykyn.	Her ear-ring in this world. [?]

(Answer: *t'ukul* 'the plant Lilium Martagon')

iʔpəpintə kōškəkata woptə,	Lying lower than a cat,
uʔptapintə inēkεte p^c*yršə.*	Standing higher than a horse. [?]

(Answer: *tuka* 'crooked rod')

kuja jilkintə nulam,	Under the sun I stand
altenəj warkam ńeʔl'em;	and blow a golden horn,
k^c*i jilkintə nulam,*	Under the moon I stand
k^c*ymyšəj warkam ńeʔl'em.*	and blow a silver horn. [?]

(Answer: *t*^{c}*aš* 'wild goose' or *k*^{c}*urujo* 'crane')

Such parallel organization of the syntactic structure of the sentences does not by itself make verse, although some implication of quantitative regularity of the phonic material is inherent in almost any parallelism. In order to speak of verse in the commonly accepted sense, a numerical regularity of the phonic material is required. This regularity consists here of a certain defined number of syllabic pulses (or at least a definite tendency for a defined number of such syllabic pulses) within certain syntactic boundaries. In Kamassian, two types of syntactic frames are important: phrase and sentence. A numerically characterized phrase in a poetic text is called a metric colon.[9] A metrically defined sentence is called a verse (line). After restoring the correct text and separating out the extraneous elements, we find that the majority of the phrases as analyzed above contain six syllabics. Deviations from the number six occur in lines two, five, seven, eight, and ten through the varying length of corresponding words. In three prefinal phrases we find trisyllabic expressions; in these we must assume missing words, as discussed above, or isochronic lengthening. The fact that the regularity is not the result of chance nor due only to the parallelism of the syntactic structures is shown by the use of the possessive suffix *-pə* throughout the poem, and the use of plural forms in the fourth and eleventh lines. These metric cola, corresponding to linguistic phrases, are further grouped into metric verses which linguistically correspond to sentences. Thus, there is a simple one-to-one correlation between the syntactic-linguistic frames on the one hand and the metric constituents on the other. The number of cola in a verse is one (in the ninth verse), two, or three (in the first and eighth). Further organization of the song-text is achieved by parallelism on various levels. The eighth verse, which matches the first, gives the impression of an attempt at a higher strophic organization, but it is not carried out.

Thus, the results of our analysis show that this Kamassian song-text has a metric structure of hexasyllabic phrase cola, with slight variations. The song begins with a three-colon line presenting the theme of the black mountains, the place of nomadic wandering left behind. This line is matched by a second three-colon line containing an association with the lost pastures of golden grass. Then there is a repetition (in a third line) of the last two cola of the first line, matched by an identically constructed fourth line; these refer to the objective circumstances of the black and the white mountains and are paralleled further by a fifth line containing a subjective reference to the diminished vital strength of the tribe. This is a transition to the two following subjective lines (the sixth and seventh), matched parallels, about the dying out of the kin. There then follows a three-colon parallel line (the eighth) matching the first line as if it were the beginning of a free strophic construction, but this is broken up immediately and this part of the poem is concluded by the subjective one-colon exclamation: "Now I do not see them!" The final couplet is constructed of two-colon lines, a parallel objective picture of the decaying nomadic hut symbolizing the end of the nomadic way of life and of the Kamassian tribe.

The metric structure at which we have thus arrived shows an inner consistency, using such poetic devices as parallelism and syllabically determined phrase-cola grouped into sentence-verses. Therefore, the Kamassian song, although possibly fragmentary, can be accepted as a good representative of Sayan-Samoyedic folk poetry of its genre. It also fits into the genetic-areal patterns of the poetry of related peoples. This verse structure is similar to that found in West Siberian Uralic and Turkic song-texts, and the poetic devices are also similar to those of other Uralic peoples, for example the Finns and Hungarians; they are also common elsewhere.

The poem is reproduced below in phonemic transcription; each colon appears by itself; the number of syllables is indicated by Arabic numbers before each line; metrical deviations are given in parentheses.

1	6	6	6	*kijen məʔlεpijem*	*sākər məjasaŋpə*	*iʔpəlε kojōpiʔ;*
2	5	3	5	*(məʔlεpinε t'ym*	*kyk noʔt'ə*	*ösērlε paʔpi!)*
3		6	6		*sākər məjasaŋpə*	*iʔpəlε kojōpi,*
4		6	6		*səri t' əlamsaŋpə*	*māla kojōpijəʔ;*
5		4	6		*kyš alwət'ə*	*iʔpəlε kojōpi;*
6		6	(3)6		*ikəʔ örenkət'ə*	*iʔpəlε māla kojōpijam,*
7		5	7		*tykanpəkət'ə*	*t'yršylε kojōpijam;*
8	7	(?)3	5	*kijen kolajlapijem*	*(?)*t^{c}*usaŋpə*	*māla kojōpi;*
9			6			*tyj təsεŋpə em ku!*
10		7	4		*iʔpəlε jātosaŋpə*	*teʔlāmpijəʔ,*
11		6	6(3)		*šytēne* t^{c}*ysεŋpə*	*pār t'emaʔtōlāmpi, kampijəʔ*

III. MORDVINIAN

This section presents the meter of Mordvinian folk poetry and places the metric description in a framework of certain assumptions of linguistic methodology and basic requirements of symbolic logic.[10] The presentation differs from the usual presentation of metrics in that it employs the axiomatic format common in mathematical and physical sciences. Formalization of this kind forces a more careful treatment of the phenomena themselves and prepares a more convenient way for comparative study. The content of the statements is, of course, identical with the usual cursive presentation.

Mordvinian is spoken by over one and a half million people in Central European Russia.[11] It is the third most widely spoken Uralic language, after Hungarian and Finnish, and is followed by Estonian. The following analysis is based on the work of two scholars, Paasonen, a Finnish linguist, and Šakhmatov, a Russian ethnographer, who collected extensive materials among the Mordvinians at the beginning of the twentieth century. There also exists a collection of Mordvinian melodies in Vienna, obtained from prisoners of war during World War I. The Paasonen and Šakhmatov materials were the basis for establishing the following syllabic patterns in Mordvinian folk songs: 4+3, 4+4, 4+5, 5+3, 5+5; 4+3+3, 4+4+3, 4+5+3, 4+4+4, 4+3+5, 4+4+5, 4+5+5, 5+3+3, 5+4+3, 5+5+3, 5+3+5, 5+4+5, 5+5+5; 4+4+4+3, 5+5+4+3. A few additional types were later discovered, and the vigorous collecting activity now taking place in the Mordvinian ASSR may contribute additional information.

The Mordvinian folk song material has been treated several times for metric purposes. Paasonen himself emphasized the regular character of these folk songs as opposed to the earlier assumption that Mordvinian folk poetry was highly irregular. Trubetzkoy, the great phonologist, contributed a few theories based on Šakhmatov's and the Viennese prisoners' materials. Then Jakobson and I published a systematic analysis of the total corpus of Paasonen and Šakhmatov, setting it in the framework of an axiomatic presentation of mathematical logic, especially as developed by Hilbert for geometry. I later set this analysis in a broader typological framework. The description that follows is based entirely on the joint article with one difference: the lines that were there taken in pairs as alternating couplets (5+5+4+3 and 4+4+4+3) are here taken as single lines. In this I follow Paasonen, in order to simplify the description.

The axiomatic method treats the subject matter explicitly by listing exactly all the primitives (i.e., the undefined terms of a system) and establishing all relationships among these basic constituents by axioms (or rules). The concept of primitives in an axiomatic system is a relative one. A notion which serves as a primitive is not necessarily a simple one. Such a notion is, rather, one that from the point of view of a closed system is assumed to be understood. For example, the notion of syllable is the subject of much discussion and controversy (see the introductory essay in this volume), but for the presentation here syllables are not further analyzed; they are simply assumed. The axioms or rules describe the relationships which exist among the given primitives. A set of definitions is introduced only to facilitate further statements; they are all derivable from the primitive rules.

A. *Constituents.*

The following linguistic constituents are necessary and sufficient to describe any Mordvinian folk song: (*a*) phonetic feature: *syllable*; and (*b*) semiotic frames: *word, colon, sentence.*

B. *Rules and Definitions.*

Rule 1: In a song there is an integral number of partial stretches which are not shorter than a colon and not longer than a sentence.

Definition 1.1: A verbal stretch as in Rule 1 is called a line.

Definition 1.2: A line within the song is assigned an ordinal number in the sequence of lines.

Rule 2: In each line there are two to four verbal stretches not shorter than a word and equal to one or more cola.

Definition 2.1: A verbal stretch as in Rule 2 is called a segment.

Definition 2.2: Lines containing two segments are called minimal, three segments, medial; four segments, maximal.

Definition 2.3: The segments in the line are identified by their ordinal number in the line; the segment with the highest ordinal number is called final, that with the lowest, initial.

Definition 2.4: Segments with the same ordinal number in different lines are called responding.

Rule 3: A segment contains three to five syllables.

Definition 3: A segment containing three syllables is called minimal, four syllables, medial, five syllables, maximal.

Rule 4.1: Responding segments contain identical numbers of syllables.

Rule 4.2: The initial segment is never minimal.

Rule 4.3: When the final segment is medial (tetrasyllabic), all segments are medial.

Rule 4.4: In maximal lines, the first two segments contain identical numbers of syllables, the final segment is minimal, and the third segment is medial.

Two metric units, segment and line, based on the linguistic primitives, (syllable, word, colon, sentence), emerge from the above axioms as constituents of the metric suprastructure. The term segment corresponds to caesura-determined parts of a verse-line. The results can be summed up in the following diagram:

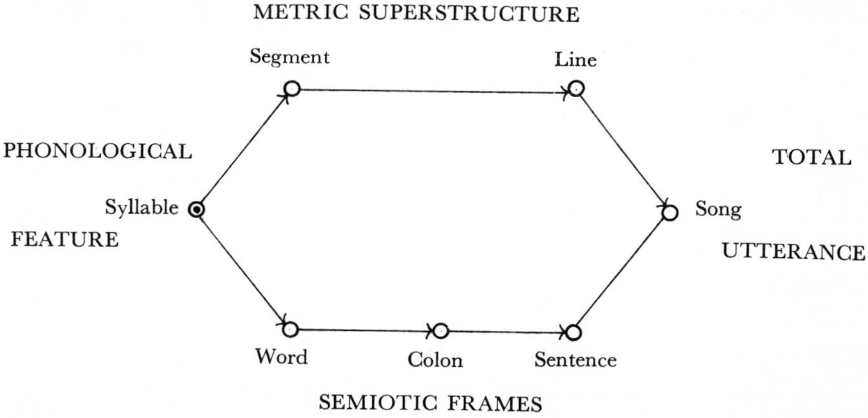

Mordvinian meter can be illustrated by the following two examples:[12] (| indicates segment boundary, || indicates line boundary)

1. Syllabic scheme 4+3:

nejan, vanan | *gornitsá,* ||
gornitśaso | *sikań stol',* ||
ve pesenze | *pure-par* ||
ombo pese | *med-parka,* ||
kuntśka vitse | *molodets.* ||
meks a simat, | *a jartsat?* ||

2. Syllabic scheme 4+4+5:

kona vidi | *patravs sóra,* | *mergəz: sorze aš!* ||
kut' videsi, | *kut'sokasi,* | *švatat tapasaž,* ||

kenərəmək, | *so ń kasəmək* | *švatat sivəntsaž.* ||
kona tirəj | *sarast matsiśt,* | *mergəz: švatan(e) aš!* ||
liśtəməkəst, | *narvaməkəst* | *kaval't salsəsaz,* ||
tolgajəmək, | *potškajəmək* | *lomat' šavəntaž* ||

An axiomatic approach permits a metric system to be evaluated as to the basic requirements posed in formal logic for axiomatic presentations, namely, the requirements of non-contradictoriness, completeness, and economy (or simplicity). In order to investigate these three logical problems we can regard the above system as a model without interpretation.[13]

Non-contradictoriness is logically indispensable in any system: otherwise all propositions including false ones could be proved within the system. Since each rule in our model refers to relationships among a different set of constituents, no contradiction can arise. This is, of course, mathematically trivial. Rules 1–2 place the metric constituents in the semiotic hierarchy by setting their upper and lower limits and determine the numerical relations between the metric constituents, segment and line (2–4), and between line and song (any integer). Rule 3 determines the numerical relations between segment and the phonetic constituent, syllable (3–5). Since these rules are either existential postulates or independent numerical assignments, no contradiction can arise in the first three rules. Rules 4.1 to 4.4 set limitations regarding the number of syllables and the arrangement of segments within the line; 4.1 gives the general rule of internal response; 4.2 gives a restriction of the initial segment (not trisyllabic); 4.3 gives a general structuring dependent on the final segment (if this latter is medial, all segments in the line, and in the song, are medial); 4.4 gives special restrictions about the maximal line. Since all these restrictions in Rule 4 are independent, there can be no contradiction.

The term "completeness" has two meanings in logic. Taken more rigorously it refers to a system where the introduction of new elements will lead to a contradiction (cf. Hilbertian geometry). Less rigorously, it refers to a system where all the existing cases are taken care of and only these are enumerated. The completeness of a system is dependent on our state of knowledge; for example, the syllabic pattern 4–5 did not occur in Paasonen's material, only in Šakhmatov's. Other types were discovered later. Completeness can be achieved by giving the general frame and adding restrictions until one accounts for the existing metric types. Another method is the simple enumeration of existing cases, but that does not give any insight into the structuring of the material. The requirements for completeness are thus met in a modest manner for our model, though the generality of the axiomatic approach guarantees that omissions are not basically significant. The model also achieves descriptive simplicity in a mathematical way, since all rules are statements about individual relations and cannot be further reduced within the framework.

Though the axiomatic method of presentation does not increase the factual coverage of the metric material, it does create a better basis for comparison between metric systems and between metrics and other linguistic fields. And it promotes a more effective interdisciplinary exchange in general. In my opinion, however, claims for a formal axiomatic methodology should not be exaggerated in metrical analysis. The introductory statement in the joint paper by Jakobson and Lotz mentioned above makes the following assertion: "The analysis of a metrical system requires the exact determination of all the constituents and their mutual relations underlying any meter of this system; the analysis must fully and unequivocally bring out which meters can and do exist and which cannot occur in the given system. Thus, the whole stock of the actual metrical forms really existing must be completely deducible from the rules established." This sounds like a modified generative-transformational statement applied to metrics. Such an approach seems, however, unfeasible for metric analysis. The aim of arriving at a full corpus of metrical schemes (cf. grammatical sentences) and excluding the non-occurring and non-permitted metrical schemes (cf. non-grammatical sentences) is not realizable. For example, after the list of Mordvinian metric schemes was compiled, based on the materials of Paasonen and Šakhmatov, a few additional metric types were discovered requiring the readjustment of the axioms (rules). In general it can be said that because of its nature, meter creates immediate countertendencies. Verse is the most idiosyncratic use of language and is subject to extreme individualistic manipulation, even in folk poetry such as the Mordvinian. Thus, the attempt to set up an "axiomatic" (i.e., rule-governed) formulation which generates all and only the existing metrical schemes of a system, results in a completely *ad hoc* explanation.

Therefore, instead of regarding the above account of Mordvinian verse as a closed explanatory system, we regard it as a descriptive statement which may perhaps be modified with the introduction of additional data or, possibly, with the expurgation of wrong data. The adjustments, nevertheless, will always be marginal, because the axioms coherently define the structural skeleton of the metric system and describe, to a large extent, the specific phenomena as well.

NOTES

1. This article was first published in a slightly different form by the Instituti Hungarici Universitatis Holmiensis, Thesis v, 1952; translated from *Ungersk dikt i svensk tolkning* (*Hungarian Poetry in Swedish Translation*) (Stockholm: Hungarian Instit., 1944), pp. 173–77.
2. Vowels with accent marks (′or ″) are always long, vowels without accents are always short; *sz, zs, cs,* represent simple sounds; *y* in old family names may denote a vowel, but otherwise it indicates the palatal articulation of the consonant phoneme. The article, *a,* can count as either a long or a short base. There are also some other arbitrary principles, especially in earlier poetry.
3. Notation is as follows: — long base; ‿ short base; ⌣ anceps.
4. A revised version of an article, "Kamassian Verse," which appeared in the *Journal of American Folklore,* 67 (1954), 369–77.
5. Surprisingly, in the 1960's an Estonian ethnographic expedition discovered two surviving Kamassian speakers, and both remembered Kai Donner's visit.
6. The text was published posthumously by Aulis Joki in *Kai Donners Kamassisches Wörterbuch nebst Sprachproben und Hauptzügen der Grammatik,* Lexica Societatis Fenno-Ugricae, 8 (Helsinki, 1944), p. 87. I was unable to locate the melody of the song in Helsinki. The melodies collected by Kai Donner and published in 1959 by Väisänen (in "Samojedische Melodien," *Mémoires de la Société Finno-Ougrienne,* 136, Helsinki, 1965) do not include the melody of this text.
7. Besides the song, the material includes thirty-one riddles, eleven tales, and two brief sacrificial prayers (pp. 85–100), and also a tale and four riddles, written down during his visit in 1912 (p. 197).
8. For further data on Uralic and other languages and for bibliography, see Wolfgang Steinitz, *Der Parallelismus in der finnisch-karelischen Volksdichtung,* FF Communications, 115 (Helsinki, 1934), and Robert Austerlitz, *Ob-Ugric Metrics,* FF Communications, 14 (Helsinki, 1958).
9. For an interesting study of the interrelation between metric constituents and linguistic units, especially in Slavic verse, see Roman Jakobson, "Studies in Comparative Slavic Metrics," *Oxford Slavonic Papers,* 3 (1952), esp. 55–57.
10. A revised version of Roman Jakobson and John Lotz, *Axiomatik eines Verssystems am mordwinischen Volkslied dargelegt,* Thesis I, Hungarian Inst. of the Univ. of Stockholm, 1941. (Trans., "Axioms of a Versification System Exemplified by the Mordvinian Folksong," in *Acta Instituti Hungarici Universitatis Holmiensis,* Series B.1, Stockholm, 1951, pp. 5–13.)
11. The Mordvinians are first mentioned by Herodotus as exceptionally skilled hunters.
12. H. Paasonen, *Über den Versbau des mordwinischen Volksliedes,* Finnisch-Ugrische Forschungen, 10 (1910), Example 1 on p. 156, and Example 2 on p. 169.
13. Among linguists, the Danish glossematicians Louis Hjelmslev and Hans Uldall have emphasized the importance of logical requirements for linguistic analysis.

SELECTED BIBLIOGRAPHY

HUNGARIAN.

Arany, János. *A magyar nemzeti versidomról* (*On the Hungarian National Verse Type*). 1856.

Gábor, Ignác. *A magyar ritmus problémája* (*The Problem of Hungarian Rhythm*). Budapest, 1925.

Gáldi, László. *Ismerjük meg a versformákat* (*Let's Learn about the Verse Forms*). Budapest, 1961.

Hegedüs, Lajos. *A magyar nemzeti versritmus* (*Hungarian National Verse Rhythm*). Pécs, 1934.

Horváth, János. *A magyar vers* (*Hungarian Verse*). Budapest, 1948.

——— *Rendszeres magyar verstan* (*Systematic Hungarian Versification*). Budapest, 1951.

Lotz, John. *Hungarian Meter.* Instituti Hungarici Universitatis Holmiensis. Thesis v, 1952.
Négyesy, László. *Magyar verstan.* (*Hungarian Versification*). 2nd. ed. Budapest, 1898.
Németh, László. *Magyar ritmus* (*Hungarian Rhythm*). Budapest, n.d.
Rákos, Petr. *Rhythm and Metre in Hungarian Verse.* Acta Universitatis Carolinae, Philologica Monographia XI. Praha, 1966. Contains a survey of research on Hungarian meter.
Szabédi, László. *A magyar ritmus formái* (*Forms of Hungarian Rhythm*). Bucuresti, 1955.
Szabolcsi, Bence. *Vers és dallam* (*Verse and Melody*). Budapest, 1959.
Vargyas, Lajos. *A magyar vers ritmusa* (*The Rhythm of Hungarian Verse*). Budapest, 1952.

MORDVINIAN.
Jakobson, Roman. "Studies in Comparative Slavic Metrics." *Oxford Slavonic Papers*, 3 (1952), 21–66.
———, and John Lotz. *Axiomatik eines Verssystems am mordwinischen Volkslied dargelegt.* Thesis I. Hungarian Inst. of the Univ. of Stockholm, 1941. Trans. "Axioms of a Versification System Exemplified by the Mordvinian Folksong." *Acta Instituti Hungarici Universitatis Holmiensis*, Series B. I (Stockholm, 1951), pp. 5–13.
Lachs, Robert. *Gesänge russischer Kriegsgefangenen.* I, i, *Mordwinische Gesänge.* (Sitzungsberichte der Akademie der Wissenschaften in Wien, philologisch-historische Klasse, Bd. 205, 2. Abh.) Vienna, 1933.
Lotz, John. "Notes on Structural Analysis in Metrics." *Helicon*, 4 (1943), 119–46.
Paasonen, Heikki. *Mordwinische Chrestomathie.* Hülfsmittel für das Studium der finnisch-ugrischen Sprachen IV. Helsingfors, 1909.
——— *Mordwinische Volksdichtung.* (Collected by H. P., ed. & trans. Paavo Ravila.) Vol. I, *Mémoires de la Société Finno-Ougrienne LXXVII*, 1938. Vol. II, *MSFOu LXXXI*, 1939. Vol. III *MSFOu LXXXIV*, 1941. Vol. IV, *MSFOu XCI*, 1947.
——— *Proben der mordwinischen Volkslitteratur.* Vol. I. Erzjanischer Teil, Fasc. 1, Erzjanische Lieder. *Journal de la Société Finno-Ougrienne*, 9 (1891). Fasc. 2, Erzjanische Zaubersprüche, Opfergebete, Räthsel, Sprichwörter und Märchen. *Journal de la Socété Finno-Ougrienne*, 12 (1894). Contains no metric material.
——— "Über den Versbau des mordwinischen Volksliedes." *Finnisch-Ugrische Forschungen*, 10 (1910).
Šakhmatov, A. A. *Mordovskij etnografičeskij sbornik.* St. Petersburg, 1910.
Trubetzkoy, N. *Zur Struktur der mordwinischen Melodien.* (Sitzungsberichte der Akademie der Wissenschaften in Wien, philologisch-historische Klasse, Bd. 205, 2. Abh., Anhang, pp. 115 ff.) Vienna, 1933.
Vaisänen, A. O. "Mordwinische Melodien." *Mémoires de la Société Finno-Ougrienne XCII*, 1948.

GERMANIC

By W. P. LEHMANN

Summary

The prosodics, or systems of versification, of the various Germanic languages have followed similar courses of development. The Germanic verse that we know shows two types of prosody: The first was built around quantity and stress; it was already being replaced when the Germanic peoples were becoming literate. The second, built around stress alone, has subsequently been the central system. Besides these major types of prosody, some poets have experimented with other principles of versification. And today there are indications that the bases of prosody may be shifting again in some of the Germanic languages; in a short sketch we can note this last shift only briefly. To understand the prosody of most Germanic verse, we must recognize two types: the quantity-plus-stress-based prosody of ancient Germanic verse; the stress-based prosody that replaced it.

Comparison of the Two Types of Prosody

The second stanza of the Old Norse *Vǫlospá* will illustrate the prosodic principles of ancient Germanic verse. (In the prosodic schemes following each line—also referred to as long line—X indicates a prosodically prominent syllable, x a non-prominent; — indicates quantity; / indicates strong stress, \ intermediary stress; the shorter spaces separate metrical segments or feet, the longer indicate a caesura.)

Ek man iǫtna, ár um borna,	$\overset{/}{\bar{X}}\mathrm{x}\ \ \overset{/}{\bar{X}}\mathrm{x} \qquad \overset{/}{\bar{X}}\mathrm{x}\ \ \overset{/}{\bar{X}}\mathrm{x}$
þá er forðom mik fœdda hofðo;	$\mathrm{xx}\overset{/}{\bar{X}}\ \ \mathrm{x}\overset{/}{\bar{X}} \qquad \overset{/}{\bar{X}}\mathrm{x}\ \ \overset{/}{\bar{X}}\mathrm{x}$
nío man ek heima, nío íviði	$\overset{/}{\bar{X}}\mathrm{xxx}\ \ \overset{/}{\bar{X}}\mathrm{x} \qquad \overset{/}{\bar{X}}(\mathrm{x})\ \overset{/}{\bar{X}}\overset{\backslash}{X}\mathrm{x}$
miǫtvið mæran fyr mold neðan	$\overset{/}{\bar{X}}\mathrm{x}\ \ \overset{/}{\bar{X}}\mathrm{x} \qquad \mathrm{x}\overset{/}{\bar{X}}\ \ \overset{/}{\bar{X}}\mathrm{x}$

I know etins,   ancient deathless
who in former times   have fathered me;
nine realms I know of,   nine well-measured
ash-tree's famed roots   the earth beneath.

Each line of Germanic verse is metrically independent. Germanic alliterative poetry was stichic, as in the Old Saxon and Old High German lines cited below. Scandinavian poetry, however, like that illustrated here, developed stanzaic structures. But in these, too, there was no metrical bond between the various lines of a stanza. Stanzaic units with formal binding principles were introduced only after Germanic verse was influenced by Latin and Romance verse.

Each line has four principal prosodic stresses, and is divided into two half-lines of two stresses each by a caesura. The stressed syllables, at least the first three, must be long, though length may be achieved by resolution. Either the vowel must be long, as in *ár* (in Old Norse texts long vowels are marked with acute accents); or, if short, the vowel must be followed in the syllable by one or more consonants, as in *mold*. Except in occasional lines, only in the fourth stressed syllable of a line may the vowel be short, as in *ne-*. The stressed syllables may be further marked by alliteration, but the binding force is stress linked with quantity.

This prosodic pattern, used throughout ancient Germanic verse whether for short poems like the Old High German *Hildebrandslied* and the Old English *Wanderer,* or for long poems like the *Beowulf,* avoided monotony through variation in internal rhythm of half-lines. Lines with even rhythm, such as the first line cited above, are infrequent. Much more common is varying rhythm, as in the second line. And as the second half-lines of the third and fourth lines illustrate, the prosodic patterns may be made up of a variety of feet. In the ancient Germanic tradition poets achieved richness of rhythm not through variation of stanza structures, or differences in length of lines, but through the varying rhythmic structure of their half-lines.

The patterning of these structures has been widely discussed. For an introduction to Germanic prosody the five types proposed by Sievers are still useful:

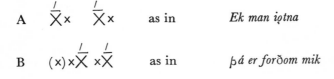

A	$\overset{/}{\overline{\times}}\,\times\quad\overset{/}{\overline{\times}}\,\times$	as in	*Ek man iǫtna*
B	$(\times)\,\times\,\overset{/}{\overline{\times}}\quad\times\,\overset{/}{\overline{\times}}$	as in	*þá er forðom mik*

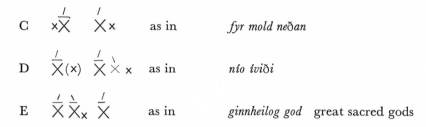

C	xX́ X́x	as in	*fyr mold neðan*
D	X́(x) X́ X̀ x	as in	*nío íviði*
E	X́ X̀x X́	as in	*ginnheilog god* great sacred gods

The prosody is based on both stress and quantity. Sievers considered the arrangement of stress central. Others, following Heusler, base their analysis primarily on quantity, and see in ancient Germanic verse a rhythm determined by units of time. Since the verse has a twofold basis, neither stress nor quantity can be disregarded. An understanding of their interplay leads to an appreciation of the achievements of the outstanding Germanic poets in manipulating a relatively fixed pattern in a variety of rhythms.

The main departure from verse built around repeated four-stress lines was developed in an Old Norse stanza structure which may be illustrated by what are probably the most widely-known ancient Germanic lines, *Hávamál* 77:

Deyr fé, deyia frændr,	X́ X́ X́x X́
deyr siálfr it sama;	X́ X́x X́x
ek veit einn, at aldri deyr:	X́x X́ xX́ xX́
dómr um dauðan hvern.	X́x X́x X́

Kine die, kin die
dies the soul itself;
I know one thing, that never dies:
the glory beyond the grave.

In this stanza short lines alternate with the normal long lines. Extra-long lines, too, with three stresses per half-line, occur in some ancient Germanic verse, as in the translation of the Beatitudes in the Old Saxon *Heliand* 1308:

Sâlige sind ôc, the sie hîr frúmono gilústid,
rîncos, that sie réhto adômien. Thes môtun sie uuérðan an them rîkia dróhtines

Blessed are also those who seek what's lawful,
the courageous, that they capably give judgments. For this they will be in the kingdom of the Lord.

Apparently poets introduced these extra-long lines to achieve an effect of solemnity. There are relatively few instances of them in ancient Germanic verse.

Auxiliary Binding Features

In ancient Germanic verse, some of the metrically prominent syllables were marked by initial rhyme, alliteration. The key alliteration falls on the third prominent syllable; the first generally alliterates; the second frequently does; the fourth alliterates only exceptionally. Each consonant, and each of the consonant groups *sp, st, sk,* can alliterate only with itself, for example *f* : *f* of line two of the stanza from the *Vǫlospa*, or *m m* : *m* of line four. All the vowels alliterate together, as do *e í*ǫ : *a* in line one of this stanza. Alliteration continuing over more than one line is infrequent, as is crossed alliteration like that in line one of the *Hávamál* stanza *d f* : *d f*.

Rhyme was occasionally used in ancient Germanic verse, but it was only decorative; in much the same way alliteration has been used in stress-based verse, as in Shakespeare, for ornament. The primary auxiliary feature of stress-based verse is end-rhyme, that of ancient Germanic verse, alliteration. But end-rhyme is less closely associated with the basis of versification than was alliteration.

Time of the Shift

The shift in prosody took place at different times in the various Germanic dialects, but the starting point was the same, as were contemporary prosodic conventions. To illustrate the prosodic principles, and the shift, in another Germanic language, we may compare a line from the Old High German *Hildebrandslied,* which observes the prosodic conventions of ancient Germanic verse, with one from recent German, which superficially follows the same pattern: the first line of Wagner's *Die Walküre*:

HL 16 *alte anti frōte dea ĕrhina wārun* X́xxx X́x xX́xx X́x
old men and wise who earlier were here

Wes Herd dies auch sei, hier muß ich rasten xX xxX Xxx Xx
Whose hearth this may be, here must I rest.

Though he uses uneven feet and alliteration, Wagner's prosody is based on stress alone. Similar examples might be given from Old Norse and the modern Scandinavian languages, as from the sparse ancient materials of the German lowlands and from Modern Dutch.

Since the various Germanic literatures parallel one another in starting with a stress-quantity prosody and shifting to one based on stress alone, the general lines of development in one language resemble those of the others. In this sketch, German will be given more space than Dutch or the Scandinavian languages. Except for details, the prosody of Dutch is very similar to that of German. The Scandinavian languages differ primarily in the time of the shift; in them the earlier Germanic prosodic conventions were maintained until the thirteenth century, and even then they were relinquished slowly. If we recognize these chronological differences, an understanding of the prosody underlying verse in one Germanic language will provide an understanding of the prosody in the other Germanic languages as well.

German Prosody in its Changes

German verse has been transmitted only since the tenth century, and even at that time a prosody centering around stress was introduced. This difference in prosody was accompanied, and underlined, by a difference in the manner of presentation to the audience. Ancient Germanic verse was designed for oral production; the audience was non-literate, as were the poets. Yet Otfrid, the first German poet to depart from ancient Germanic prosody, informs us that his verse was composed to be read. Whether or not subsequent poets also directed their verse at a literate audience, the availability of writing affected their verse, possibly most fundamentally by providing an opportunity for longer prosodic units. In ancient Germanic verse the longest prosodic unit was the line. But with the introduction of writing, poets joined together a number of lines into prosodic units; Otfrid himself used an acrostic to unite several long sequences, one of ninety-six lines. His normal prosodic unit was the rhymed couplet, consisting of two lines with four stresses each:

.v.3	*Tho quam bóto fona góte, éngil ir hímile,*	Xx Xx Xx Xx Xx X Xx X
	bráht er therera uuórolti diuri árunti.	Xx Xxx XxX X X X xX

> Then came a messenger from the Lord, an angel out of heaven;
> he brought down to this world a priceless report.

(Otfrid's rhymes—*góte: hímile, uuórolti: árunti*—may seem rude in comparison to modern conventions. Similar rhymes are found in Celtic and medieval Latin verse.)

This couplet is also the prosodic unit of Middle High German epic verse, for example, Gottfrid's *Tristan and Isolde*:

1	*Gedæht man in ze guote niht*	xX xX xX xX
	von den der werlde guot geschicht,	xX xX xX xX
	so wære ez allez alse niht,	xX xX xX xX
	swaz guotes in der werlt geschicht.	xX xX xX xX

> If those men were to count as nought
> by whom good to the world is brought,
> then everything would be as nought
> the good that to the world is brought.

The prime difference between Otfrid's prosody and that of Gottfrid, between Old High German versification and Middle High German, is increased strictness in prosodic and rhyming conventions; besides internal development toward an alternating rhythm, the influence of French courtly verse introduced to German verse greater regularity than had the prosodic conventions which Otfrid took over from late Latin verse.

Introduction of Complex Stanza Forms into German

Literacy had brought with it an increased possibility of borrowing from other verse. After the initial borrowing from Latin verse, the most far-reaching influence came from the courtly culture of France in the twelfth and thirteenth centuries. Besides attention to even rhythm and pure rhyme, this influence led to the introduction of complex stanzaic forms. Courtly lyric verse was accompanied by song; some melodic patterns were taken over completely by German poets, and with them prosodic requirements for intricate stanzas. A stanza of Walther von der Vogelweide will illustrate this complexity, as well as the regularity of rhythm and rhyme:

LI.xxix	*Wol dir, meie, wie du scheidest*	Xx Xx Xx Xx
	allez âne haz!	Xx Xx X
	wie dû walt und ouwe kleidest,	Xx Xx Xx Xx
	und die heide baz!	Xx Xx X
	diu hât varwe mê.	Xx Xx X
	"dû bist kurzer, ich bin langer,"	Xx Xx Xx Xx
	alsô strîtents ûf dem anger,	Xx Xx Xx Xx
	bluomen unde klê.	Xx Xx X

Hail, oh May, who now restorest
everything so well!
How you clothe the field and forest,
and every blooming dell!
Color they have more.
"You are shorter, I am longer."
So the flowers think they're stronger
Than clover evermore.

German verse has subsequently adopted stanza forms from other cultures too—the sonnet form from Italian, and other stanza forms from Spanish and French; various ode forms from Greek and Latin; Oriental forms from Persian and Indic—but without major prosodic innovation. The imported stanzaic patterns fostered variation in externals, such as length of line, distribution of rhyme, type of meter, but no change in the basic prosodic conventions. In the only major prosodic shift beyond the introduction of stanzas, poets may continue beyond them to handle an entire poem as a prosodic unit, for example, Goethe in the closing stanzas of his *Mailied*:

So liebt die Lerche	Like me the lark
Gesang und Luft	Loves song and air,
Und Morgenblumen	And morning flowers
Den Himmelsduft,	The heavens fair,
Wie ich dich liebe	So I love you
Mit warmem Blut	With heart's warm blood,
Die du mir Jugend	You give me youth,
Und Freud' und Mut	Joy, hardihood,

Zu neuen Liedern	Yourself to song
Und Tänzen gibst.	And dance you give.
Sei ewig glücklich,	Be ever happy,
Wie du mich liebst!	Love while you live.

After establishing his four-line stanza, Goethe breaks through it, as many poets have broken through the sonnet form. But apart from this striving to establish longer units, Goethe's prosody, like that of Otfrid, Gottfrid, Walther von der Vogelweide, and later poets, is based on stress, with rhyme as an optional auxiliary, and variation in length of prosodic units.

As Walther's poem illustrates, in Middle High German lyric poetry considerable variety was permitted in length of line and also in type of feet. In German verse after the seventeenth century greater regularity in both dimensions is aimed at. To designate each, terminology which had originated to describe the quantitative verse of Greek was introduced, often to the confusion of early prosodists. But the rhythms were those used in earlier verse, as the examples given above illustrate. Most lines of German verse begin with a metrically non-prominent syllable and end with a prominent, for example, Goethe's *Gesang und Luft* (xX xX). Such lines are often called iambic; and since this line consists of two iambs it is said to be in iambic dimeter. Stanzas beginning with a prominent syllable, known as trochaic, are less frequent, for example Heine's *Romanzero:*

Täglich ging die wunderschöne. Xx Xx Xx Xx

Daily went the wondrous beauty.

Even less frequent are lines with several weakly stressed syllables preceding or following a stressed, such as the following line from the last part of Goethe's *Faust* (dactyl):

Alles vergängliche Xxx Xxx

Everything perishable.

Means of Achieving Variety in German Versification

In Modern German verse variety has been attempted (1) by selecting lines of different length (though as in English, lines of five feet are very widely used), (2) by varying the position of the caesura, (3) by shifting the stress locations in individual feet after establishing a pattern, (4) by the selection of internal patterns of vowels and consonants, (5) by ending lines not only on stressed syllables (masculine rhymes), but sometimes on unstressed syllables (feminine rhymes), as in the final words spoken by Maria Stuart in Schiller's play, v.ix.43–45:

Kniet zu den Füssen der Elisabeth!	X xxX xX xX xX
Mög' Euer Lohn nicht Eure Strafe werden!	xX xX Xxx Xx Xx
Lebt wohl! Jetzt hab' ich nichts mehr auf der Erden.	xX Xxx Xx Xx Xx

Kneel at the feet of Queen Elizabeth!
And may your prize not turn into your pain!
Farewell! On earth I now have nothing more to gain.

Visual Forms

The use of writing gave poets an awareness of designing prosodic forms visually, and also a possibility of precisely maintaining prosodic patterns of the past. But neither conservatism nor visual forms yielded great poetry in Germanic.

The ancient Germanic poets also maintained traditions from the past; even though it did not appear until the thirteenth century, Snorri's poetic handbook, the *Háttatal*, suggests as much. But alliterative verse differs so greatly in rhythm in the various Germanic dialects that we must assume that the spoken language rather than any rigid pattern determined the rhythm of individual lines, whether in Scandinavia or in England or on the continent. Literate poets on the other hand may follow patterns set primarily by the written language; one unfortunate example is given by the *Meistersinger*, ridiculed by Wagner. Like their frozen prosodic patterns, verse based on visual shapes has received little distinction; an example is Philip von Zesen's *Palm-tree*, with lines varying in length to achieve a shape resembling a tree. Some recent poets have also used visual arrangements to support their prosody, for example, Arno Holz; but they have not been the most influential poets nor have their visual patterns been generally admired. Visual patterns have been most successful when, as in Dylan Thomas' *Vision and Prayer* poems, they are auxiliary to other formal patterns.

Dutch Prosody

Since the history of Dutch prosody parallels that of German, only a few examples of Dutch verse will be given here. The Flemish poet Heinrich von Veldeke preceded the great German medieval poets in using the forms of courtly verse. As a portion of one of his lyric poems will illustrate, he observes as great regularity of rhythm and rhyme as they do. (As with Gottfrid above, I quote the edited texts, which provide "regular" forms that the poet may not have used; as indicated below, some *-e* endings should be elided in the scansion.)

Tristant mûste âne sînen danc	Xx Xx Xx X
stâde sîn der koninginnen,	Xx Xx Xx Xx
want poisûn heme dâ tû dwanc	xXx Xx Xx X
mêre dan dî cracht der minnen.	Xx Xx Xx Xx

Tristan knew no other right
than give the queen his adoration,
when driven by the poison's might
even more than by the power of passion.

Dutch verse also parallels German in variety of stanzaic forms and rhythmic lines. To illustrate a pattern more successful in Dutch than in German we may cite some alexandrines from Vondel's *Geboortklock*:

Om wie ick 't leven lieve, en sonder welcke ick niet	xX xX xX xX xX xX
De majesteyt der sonne aenschou als met verdriet	xX xX xX xX xX xX

For whom I love this life, without whom I'll abstain
From gazing at the glory of the sun, except with pain.

In Dutch verse today, for example, Verwey's *Meidag*, the prosody is parallel to that of German and the other contemporary Germanic languages:

Hoe nabij,	X xX
Hoe als eerst,	X xX
Glanst het bosje en straalt de wei,	X xXx xX xX
Schalt de leeuwrik die met zang de lucht beheerst.	X xXx x xX xX xX

How nearby,
How anew,
Gleams the wood, the lea shines too,
Sings the lark whose song fills all the sky.

Scandinavian Prosody

From Scandinavian verse we may quote examples which illustrate for the older period how the ancient Germanic prosody became increasingly intricate, and for the modern period how prosodic conventions have approximated those in the other Germanic languages.

Verse of the *Edda,* as illustrated above, was modified by additional rhythmic and metrical requirements to become some of the most prosodically complex ever found in poetry, the Skaldic forms. The first example in Snorri's *Háttatal* will illustrate its complexities:

Lætr sá'r Hákon heitir,	X́x X́x X́x
hann rekkir lið, bannat,	X́͡Xx X́ X́x
jǫrð kann frelsa, firðum	X́x X́x X́x
friðrofs, konungr ofsa.	X́x X́x X́x

Powerful Haakon, hero:
he sends armies reeling,
His might brings freedom; fighters'
fierce scourge; king of courage.

Each line consists of a fixed number of syllables, in this stanza six. Besides the alliteration binding successive lines, each line must have internal rhyme, either consonantal: *lætr, heitir;* or syllabic: *hann, bann.* Stylistic requirements, which are not discussed here, combined with the prosodic requirements to lead to a poetry so rigid that much of Skaldic verse is scarcely distinguished for its content.

These requirements, of combining stress with quantity and alliteration with rhyme, were maintained in the medieval Icelandic ballads (*rímur*). These are stricter in form than are the ballads in the other Germanic languages, as the first stanza of Einar Gilsson's *Rime of Olaf* of the fourteenth century will illustrate:

Ólafr Kóngur örr og fríðr	X́ X́x X́x X́
átti Noregi að ráða	X́x X́͡Xxx X́x
gramr var æ við bragna blíðr	X́x X́x X́x X́
borinn til sigrs og náða	X́͡Xx X́x X́x

Olaf, King of favors, the Fair,
  Owned all Norway to police,
Bearing the bold within his care,
  Born for triumph and peace.

In recent Scandinavian poetry, as in Dutch poetry, the prosody is parallel with that in other Germanic dialects, for example, in Ibsen's *Peer Gynt* I.159–60:

P. G.:	*Hvor er sneen fra ifjor?*	Xx Xx Xx X
ASE:	*Du skal tie for din moer!*	Xx Xx Xx X

Where are all the snows of yore?
Your mother bids you say no more.

The parallelism in prosody in the various Germanic languages might well be expected when we find that a Norwegian poet ends one of his acts (*Peer Gynt,* Act IV) with a line in another language:

Es lebe hoch der grosse Peer!	xX xX xX xX

All hail and honor, mighty Peer!

A stanza of Fröding's will illustrate how the prosody of recent Swedish verse is also comparable to that of German:

Hör, hur det ljuder kring myr och mo:	X xxX xxX xX
Lilja—mi Lilja—mi Lilja—mi ko!	Xx xXx xXx xX
Eko vaknar i bergigt bo,	Xx Xx xX xX
svarar ur hällarne	Xxx Xxx
langt norr i fjällarne	Xxx Xxx
Lilja—mi Lilja—mi ko!	Xx xXx xX

Hear, how the sound goes round moor and mow:
Lilja—my Lilja—my Lilja—my cow!
Farms in the hills giving echoes now,
Answering from all the halls
Far north from all the hills
Lilja—my Lilja—my cow!

In all of this verse, German, Dutch, Scandinavian, whatever the stanza, the length of line, the use of rhyme, or the distribution of weakly stressed syllables, prosody is based on stress.

Recent Developments

In some recent poetry the prosody is not based solely on stress, but may also be based on stress phrases; its rhythm may therefore be composite, determined by stresses and junctures, not stress and quantity. A foretaste of this prosody may be found in the free rhythms of the nineteenth century, such as some of Heine's verse; for example, *Die Nordsee* I.viii:

Es wütet der Sturm,	xX xxX
Und er peitscht die Wellen,	xxX xXx
Und die Well'n, wutschäumend und bäumend,	xxX XXx xXx
Türmen sich auf, und es wogen lebendig.	XxxX xxXx xXx

Now rages the storm,
And it whips the waves,
And the waves, rage-frothing and wroth,
Tower on high, and they thunder resounding.

In spite of such verse, the underlying prosody of most verse in the nineteenth century did not depart from a basis in stress alone.

In recent verse, again, poets sometimes base their rhythm on junctures as well as stresses. Brecht's *Vom ertrunkenen Mädchen,* for example, has lines with five stressed syllables. In the last stanza, however, the units come to be bounded by junctures, much as in some of Pound's verse:

xii *Als ihr bleicher Leib im Wasser verfaulet war,*
xxXxX xXx xXxX
Geschah es (sehr langsam), dass Gott sie almählich vergass,
xXx xXx xX xxXxxX
Erst ihr Gesicht, dann die Hände und ganz zuletzt erst ihr Haar.
XxxX xxXx xxxXx xX
Dann ward sie Aas in Flüssen mit vielem Aas.
Xxx X xXx xXxX

When in the waters her pale body had turned to mush,
It happened (quite slowly) that God her gradually forgot,

First her face, then her hands, finally also her hair in the slush,
All became rot, in rivers with lots of rot.

This move towards a new type of composite rhythm is still hesitant. It has been confused occasionally with the totally different prosody of ancient Germanic verse. Fortunately, students of prosody today can base their judgments about prosody on close analyses of recordings made by expert readers, often the poet himself. With these possibilities each student may determine for himself the bases of contemporary prosody.

SELECTED BIBLIOGRAPHY

Andreas Heusler. *Deutsche Versgeschichte mit Einschluss des altenglischen und altnordischen Stabreimverses*. Vol. I. Berlin & Leipzig: de Gruyter, 1925. 2nd unchanged ed., 1956.

Lee M. Hollander. *The Skalds*. A Selection of Their Poems, With Introduction and Notes. New York: Princeton Univ. Press, 1947. Reissued by Univ. of Michigan Press: Ann Arbor, 1968.

W. P. Lehmann. *The Alliteration of Old Saxon Poetry*. Norsk Tidsskrift for Sprogvidenskap. Suppl. Bind III. Oslo: H. Aschehoug, 1953. Especially for the survey of previous scholarship.

——— *The Development of Germanic Verse Form*. Austin: Univ. of Texas Press and Linguistic Society of America, 1956. Rpt. New York: Gordian Press, 1971.

Th. Möbius. *Hattatal Snorra Sturlusonar*. Halle: Buchhandlung des Waisenhauses, 1879.

Gustas Neckel and Felix Niedner. *Die jüngere Edda*. Thule. Vol. XX. Darmstadt: Wissenschaftliche Buchgesellschaft, 1966. Contains a translation of the Háttatal and of Snorri's treatise on alliterative verse.

Eduard Sievers. *Altgermanische Metrik*. Halle: Niemeyer, 1893.

CELTIC

By CHARLES W. DUNN

> Lo, bards coming to chant a song to Arthur. But never a man was there might understand that song . . . except that it was in praise of Arthur.
>
> *The Dream of Rhonabwy.*[1]

The poetry composed in the various Celtic languages—Irish, Manx, Scottish Gaelic, Welsh, Cornish, and Breton—is of interest to any student of literature both for the archaism of its earliest forms and for the extreme complexity of its later medieval developments. The verse in which the Gauls (and other Continental Celts) preserved their lore is lost beyond recovery, since it was transmitted orally and never committed to writing; but the remains of the most ancient poetry of Ireland, and to a lesser extent that of Wales, reflect what may well have been a common prosodic system brought by Celtic-speaking settlers from the Continent.

Surviving verse dates back only to the sixth century A.D., at the earliest, by which time the inherited Indo-European pitch and stress systems had been modified so that Irish words, apart from unstressed connectives and particles, bore emphatic initial stress. Archaic examples, however, still maintain a common Indo-European cadenced system of prosody, similar to that of Vedic Sanskrit, Greek, and Slavic.[2]

Irish Cadenced Verse

Irish cadenced verse (1) contains a fixed number of syllables per line, (2) requires no fixed position of stress in the initial portion of each line, (3) contains a break (merely a word boundary, not necessarily a syntactic caesura) at a fixed point in the line, (4) carries a fixed cadence at the end of each line, predominantly of the stress pattern /x x x or /x x /x. Alliteration is used optionally, but with great frequency, to bind stressed words together in the line and to link one line with another. Rhyme is used very rarely, probably as a decoration in place of alliteration. Strophic divisions are indicated by shortened lines.

Examples occur in legal recitals, in invocations, and in the exclamatory "rhetorics" embedded within prose narratives.[3] *The Tract on Taking Possession* (Watkins, p. 221), for instance, begins with a series of typical seven-syllable lines, all of the same cadenced pattern as the first:

To-combacht selb sóertellug. ʹ5 6 7

Property has been recovered by privileged occupation.

This identical pattern appears in the most archaic portions of the earliest version of the Deirdre legend (*The Exile of the Sons of Uisliu*) (Watkins, p. 222). When the unborn child cries out within her mother's womb, the terrified father-to-be asks:

Cía deilm dremun derdrethar, ʹ5 6 7
dremnas fot broinn búredaig? ʹ5 6 7

What is the violent uproar which resounds and rages within your roaring womb?

Despite the simplicity of its fundamental principles, Irish cadenced verse shows a wide range of variations. *The Ode to Poetic Inspiration* (Watkins, p. 239), for instance, consists of four-syllable lines with a two-syllable cadence and begins with a three-syllable line as a strophic marker:

Fo chen aí, ʹ3
ingen soïs, ʹ3 4
sïur chélle ʹ3 4

Hail to poetic inspiration, daughter of true knowledge, sister of prudence.

In contrast, *The Ode to Judgment* (Watkins, p. 242) is built upon an eleven-syllable line with a three-syllable cadence following an initial portion of eight syllables divided by a break into two parts:

Fo cen breth breithemun brighach n-imglinde. ʹ9 10 11

Hail to the judge's judgment mighty and doubly secured.

Irish Rhyming Syllabic Verse

By the sixth century the obsolescent form of cadenced verse had already begun to yield place to a new poetic form built upon a device that was destined to dominate the Golden Age of Irish poetry (the eighth to the tenth centuries) and to hold sway in both Ireland and Scotland till the end of the medieval period. This device may best be called generic rhyme.[4] Its immediate source has not been definitely established. It may have arisen from imitation of the rhyme found in medieval Latin hymns, but this assumption is dubious, since the closest Latin parallels occur in hymns composed by Irish-speaking poets.[5] The peculiarities of Irish rhyme, moreover, are shared by Welsh rhyme and may stem from a common Celtic development.

Rhyming verse is built upon the foundation of cadenced verse, but, by the twelfth century, the professional bards had attained in the new form an extraordinary complexity. The following melodious stanza illustrates how apparently effortlessly a gifted poet could satisfy the manifold requirements of his meter. The extract is taken from an elegy composed early in the thirteenth century by Muireadhach Albanach Ó Dálaigh:[6]

M'anam do sgar rioms' a-raoir— '7
calann ghlan dob ionns' i n-uaigh. '7
Rugadh bruinne maordha mín '7
is aonbhla-lín uime uainn. '7

My soul was shorn from me last night—a pure body which I loved, in the grave. A gentle, noble breast was taken from us, with but a linen shroud about it.

The four essential features of cadenced verse are still relevant: (1) each line contains a fixed number of syllables—seven; (2) stress is free in the initial portion of each line; (3) there is a break at a fixed point in the line—after the sixth syllable; (4) there is a fixed cadence at the end of each line—a stress on the final, seventh syllable. Alliteration has now, however, become an obligatory feature; each line must contain a pair of adjacent, stressed alliterating words (*rioms', raoir; ionns', uaigh; maordha, mín; uime, uainn*). (Any vowel may alliterate with itself repeated or with any other.)

In place of strophic divisions, lines are now connected in stanzas by generic rhyme between any one member of a phonetic group and itself repeated or any other member of the same group, according to the following distribution (phonetic equivalents have been added to explain the spelling):

(1)	*p* [*p*]	*c* [*k*]	*t* [*t*]			
(2)	*ph*/*f* [*f*]	*ch* [*x*]	*th* [*θ*]			
(3)	*b* [*b*]	*g* [*g*]	*d* [*d*]			
(4)	*bh* [*v*] *mh* [*ṽ*]	*gh* [*g̵*]	*dh* [ð]	*l* [*l*]	*n* [*n*]	*r* [*r*]
(5)	*m* [*m*]			*ll* [*L*]	*nn* [*N*]	*rr* [*R*]
(6)	*s* [*s*]					
(7)	*Any final vowel* (*with itself only*)					

Groups (4) and (5) are frequently not differentiated. In all cases, the vowels preceding rhyming consonants must be identical.

In the measure here illustrated (The Great Quatrain—*Rannaigecht Mór*), the last word of the second line must form generic rhyme with the last word in the fourth line (*uaigh, uainn*). In terms of this principal rhyme-scheme the stanza may seem not to differ essentially from the popular English ballad measure (-x -a: -x -a), but external-internal and internal-internal rhymes are also required. The last word in the third line must rhyme with some internal word in the fourth line (*mín, lín*); and the other internal stressed words in the fourth line must rhyme with internal stressed words in the third line (*aonbhla, maordha; uime, bruinne*). Similarly, though here external-internal rhyme is not required, every internal stressed word in the second line must rhyme with some internal stressed word in the first line (*calann, anam; ghlan, sgar; ionns', rioms'*).

Furthermore, the system of full generic rhyme is complemented by a system of near generic rhymes or consonances. Somewhat as with the Old Norse near-rhyme pattern known as *skothending,* the final words in the first and third line (*raoir, mín*) must consonate and must not assonate with the final, fully rhymed words (*uaigh, uainn*) in the second and fourth lines. That is, they must agree in their generic consonants and must differ in the preceding vowels.

Many different kinds of stanzas were constructed, varying according to the number of syllables required in each line, the pattern of stress required at the end of the line, and the regulation of alliteration, rhyme, and consonance.[7] Not all were of equal ornateness. The commonly used Cut Stanza[8] (*deibide*) is, for instance, distinctly less exacting than the Great Quatrain illustrated above:

Deibide scaílte na scél— '7
ní h-íside nád aithgén. '6 7
's í seo ind aiste bláith bras '7
i ngnáthaighther in senchas. '6 7

The Cut Stanza, consonance-free, used in tales—'tis this one that I am not unfamiliar with. This is the smooth, swift meter in which tradition is customarily cast.

Here the final stressed syllable in the first line rhymes with an unstressed final syllable in the second; and similarly the final syllable in the third line with an unstressed final in the fourth. Consonance is not relevant; internal rhymes are not required; and alliteration is optional.

Irish and Scottish Gaelic Assonanced Verse

With the gradual extinction of the bardic tradition, a popular verse form arose, originating doubtless from the rhythm of the occupational songs of the people. Syllabic count became irrelevant, stress became fixed throughout the entire line and not just in the cadence, and rhyme was abandoned. Symmetrically stressed assonances became the determining feature. The following stanza composed in Scottish Gaelic by an eighteenth-century Jacobite provides an elaborate example:[9]

1 2 3 4 5
Mo chreach, Teàrlach ruadh bòidheach bhith fo bhinn aig Rìgh Deòrsa nam biasd!

1 2 3 4 5
B'e dìteach na còrach, an Fhìrinn 's a beòil foipe sios;

1 2 3 4 5
Ach a Rìgh, ma's e 's deòin leat, cuir an rìoghachd air seòl a chaidh dhinn,

1 2 3 4 5
Cuir rìgh dlìgheach na còrach ri linn na tha beò os ar cinn.

Alas that the bonnie, red-haired Charles should be at the mercy of George of the beasts! *That* would be a denial of justice, a stifling of the lips of truth. But, O Lord, if it be your will, restore the kingdom to the course we have lost; restore the rightful king over us in the generation of the living.

Here, with the exception of the first stressed word in the first line, assonance occurs in exactly the same sequence in each line: *ì ò i ò i.*

Variations of this kind of verse have remained popular down to the present day in Gaelic poetry.

Welsh Rhyming Syllabic Verse

Early Welsh poetry preserves many of the features found in early Irish.[10] There are no remains of ancient cadenced verse, but the poetry attributed to Aneirin and Taliesin, dating back perhaps to the late sixth century, corresponds closely to Irish rhyming syllabic verse. The following lines from *The Gododdin* are typical:[11]

Gwyr a aeth Gatraeth; buant enwawc. '8 9
Gwin a med o eur vu eu gwirawt. '8 9

Men went to Catraeth; renowned were they. Their drink was wine and mead from gold.

The survivals of a common Celtic poetic tradition are evident: (1) each line contains a fixed number of syllables—nine; (2) stress is free in the initial portion of each line; (3) there is a break at a fixed point in the line—after the seventh syllable; (4) there is a fixed cadence at the end of each line—a stress on the eighth syllable and a non-stress on the ninth. Alliteration is optional but frequent, occurring between stressed words which are not necessarily, as in Irish usage, adjacent. Lines are organized in strophes (a heritage, presumably, from earlier cadenced verse) connected by one common generic rhyme (*enwawc, gwirawt*) running throughout the strophe. Internal rhyme is used as an optional decoration (*aeth, Gatraeth,* and, perhaps, *gwin, gwir-*).

Internal rhyme was also used, sporadically in *The Gododdin* and systematically in later verse, to supply variation in the pattern of the strophe, as in Meilyr's praise of Bardsey (twelfth century):[12]

Ynys Veir virein, ynys glan y glein,— '10
Gwrthrych dadwyrein ys kein yndi. '8 9

Island of comely Mary, holy island of the Saints—blissful therein it is to contemplate resurrection.

Here the basic pattern of consecutive nine-syllable lines rhyming in *-i* (*yndi*) is varied by a ten-syllable line, the final syllable of which forms a rhyme (*glein*) with an internal syllable of the same line (*virein*) and also with two internal syllables in the following rhyming line (*dadwyrein, kein*).

Welsh Cynghanedd (Harmony)

Despite the many similarities between early Welsh and early Irish verse, at the acme of their achievement in the fourteenth century the Welsh bards developed a measure very different from the strict meters in which their Irish contemporaries were composing. Dafydd ap Gwilym's apostrophe to the seagull (fourteenth century) illustrates its complex effects:[13]

Yr wylan deg ar lanw dioer, '7
Unlliw ag eiry neu wenlloer, '6 7
Dilwch yw dy degwch di, '7
Darn fel haul, dyrnfol heli. '6 7

Fair seagull on the certain tide, of color like snow or the bright moon, spotless is your beauty, a patch like sunlight, gauntlet of the sea.

Some traditional features still remain: (1) each line contains a fixed number of syllables—seven; (2) stress is free in the initial portion of each line; (3) a break occurs at a fixed point—alternately after the sixth and fifth syllables; (4) the cadence at the end of the line is fixed—alternately a stressed monosyllable and a penultimately stressed disyllable.

The requirements of decoration, however, have been elaborately systematized upon the basis of previous optional devices. Generic rhyme has disappeared. Identical rhyme is now required between the alternate stressed and unstressed final syllables in each couplet (*'dioer, 'wen-lloer; 'di, 'he-li*).

Internally, also, each line must be decorated by internal harmony (*cynghanedd*). Welsh prosodists distinguish four types, but these involve only two essentially different principles, either internal rhyme or internal consonantal linkage. Rhyme may be used in two different ways. The sixth syllable, if stressed, may form a rhyme with any syllable within the line (not illustrated above); or two internal words may rhyme, provided that the second alliterates with the last word in the line (*degwch* rhymes with *dilwch* and alliterates with *di*). As an alternative, a special form of alliteration is applied, in which consonants (not necessarily initial) are linked in matching sequences. The consonant under the final stress, along with any additional number of consonants occurring in series before it, may alliterate with a consonant in the first part of the line along with a similar series of preceding consonants. In the first line above, the sequence is R L N D–R L N D; in the second, merely N LL–N LL; in the fourth, in which every consonant is included, D R N F L L–D R N F L L.

In this alliterative system, somewhat as with Irish consonance, the final consonant under stress must be associated with a vowel different from the vowel with which the corresponding consonant in the first half is associated: (D) *deg, dioer;* (N) *un, wen;* (L) *haul, heli.* Thus, though the overall effects of Welsh *cynghanedd* are new, the techniques are evolutionary rather than revolutionary; and Dafydd's spectacular Welsh couplets, just as much as Ó Dálaigh's polished Irish quatrains, are founded upon that primitive metrical drum-beat, the Indo-European cadence.

Cornish and Breton Syllabic Verse

The scanty remains of early Cornish and Breton poetry indicate a development almost completely identical with the earlier stages of Welsh. The following couplet from the Breton *Fifteen Joys of Mary* (fifteenth century),[14] for instance, not only rhymes a final stressed syllable with a final unstressed syllable but also contains a loose variety of *cynghanedd* in each line:

Guerches, so roänes e-n neff,	'8
och pep pirill mir ma eneff.	'7 8

Virgin, who are queen in Heaven, against each peril guard my soul.

Here *guerches* rhymes with *roänes,* and, according to Breton usage, *pir-* with *mir.*

Parallels of a different kind also appear in Cornish verse, as in the following portion of a stanza contained in *The Three Maries* (fifteenth century):[15]

Ellas, ow holon yu claf.	'7
Ny won vyth p'ur y'n gwelaf	'6 7
Nep yu Dew pur.	'4

Alas, my heart is stricken. I know not ever when I shall see him who is very God.

Here the final stressed syllable in the first line rhymes with the final unstressed syllable in the next line, and the third line rhymes with another corresponding line elsewhere in the stanza.

Celtic Aesthetics

The more recent developments in Celtic prosody are of minor interest for comparative purposes; in general, the folk poets have followed debased forms of older modes, and educated poets have imitated contemporary common European trends. Historically, the peculiar and supreme Celtic achievements in the realm of prosody clearly lie in Irish syllabic verse and in Welsh *cynghanedd.* The complexity of these forms raises a central question concerning aesthetic values. Simply stated, the question is, how effective are these intricate measures?

Obviously, metrical virtuosity cannot in itself guarantee good poetry. The more intricate forms of Celtic verse, however, make such peculiar demands on the poet that inexperienced readers are likely to find some difficulty in discriminating between virtuosity and genius. The bard has no Wordsworthian concern for the "language really used by men." He strains syntax; he contorts and intertwines sentences; he relies upon context to imply essential connectives and verbs which he has omitted because he could not make them scan; and he supplies artificially constructed compounds, empty epithets, and formulaic phrases which do scan. Sometimes, indeed, even Dafydd ap Gwilym's brilliant metaphorical sequences seem to be inspired more by the requirements of consonantal linkage than by a poetic search for precision in meaning.

The infatuation of the bards with intricate ornamentation is explicable, even if disturbing to the modern critic. Traditionally, members of the various bardic orders were aristocratic professionals, trained in an esoteric art which was directed towards an exclusive audience. Their repertoire was limited primarily to conventional eulogies, elegies, and satires. They proudly practiced their art, not as an exercise in self-expression, but as a self-sufficient social ritual; and the chief outlet for their virtuosity lay in the craftsmanship of their decorations. Characteristically, the very treatises which they compiled concerning prosody, grammar, and syntax serve as showcases of their knowledge and not as explanatory introductions.[16]

The bardic craft was, in fact, closely akin to that of the Celtic jewelers and manuscript illuminators; and to it one may well apply the reservations expressed by an archaeologist concerning the illumination in *The Book of Kells:* "Its mysterious motives . . . achieve too fully the aims of an art which was non-classical, non-representational, non-humanistic, and which was destined to remain outside the main stream of European culture."[17]

The cultural separation of the Celtic tradition is hard to bridge. Gerard Manley Hopkins, Wilfrid Owen, and Rolfe Humphries, among others, have introduced Celtic prosodic features into English;[18] but there is a great difference, for instance, between the occasional use of near-rhymes and the systematic application of generic rhyme. Douglas Hyde and T. Gwyn Jones have attempted to prepare translations which match feature for feature, but they willingly admit their limitations;[19] and, even if anyone could succeed, the English-speaking listener would, unless indoctrinated, be unable to hear the effects. Furthermore, the specialist who can readily understand the language and poetic technique sometimes finds that he particularly admires the very poems which the bards would have regarded as the most unpolished.

Despite a commonly held romantic assumption, the voice of poetry is not universal, and the literary critic who would truly appreciate the achievement of the Celtic bards must, therefore, train himself in what must certainly be the most exacting standards of prosody known in the history of Western literature.

NOTES

1. *The Mabinogion,* trans. Gwyn Jones and Thomas Jones (London: Everyman, 1949), p. 151.
2. Calvert Watkins, "Indo-European Metrics and Archaic Irish Verse," *Celtica,* 6 (1963), 194–249.
3. The so-called "rhetoric" should properly be identified by the native Irish term *roscad,* which includes, as Proinsias Mac Cana has shown, in "On the Use of the Term *Retoiric,*" *Celtica,* 7 (1966), 65–90, several differing metrical forms of various antiquity; some of these have not yet been adequately analyzed.
4. Charles W. Dunn, "Celtic Prosody," *Encyclopedia of Poetry and Poetics,* ed. A. Preminger (Princeton: Princeton Univ. Press, 1965), p. 110. Examples appear in *Early Irish Lyrics,* ed. and trans. Gerard Murphy (Oxford: Oxford Univ. Press, 1956), and in *A Golden Treasury of Irish Poetry,* ed. and trans. Frank O'Connor and David Greene (London: Macmillan, 1967).
5. R. Thurneysen, "Zur irischen Accent- und Verslehre," *Revue Celtique,* 6 (1883–85), 336 ff., advanced the theory of Latin origin, supported most recently by Gerard Murphy, *Early Irish Metrics* (Dublin: Royal Irish Acad., 1961). Doubts on various grounds have been expressed by Kenneth Jackson, "Incremental Repetition in the Early Welsh *Englyn,*" *Speculum,* 16 (1941), 304–21; Watkins, pp. 247–48; and James Travis, "The Indigenous Origin of Old-Irish Verse Ornament and Verse Forms" (typescript).

6. Osborn Bergin, ed. and trans., "Unpublished Irish Poems," *Studies: An Irish Quarterly Review,* 13 (1924), 427–30. This poem survives only in the version recovered from oral tradition in Perthshire in the sixteenth century, which was recorded in crude phonetics in *The Book of the Dean of Lismore*. In some places the manuscript does not seem to contain the correct syllabic count. Oral transmission could preserve such carefully wrought compositions intact only so long as the reciters were themselves trained in the requirements. For a diplomatic edition, see E. C. Quiggin, *Poems from the Book of the Dean of Lismore* (Cambridge: Cambridge Univ. Press, 1937), pp. 42–43. (Stanza 1, line c, for instance, is recorded as *a brwne ni,* i.e., *a bruinne* 'her breast'; here the *a* is hypermetrical; the composer undoubtedly intended *bruinne* 'a breast.') On the date for the evolution of "strict verse" (*dán díreach*), see Brian Ó Cuív, "Some Developments in Irish Metrics," *Éigse,* 12 (1967–68), 273–90.
7. See the convenient metrical list in Murphy, *Metrics*, pp. 74–76.
8. Murphy, *Metrics*, p. 65.
9. John Roy Stewart, "Culloden Day," in *Highland Songs of the Forty-Five,* ed. and trans. John Lorne Campbell (Edinburgh: John Grant, 1933), p. 168. The otherwise very useful comment on meter (p. xxix) misprints the stress in the fourth line, as an examination of the music (p. 303) will prove.
10. In breaking away from the inherited Indo-European pitch and stress systems, Welsh developed a stress system different from that of Irish initial stress. All polysyllabic words in Welsh took penultimate stress. Monosyllables and disyllables in the two languages thus retained identical initial stress patterns (′x or ′x x); only trisyllables (Ir. ′x x x, Welsh x ′x x) and longer words—all relatively infrequent in usage—presented differing prosodic patterns in the two languages.
11. *Canu Aneirin*, ed. Ifor Williams (Cardiff: Univ. of Wales Press, 1938), p. 10. For translations of Welsh poems referred to, see Joseph Clancy, *The Earliest Welsh Poetry* (London: Macmillan, 1970) and *Medieval Welsh Lyrics* (London: Macmillan, 1965).
12. *Hen Gerddi Crefyddol*, ed. Henry Lewis (Cardiff: Univ. of Wales Press, 1931), p. 22.
13. *Gwaith Dafydd ap Gwilym*, ed. Thomas Parry (Cardiff: Univ. of Wales Press, 1952), p. 313.
14. *Trois Poèmes en Moyen-Breton*, ed. and trans. Roparz Hemon, Mediaeval and Modern Breton Series, No. 1 (Dublin: Instit. for Advanced Studies, 1962), st. 193; see p. xi.
15. *An Tyr Marya*, ed. and trans. R. M. Nance and A. S. D. Smith, Extracts from Cornish Texts, No. 2 (Marazion: F. Worden, 1951). The usual handbooks are quite misleading when they say of the Cornish *Ordinalia*, from which this extract is taken, that the lines are "of seven syllables with four stresses." *The Legend of the Rood*, trans. F. E. Halliday (London: Gerald Duckworth, 1955), p. 50, e.g. The poets considered only the placement of the final stress and the total number of syllables, not the total number of stresses.
16. For a bibliography of the Irish treatises, see Murphy, *Metrics*, pp. v-vi. One of these, composed ca. A.D. 800, is the earliest prosodic study written in a Western European vernacular. All the extant Irish bardic metrical, grammatical, and syntactical tracts deserve fuller study in respect to their methods, sources, and analogues. An important contribution is Brian Ó Cuív, "Linguistic Terminology in the Mediaeval Irish Bardic Tracts," *Transactions of the Philological Society* (London), 1965, pp. 141–64. For the Welsh, see Thomas Parry, "The Welsh Metrical Treatise Attributed to Einion Offeriad," *PBA*, 47 (1961), 177–95.
17. Máire and Liam de Paor, *Early Christian Ireland* (New York: Praeger, 1958), p. 129.
18. David Bell, "The Problem of Translation," in *Dafydd ap Gwilym: Fifty Poems*, trans. H. I. Bell and David Bell (Y Cymmrodor, 48) (London, 1942), pp. 81–94, 97; Annemarie E. Towner, "Welsh Bardic Meters and English Poetry, "*MR*, 6 (1965), 614–24.
19. Hyde, *Filidheacht Ghaedhealach: Irish Poetry* (Dublin: M. H. Gill, 1902); Jones, quoted by David Bell in *Dafydd Fifty Poems*, pp. 79–80, and see further, p. 95.

SELECTED BIBLIOGRAPHY

Many questions regarding Celtic prosody still remain unanswered. What prosodic features, for instance, are shared by all the Celtic languages, which features are descended from a common Celtic tradition, which are borrowed from alien tradition, what has been the effect on prosody of the widespread custom of oral composition and oral transmission, and how has prosody accommodated itself to various singing, chanting, and recitational styles? Despite these limitations of knowledge and the rapid advances of scholarship, the following works can still be recommended as useful guides.

GENERAL. *Encyclopedia of Poetry and Poetics*. Ed. Alex Preminger. Princeton: Princeton Univ. Press, 1965. Articles on "Celtic Prosody," supplemented by articles on "Breton Poetry," "Cornish Poetry," "Irish Poetry," "Scottish Gaelic Poetry," "Welsh Poetry." Literary as well as linguistic surveys of the various traditions; useful bibliographies.

IRISH. Gerard Murphy. *Early Irish Metrics*. Dublin: Royal Irish Acad., 1961. Invaluable though outdated. See review by Brian Ó Cuív, *Éigse*, 10 (1962–63), 238–41.

SCOTTISH GAELIC. *Bardachd Ghaidhlig*. Ed. William J. Watson. Glasgow: Commun Gaidhealach, 1959.

WELSH. Joseph Loth. *La Métrique galloise*. Paris: Albert Fontemoing, 1900–02. 2 vols. Illustrations of all Welsh meters, including comparison with Cornish, Breton, and Irish.

ITALIAN

By A. BARTLETT GIAMATTI

> . . . we do not find any [Italian poets] who, reckoning a line by syllables, have exceeded eleven syllables or used less than three. And while Italian poets have used the *trisillabo* and the *endecasillabo,* and all those [lines] in between, they most frequently use the *quinario,* the *settenario,* and the *endecasillabo;* and after these, the *trisillabo* before the others.
>
> *De Vulgari Eloquentia* II.v.2.[1]

As Dante says, Italians have always regarded their verse as syllabic; that is, they classify lines of poetry according to the number of syllables the lines contain. The syllabic verse of Romance languages like Italian is thus conventionally contrasted with the accentual stress verse of a Germanic language such as English. This distinction, however, is often less revealing than it seems, much less than, for instance, the distinction between quantitative and qualitative verse. For, as will become apparent, accentual stress occurs in Italian verse, though in comparison with English verse the Italian has a much more limited, or at least less perceptible, accentual prescription. When Dante says Italian poets have favored above all others lines of three, five, seven, and eleven syllables, he implies what he later explicitly states: "Lines of an even number of syllables are used only rarely by us because of their rudeness . . ." (*DVE* II.v.7). He explains the "rudeness" (*ruditas*) of lines of an even number of syllables by a Pythagorean doctrine of numbers he has derived from Aristotle's *Metaphysics* by way of St. Thomas Aquinas. What he means by "rudeness" is rhythmic monotony, a predictable pattern of stress that renders these lines of an even number of syllables fit only for lower, more "popular" poetry. Thus Dante recognizes stress patterns as an important element in Italian verse even as he uses the (already traditional) terminology of syllabic computation.[2]

The reasons for the difference in the accentual element between Italian and, say, English lies in the natures of the languages. The weaker stress patterns in Italian derive from the fact that the unstressed Italian vowel has much greater clarity or shape than its English counterpart. Hence, in Italian, the difference in stress between the tonic and atonic vowels is comparatively slight. By the nature of the English language, on the other hand, the relative obscurity of the unstressed vowel causes the stressed vowel to stand out in much sharper relief.

With these qualifications in mind, we will survey traditional Italian metrics, a system in which lines of poetry must have a certain number of syllables and where, within the line, the stressed syllables must occur in certain positions. Naming lines of Italian verse after the number of syllables they contain involves some preliminary considerations, the first of which is the computation of syllables.

In counting syllables in Italian verse, special rules to observe are those governing elision and hiatus, which concern the computation of syllables at word boundaries, and dieresis and syneresis, which concern the computation of syllables within a word.[3]

Elision (*elisione* or *sinalefe*) occurs between two atonic syllables, or, more rarely, between an atonic syllable and tonic syllable. Thus, the opening line of Giacomo Leopardi's (1798–1837) "La sera del dì di festa,"

Dolce‿e chiara‿è la notte‿e senza vento,

has eleven, not fourteen syllables. However, no elision can occur when the first vowel is tonic or when both are tonic. "Ella giunse e levò—ambe le palme" (Dante).

Hiatus (*iato* or *dialefe*) occurs when the first of the two vowels is tonic, or both are. Dante's line,

Là—onde invidïa prima dipartilla,

has both hiatus and elision. In the "ia" of *invidia,* there is also dieresis.

Dieresis (*dieresi*) occurs ordinarily in the separation of two adjacent vowels within a word to form two distinct syllables. Dieresis is sometimes marked by ¨: "Dolce color d'orïental zaffiro" (Dante). *Oriental,* a trisyllable in prose, is here a quadrisyllable. No dieresis should occur, however, in the case of Italian diphthongs derived from a Latin simple vowel (or from *ae*).[4]

Syneresis (*sineresi*), the contraction within a word of two adjacent vowels belonging to different syllables into one syllable, occurs ordinarily in all cases where dieresis may not. Two examples of syneresis occur in the eleven-syllable line of Petrarch, "Morte bella par*ea* nel *suo* bel viso." However, no syneresis may occur at the end of a line: "Vago augelletto che cantando va-i" (Petrarch). Nor should syneresis occur when in the same word *a, e,* or *o* is followed by a stressed vowel (as in *a-ereo; be-ato; so-ave*).

The following line of the Tuscan humanist Agnolo Firenzuola (1493–1543) shows both dieresis and syneresis in two uses of the same word: "O vi-ole formose o dolci vio-le." Poets may or may not recognize the "rules" for dieresis and syneresis, though from Petrarch on they have tended to stay closer to these "rules" than poets before Petrarch. In the earlier poets, particularly Dante, one will find many more examples of exceptional dieresis and syneresis.

One other element must be understood in order properly to reckon syllables in Italian poetry. The Italians distinguish three kinds of words and accordingly three kinds of lines. A line may be *piano* and end with a word stressed on the penultimate syllable; *sdrucciolo* and end with a word stressed on the antepenultimate syllable; or *tronco* and end with a word stressed on the last syllable. The following three lines from the "Cinque Maggio" of Alessandro Manzoni (1785–1873) are (in order) *piano, sdrucciolo,* and *tronco*:

Orma di piè mortale	Track of mortal foot
La sua cruenta polvere	Will come to trample
A calpestar verrà.	Its bloody dust.

All three lines are *settenari,* or lines of seven syllables, and that, allowing for the syneresis in *piè,* is the number of syllables in line one. But if we allow for the dieresis in *cru-enta,* line two has eight syllables, and line three has only six syllables. How can lines two and three be considered seven-syllable lines? In the reason lies a fundamental rule of Italian metrics: In theory, there must be one, and only one, unstressed syllable after the last stressed syllable. Thus, in theory, all lines are *piano.* And, in fact, because most Italian words are paroxytones, most lines are *piano* (and most rhymes are "feminine").

All lines in Italian poetry receive their name as *piano* lines. When a line is *sdrucciolo,* like line two above, the second unstressed syllable is ignored in the computation of syllables; when a line is *tronco,* like line three above, the Italians silently assume an unstressed syllable after the stressed syllable (an unstressed syllable which often was once there). Thus Manzoni writes his

Ode on Napoleon's death in lines which metrically are counted as seven-syllable lines, but which actually contain from six to eight syllables. Because the Italians consider the *piano* normative, they may seem to have constructed a fiction when they count syllables which are not there (*tronco*) or ignore syllables which are there (*sdrucciolo*). However, this system applies only to the classification of lines. Melodically, within the framework and meaning of the poem, the actual number of syllables counts very much.

The Italians think of their lines of verse in two groups, the *versi brevi* or "short lines" and *versi lunghi* or "long lines." We will first consider the *versi brevi,* lines of three, four, five, six, and seven syllables.

The *ternario* (ternary) is a three-syllable line with a stress on the second syllable. A number of commentators deny its very existence,[5] while others consider it only a fragment of a longer line (one of six- or nine-syllables). But the Notary, Giacomo da Lentini (ca. 1200–50), used *ternari* mixed with *senari*:

Dal core mi vene	From the heart she comes
Che gli occhi mi tene	For she holds my eyes
/	
Rosata.	Rosata.

And Dante certainly considered the *ternario* a line in *DVE* II.v.2 and 7. In our own day, Giuseppe Ungaretti (1888–1970) wrote his imagistic "Mattina" in *ternari*:

/	
M'illumino	I am illuminated
/	
d'immenso.	by immensity.

The *quaternario* or *quadrisillabo* (quaternary) is a four-syllable line with a stress on the third syllable, and a weaker stress on the first.

	\ /	
(1) 3	*Nelle luci*	In your
	\ /	
(1) 3	*Tue divine*	Divine lights
	\ /	
(1) 3	*Pace alfine*	The heart enjoys
	\ /	
(1) 3	*Gode il cor.*	Peace at last.

(Pietro Metastasio, 1698–1782)

Often the *quaternario* is used with the *ottonario,* as here by Giosuè Carducci (1835–1907), where the short line undercuts the expectations raised by the long line in various ways:

Il poeta, o vulgo sciocco,	The poet, o vulgar crowd,
un pitocco.	is a louse.

The *quinario* (quinary) is a five-syllable line, with a principal stress on the fourth syllable, and perhaps a weaker stress on the first or second.

(2) 4	*O prima ed ultima*	O first and last
(1) 4	*Cura e diletto*	Care and delight
(2) 4	*Di madre amabile*	Of dear mother
(1) 4	*Bel pargoletto.*	Lovely little child.

(Vincenzo Monti, 1754–1828)

The *quinario,* a very old and popular line in Italian verse, was used in combination with the *settenario* and the *endecasillabo* before it was used alone. In the lines of Jacopone da Todi (ca. 1230–1306), it is used with *settenari:*

(1) 4	*Haggi pietanza*	Have pity
(1) 4	*Di me peccatore*	On me the sinner
	Che so stato in errore	For I have been in error
	Lungo tempo passato.	A long, long time.

The *senario* (senary or senarius) is a six-syllable line, almost always an actual *piano,* with principal stresses on the second and fifth syllables.

Se resto sul lido	If I remain on the shore,
Se sciolgo le vele.	If I loosen the sails.

(Metastasio)

This line is rarely *sdrucciolo.* An example of the rare exception is the fifth line of every stanza of "Sopra una conchiglia" by the literary scholar and poet Giacomo Zanella (1820–88):

Sul chiuso quaderno	On the closed notebook
Di vati famosi,	Of famous bards,
Dal musco materno	You rest far from
Lontano riposi,	The maternal moss,
Riposi marmorea	You rest marmoreal,
Dell'onde già figlia	Once daughter of the waves,
Ritorta conchiglia.	Twisted shell.

There can also be principal stresses on the third and fifth syllables, with perhaps a weaker stress on the first—as in these lines of the prosodically adventurous Gabriello Chiabrera (1552–1638):[6]

(1), 3, 5	*Dolci miei sospiri,*	My sweet sighs,
(1), 3, 5	*Dolci miei martiri,*	My sweet pains,
(1), 3, 5	*Dolce mio desio,*	My sweet desire,
3, 5	*E voi dolci canti,*	And you sweet songs,
3, 5	*E voi dolci pianti,*	And you sweet plaints,
3, 5	*Rimanete addio.*	Fare ye well in God.

The *settenario* (septenary or heptasyllable), a seven-syllable line, is the most favored in Italian poetry after the *endecasillabo.* With the *endecasillabo* and the *quinario,* the *settenario* was used at the beginnings of Italian literature in ballads, *canzoni,* and some sonnets. The *settenario* has a principal stress on the sixth syllable, and another principal stress on either the first, second, third, or fourth syllable. In the following stanza from the "All'Amica Risanata" of Ugo Foscolo (1778–1827), the *settenario,* used with an *endecasillabo,* displays all the possibilities:

2, 6	*O quando l'arpa adorni*	O when you adorn the harp
4, 6	*E co' novelli numeri*	Both with the new numbers

3, 6	*E co' molli contorni*	And the soft lineaments
3, 6	*Delle forme che facile*	Of the forms that pliant raiment
1, 6	*Bisso seconda, e intanto*	Shows forth, and amid
	Fra il basso sospira vola il tuo canto.	The deep sighing your song takes flight.

In the nineteenth century, many poets, particularly Monti, followed eighteenth-century practice and never stressed the first syllable, and allowed stress only on the second or fourth syllable and on the sixth. But Foscolo found a liberating model in the great satirist Giuseppe Parini (1729–99), who had stressed the first syllable: (1, 6) "Sopra i gigli di pria," and even the fifth syllable: (5, 6) "Con un dondolio lento," though here he had a predecessor in Dante, in his *canzone* "E m'incresce di me sì duramente":

	La mia persona pàrgola sostenne	My child-like self sustained
5, 6	*Una passïon nuova*	A new passion
	Tal ch'io rimasi di paura pieno.	Such that I was full of fear.

Many writers on Italian metrics consider these *versi brevi* or "short lines" as only parts or hemistichs of *versi lunghi* or "long lines." Pernicone, for instance, argues that the *ternario* is half a *senario* or part of a *settenario* or of the eleven-syllable *endecasillabo*; that the *quaternario* is a hemistich of an *ottonario*; that the *quinario* is an *a minore* hemistich of an *endecasillabo*. (For *a minore* and *a maiore*, see the next paragraph.) He also suggests that the *senario piano* is a shortened *ottonario*, and the *senario sdrucciolo* corresponds to the second hemistich of an *endecasillabo*, while the *settenario* and the *ottonario* are hemistichs of longer lines of fourteen, fifteen, or sixteen syllables.[7]

Long lines of eight syllables or more can, therefore, be seen as combinations of various short lines. Some writers carry the combinations to great lengths and make much use of the terms *a minore* and *a maiore*, which refer to lines beginning with either a short or a long hemistich. And while *a minore* and *a maiore* are terms generally used to refer only to types of the *endecasillabo*, they can be, and often are, used in reference to the *ottonario*, the *novenario*, and the *decasillabo*.

There are two basic rules concerning long lines made from short lines.

The first is that at the junction of the short lines, a syllable is lost. This syllable is lost through elision or through syneresis where one expects dieresis; through a shortening of the second short line; or because the first short line is *tronco*. Therefore, each long line has always one syllable less than the sum of its parts, that is, than the sum of its short lines. As a result, we can speak of a "caesura" in the long line at the point of junction of the short lines. The Italians refer to the point of junction as the point of "fusion," and the union of the two short lines as the "fusion" of the short lines.

The second rule concerning a long line is that it will have at least two principal stresses. One stress in the long line will be on the line's last tonic syllable, and the other on the tonic syllable immediately preceding the caesura or point of fusion. We should add that the caesura will move in accordance with the type of long line, or, put another way, with the combination of short lines. Because of the various ways of unifying two short lines in one long line, the caesura will be of varying "strengths."[8]

The long lines are those of eight, nine, ten, and eleven syllables. The *ottonario* or octosyllabic line was much used at the beginnings of Italian literature, particularly, though not exclusively, for goliardic and religious verse.[9] Like all lines of an even number of syllables, it is associated with popular poetry or—because of its accentual regularity—with monotony. It depends on your point of view. The *ottonario* fell into relative disuse after the Middle Ages, though it had a revival during the nineteenth century in the hands of poets like Manzoni, Giovanni Berchet (1783–1851), and Carducci.

The *ottonario* can be stressed on the first, third, fifth, and seventh syllables—as it is here by Tommaso Grossi (1791–1853), who was much influenced by Manzoni: "Rondinella pellegrina." But that would soon pall, and does. Lorenzo de' Medici (1449–92) preferred to stress the third, fifth, and seventh syllables: "Giovanetti e donne amanti." The most common form is stressed on the third and seventh syllables:

Bell' Italia, amate sponde,	Beautiful Italy, beloved shores,
Pur vi torno a riveder.	So I return to see you again.
	(Monti)

Here one might also stress the first syllable, as in Manzoni's line where the fourth and seventh syllables are also stressed:

Terra di sangue ora intrisa.

An effort to vary the regularity of the *ottonario* by stressing the second and seventh syllables was made by Giulio Rospigliosi (1600–99), poet and diplomat, who, as Clement IX, occupied himself with combatting Jansenism.

D'abisso le forze abbatte	She casts down the forces of the abyss,
Pugnando suo vivo zelo	Fighting its lively zeal,
E s'ella combatte al cielo,	And if she battles in heaven,
Il cielo per lei combatte.	Heaven battles for her.

Of the *novenario* (novenary) Dante said, it "seemed a trisyllable [*ternario*] repeated three times, and either was never held by us in high esteem or fell into disuse because it displeased" (*DVE* II.v.7). Dante's comment is accurate; the rhythm of the *novenario* is predictable and rigid, and it is the only line of an odd number of syllables to share this feature with lines of an even number. Nevertheless, Dante himself used the line once, in his lyric "Per una ghirlandetta" (along with *settenari*), and there we can see the basic form of the *novenario*: stress on the second, fifth, and eighth syllables: "I' vidi a voi, donna, portare."[10]

The *novenario* was revived once by Chiabrera, as part of what Levi calls Chiabrera's aspiration to be "the Christopher Columbus of our poetry," and then again by Carducci, from whom Giovanni Pascoli (1855–1912) and Gabrielle D'Annunzio (1863–1937) took it. The following examples show some of the variations poets have found by using weaker stress and by stressing the third syllable. In the first example, the distinguished physician and poet Francesco Redi (1626–98) exploits the frivolity of a regular pattern of stronger and weaker stresses.

(1), 3, (5), 8	Corri, Nina, prendi una conca	
(1), 5, 8	Vengono farfalle di neve	(D'Annunzio)
(3), 5, 8	Tremolando a coppie ed a sciami	(D'Annunzio)

The *decasillabo* (decasyllable), a ten-syllable line, shares the character of all lines with an even number of syllables—a rigid pattern of stress—and thus meets their customary fate: favor in the Middle Ages, then only occasional use until revival in the nineteenth century.[11] It is rhythmically the heaviest of all Italian meters. The *decasillabo* is stressed on the third, sixth, and ninth syllables. Among other things in this meter, Manzoni wrote all

128 lines of the Chorus of Act II of *Il Carmagnola*: "S'ode a destra uno squillo di tromba." This is the first line; the other 127 sound the same.

The eleven-syllable line, *endecasillabo* (hendecasyllable), is one of Italy's national monuments.[12] Dante called it the "most famous" line, and said it had a certain association with the *settenario*. He advised that, while its supremacy should be maintained, the *endecasillabo* appeared in an even better light when used with the *settenario* (*DVE* II.v.5), and it often has been, as well as with the *quinario*.

The *endecasillabo*, unlike its French counterpart the *décasyllable* (which it may antedate), has a very flexible caesura. The line can be thought of as being formed of a *quinario piano* and a *settenario piano* (the *a minore* form, which Levi says sounds better) or of a *settenario piano* and a *quinario piano* (the *a maiore* form). If one thinks of all the possible combinations, including *sdrucciolo* and *tronco* lines, the ways of making an *endecasillabo* grow like dragon's teeth: Guarnerio has forty-eight combinations of *a minore* and *a maiore* lines; Fraccaroli, eighty-seven; Levi, who adds the *senario*, comes up with 828 combinations. Pernicone's assertion that the *endecasillabo* has a rhythm of its own which is not the result of combined lines is not only sensible but something of a relief.[13] The higher mathematics does remind us, however, of the immense variety the *endecasillabo* can achieve. There is always a stress on the tenth syllable; after that—in its most common form—it has a stress on either the fourth or the sixth syllable. In the Ferrara Inscription of 1135, we have the first recorded *endecasillabi*, and in the Inscription's second and third lines we have the two basic patterns already established:

	Li mile cento trenta cenqe nato	In the year 1135 was born
4, 10	*fo questo templo a S. Gogio donato*	This temple to Saint Gogio
6, 10	*da Glelmo ciptadin per so amore*	Given by citizen William out of his love,
	e tua fo l'opera Nicolao scolptore.	And it was your work, Nicholas the sculptor.

The second line is *a minore*; the third, *a maiore*.[14]

The *endecasillabo* can have from two (as above) to five stressed syllables, though as Boyde properly notes with regard to Dante: "stresses in the ninth position are not common and those in the fifth very rare indeed, as both would tend to 'interfere' with the all important fixed and dominant stresses" (*Dante's Lyric Poetry*, I, liii).

The examples below are meant to indicate only some of the line's possibilities, including some of its rarities. Not included are the standard four, ten and six, ten patterns.

4, 8, 10	O cameretta, che già fosti un porto	(Petrarch)
4, 7, 10	E se venite da tanta pietate	(Dante)
1, 4, 7, 10	Quanto si gode, lieta e ben contesta	(Michelangelo)
2, 6, 7, 10	Col falso lor piacer volser miei passi	(Dante)
2, 4, 6, 8, 10	E caddi come corpo morto cade	(Dante)

The rare *endecasillabo* with a stress on the ninth syllable does occur in both Dante and Petrarch; in one case the insistent, adjacent stress forces us to fix on Count Ugolino, in the other on Madonna Laura:

(2), (4), 9, 10 *Che furo all'osso, come d'un can, forti.*

Posta a bagnar un leggiadretto velo
2, 6, 9, 10 *Che all'aura il vago e biondo capel chiuda.*

Who was on the bone, like a dog, strong

Set to moisten a pretty little veil
That keeps from the breeze her free blond hair.
(*Canz.*, lii)

In the sonnet "Sì lungiamente m'ha tenuto amore" (*Vita Nuova*, XXVIII), Dante puts a stress on the fifth syllable: (2, 4, 5, 8, 10) "Che fa li miei spiriti gir parlando."

Here we may also mention the most famous species of the *endecasillabo,* the *verso sciolto.* This unrhymed *endecasillabo* was called *sciolto* by Giangiorgio Trissino (1478–1550) because it was "loosed" or "freed" from rhyme. It corresponds to what in English we call "blank verse," for which it was a model. *Versi sciolti* appear in thirteenth- and fourteenth-century Italian poetry—though one must always distinguish between those poets who cannot rhyme and those who do not want to. But *versi sciolti* are really a development of the sixteenth century and its efforts to approximate classical meters in Italian.[15] Trissino used *endecasillabi sciolti* to approximate Latin hexameters in his tragedy *Sofonisba* (1515; pub. 1524) and in his epic *L'Italia liberata dai Goti* (begun 1527; pub. 1547–48). In the second decade of the sixteenth century, Ludovico Ariosto (1474–1532) was rewriting his early prose comedies *La Cassaria* and *Il Negromante* in *endecasillabi sciolti sdruccioli* in an effort to imitate Latin iambic trimeter. The *endecasillabo sciolto* was then used by Torquato Tasso (1544–95) in his *Le Sette giornate del mondo creato* (1594; partial ed. 1600; complete ed. 1607) as well as by Annibale Caro (1507–61) in his famous translation of the *Aeneid* (pub. 1581). The association of the line with drama was assured by Vittorio Alfieri (1749–1803), and it was used for all kinds of narrative verse by Parini and Foscolo, Manzoni and Monti. Since Caro's *Aeneid*, the *endecasillabo sciolto* has been the medium for most of the great translations from the Greek and Latin into Italian.[16]

Lines longer than the *endecasillabo* do exist, and we will speak of the *dodecasillabo* in a moment. Burger cites some lines of thirteen syllables from an early *pastorella* (p. 63) and Mari, some of the same length from the sixteenth century (p. 20). Lines of thirteen syllables, however, are very rare, and it could be argued that they are simply combinations of various shorter lines. We will end our survey with some remarks about a group of lines which are in fact clearly recognized as combinations.

These are the *versi accoppiati* or *versi doppi* ("coupled" or "doubled" lines). Unlike *versi lunghi,* made from two *versi brevi* (see above, page 154), these lines are not the product of "fusion"—and hence, the loss of a syllable in the process—but of the grammatical coupling of two lines. All *versi accoppiati* are formed by the coupling of two shorter lines. They admit neither hiatus nor elision; and they all have a fixed caesura. To avoid hiatus, the first member of a *verso accoppiato* must be a *piano* or a *sdrucciolo,* but not a *tronco,* and the second member must begin with a consonant.

The *quinario doppio* (double quinary), a ten-syllable line, is like the *decasillabo,* unless the first member is *sdrucciolo.* It is stressed on the fourth and ninth syllables, and perhaps on the second and sixth.

4, 9 Or si comincia || lo duro pianto (Jacopone da Todi)

2, 4, 6, 9 Al mio cantuccio || donde non sento (Pascoli)

The *senario doppio* (double senarius) or *dodecasillabo* (dodecasyllable) will make a twelve-syllable line only if the first *senario* is *piano* and the second begins with a consonant. It is stressed on the second, fifth, eighth, and eleventh syllables. Manzoni, who liked this sort of thing, used the line in the first chorus of Act III of *L'Adelchi*:

Dagli atri muscosi, || dai fori cadenti,	From the mossy atria, from the crumbling fora,
dai boschi, dall'arse || fucine stridenti.	From the woods, from the scorched, clanging forges.

Another form of the *dodecasillabo* (akin to the *senario doppio*) is made of an *ottonario* and a *quaternario* and is stressed on the third, seventh, and eleventh syllables. Carducci used it to translate Klopstock: "Quando il tremulo splendore della luna"; and it occasionally occurs in the Middle Ages.

The *settenario doppio* (double heptasyllable) is also called the *alessandrino* after the French alexandrine, which first appeared in France in the *Pèlerinage de Charlemaegne à Jerusalem* and the late twelfth-century *Roman d'Alexandre,* whence the French line derives its name. The *settenario doppio* is also called the *martelliano,* after the Bolognese poet Pier Jacopo Martelli (1665–1727), who re-introduced the line into cultivated verse. The line was widely used in the Middle Ages and developed differently in the North of Italy and the South, but the usual form is the Southern, a *settenario sdrucciolo* followed by a *settenario piano.*[17]

Though Dante did not mention this line (or any of the *versi doppi*) in his discussion in *DVE* II.v. he knew it, for at *DVE* I.xii.6 he cites the third line of the most famous example of the *settenario doppio,* Cielo d'Alcamo's *contrasto*:

3, 6, 12, 14 Rosa fresca aulentissima || c'appar inver la state.

This line was also used with slightly different stress later in the drama:

2, 6, 8, 13 La sera o la mattina || sentesi in ogni loco (Goldoni)

and elsewhere:

2, 6, 8, 13 Su i campi di Marengo || batte la luna; fosco. (Carducci)

In these two examples both hemistichs are *settenari piani.*

The *ottonario doppio* (double octosyllable), a very rare line, is made of two *ottonari piani*. Carducci used it in his *La Sacra di Enrico V:*

3, 7, 11, 15 Quando cadono le foglie, ‖ quando emigrano gli augelli.

In closing, we may briefly note that to some it has seemed that since the end of the nineteenth century a "crisis" has occurred in traditional Italian versification. For example, as forces disrupting traditional meters, Pernicone points to the influence of French *symbolisme,* of *vers libre,* and of the Futurists. He cites Carducci's statement of 1875—"Odio l'usata poesia" ("I hate shopworn poetry")—as well as the cry of Domenico Gnoli:

A noi, giovani, apriamo i vetri,	Let's open the windows, boys,
rinnoviamo l'aria chiusa	Let's get some fresh air

and the rhythmic irregularities of D'Annunzio. He further notes that Giuseppe Ungaretti felt compelled to write a "Difesa dell'endecasillabo" (in *Corrente,* Milano, 15 June 1939) and that the opening lines of Eugenio Montale's "La casa dei doganieri": "Tu non ricordi la casa dei doganieri" and of Salvatore Quasimodo's "Color di pioggia e di ferro": "Dicevi: morte, silenzio, solitudine," betray impulses which have little to do with traditional metrical forms (pp. 342–45). All this is doubtless true, but suffice it to say that "crises" of one sort or another have been common in the history of Italian metrics. The advent of the *verso sciolto,* or each revival of classical quantitative prosody, has represented such a crisis. Because the weight of tradition in Italian metrics, as in every phase of Italian poetry, is very heavy indeed, what seems a "crisis" may be only change. And change is not necessarily new or lamentable.

NOTES

1. I wish to thank Thomas G. Bergin of Yale University and Dante della Terza and Paolo Valesio of Harvard University for generous assistance and advice.—*De Vulgari Eloquentia* (hereafter *DVE*) is translated from the standard edition of A. Marigo, *Opere di Dante*, ed. M. Barbi, VI (Firenze, 1938). For full reference for all abbreviations and works cited in these notes, see the selected bibliography at the end. The works noted there are those which I found particularly useful and from which I drew most of my examples. After Dante, treatises partially or wholly on prosody include: Francesco da Barberino, *Documenti d'Amore* (ca. 1306–13); Antonio da Tempo, *Summa Artis Rytmici Vulgaris Dictaminis* (1332), paraphrased by Gidino da Sommacampagna, *Trattato de li Rithimi Volgari* (shortly after 1350). Francesco Baratella's *Compendio dell'arte ritmica* (1447) and da Tempo's *Summa* were the sources for the four-page handbook of the 1480's by Guido Peppi (called Guido Stella), "Modo et regula

da fare versi vulgari rhithimi," and an untitled treatise on metrics and rhythm by Bastiano di Giannozo da Magnale (1518). Overshadowing all were two works: Mario Equicola, *Institutioni al comporre in ogni sorte di rime della lingua italiana* (1541; composed, 1525), and Giangorgio Trissino, *Poetica*, Books I–IV (1529; Books V–VI published posthumously, 1563). For further bibliography and discussion, see Pernicone, "Storia e svolgimento della metrica," p. 349, and C. Dionisotti, "Ragioni metriche del Quattrocento," *Giornale Storico della Letteratura Italiana*, 124 (1947), 2–34.

2. For Dante's Pythagorean doctrine, see *DVE* II.v.7 and I.xvi.5 and Marigo's notes, pp. 203–204; 141. For theories of Italian meters as derived from Latin quantitative verse through medieval Latin accentual verse, see Pernicone, pp. 300–08, and Burger, "Recherches sur la structure et l'origine des vers romans," passim; Pernicone sees the fundamental rhythms of Italian lines with an even number of syllables as trochaic (from trochaic tetrameter acatalectic), and of lines with an odd number of syllables as iambic (from iambic tetrameter catalectic); Guarnerio, *Manuale di versificazione italiana*, pp. 49 ff., regards Italian lines as either anapestic-dactylic or iambic-trochaic.

3. For other metrical terms: *aferesi, sincope, apocope*, which diminish the number of syllables; *protesi, epentesi, paragoge*, which increase the number; and *diastole* and *sistole*, which modify the stress, see Guarnerio, pp. 35–38, and Levi, "Della versificazione italiana," pp. 516–25.

4. No dieresis should occur when a) diphthongs *ie* and *ou* derive from Latin short *e* or *o* (L. *homo* > It. *uomo*; L. *tenet* > It. *tiene*); b) when *ie* derives from Latin *ae* (L. *saepes* > It. *siepe*); c) when in two vowels, the first is *i* deriving from Latin *l* in the consonantal groups *pl, bl, fl, cl, gl, tl* (L. *planta* > It. *pianta*; L. *flumen* > It. *fiume*; L. *clarus* > It. *chiaro*; L. *glans, glandis* > It. *ghianda*; L. *vetulus, vet'lus* > It. *vecchio*); d) when unstressed *i* or *u* before a vowel has the value of a consonant (It. *acqua*; *equo*); e) when *i* is only orthographic, to indicate the sound of the preceding consonant (*lasciare*; *figlio*; *giovane*; *goccia*); f) when Latin *ri* plus a vowel become Italian *j* or *i*, which is consonantal (L. *librarius* > It. *librajo*). An instance not covered by the principle above: no dieresis should occur when *i* was originally preceded by *b, p, m,* or *v* in Latin; these consonants are doubled in Italian (L. *rabies* > It. *rabbia*; L. *sapiam* > It. *sappia*; L. *vindemia* > It. *vendemmia*); to the Latin consonants preceding *i*, Maruffi, *Piccolo manuale di metrica italiana*, p. 6, would add *c* and *g*. One should add that parallel to the doubled consonant forms, there existed in Old Italian (and later), learned variants with the simple consonant, and these variants played an important role in poetry. The best general discussion of these matters is D'Ovidio's, in *Versificazione romanza*, pp. 1–76.

5. Mari, *Riassunto e dizionarietto*, pp. 14–15, ignores the *ternario* completely; Maruffi, p. 10, and Levi, p. 467, argue it does not exist because (Levi) "it lacks that renewal of beat which is the essence of rhythm" (and he cites G. Fraccaroli, *D'una teoria razionale di metrica italiana*, Torino, 1882, p. 1).

6. Maruffi, pp. 11–12, and Guarnerio, pp. 55–56 and 71–72; Maruffi also discusses the rhythmic irregularity of the 2, 5 form (because of its possible derivation from the *settenario*); Guarnerio, p. 69, cites still another form, stressed principally on the first and fifth syllables, with weaker stress on the third.

7. Pernicone, "Storia e svolgimento della metrica," p. 306, also p. 304.

8. Mari, pp. 16–17, whom I follow very closely; see also Guarnerio, pp. 88–93, on the *endecasillabo*.

9. Federzoni, *Dei versi e dei metri italiani*, pp. 23–24 n., cites Dante's "Per una ghirlandetta" (for which, see above, p. 156), written in nine-syllable lines, and shows how it was reduced to a popular song in *ottonari*. Boyde, in his note in *Dante's Lyric Poetry*, I, lii, says Dante "never used" lines with an even number of syllables; but as Levi (p. 474) shows, Dante used an *ottonario* with stresses on the first, fourth, and seventh syllables ("Fiéra crudéle e divérsa").

What Dante said in *DVE* II.v.7 was that lines of an even number of syllables "non utimur nisi raro," which is different from saying "never."

10. Text of Dante from *Dante's Lyric Poetry*, ed. Foster and Boyde, I, 38; for commentary on this poem's prosody, see II, 63–64. For a *novenario* with the pattern (1), 3, (6), 8, see Guarnerio, pp. 58–59 and 68–69; he also notes, pp. 79–81, a *novenario* with stress on the fourth and eighth syllables, with a caesura after the fourth or fifth.

11. Guarnerio, p. 73, notes a *decasillabo* of Chiabrera's which is stressed 3, 7, 9—though Maruffi, p. 16, reads the same line 1, (3), 5, 7, 9.

12. On the origins of the *endecasillabo*, see Pernicone, pp. 304–06 and the additional bibliography there and in his note, p. 349; also Burger's chapter on "Le Décasyllable," pp. 20–29, esp. pp. 25–29 for the various forms of the Italian line. There is also the older work of W. Thomas, *Le Décasyllable roman*, Travaux et Mémoires de l'Université de Lille, N.S. I, 4 (Lille, 1904); pp. 65–88 consider the *endecasillabo.* I have not been able to see S. D'Arco-Avalle, *Preistoria dell'endecasillabo* (Milano-Napoli, 1963). Guarnerio, pp. 53–54, 88–101, and Levi, pp. 483–90, have detailed discussions, while Boyde, I, li-liv, has excellent remarks on the *endecasillabo* and Dante's use of it. For a linguist's perspective, see G. E. Sansone, "Per un'analisi strutturale dell'endecasillabo," *Lingua e stile*, II, 2 (1967), 179-97. See also A. Monteverdi, n. 14, below.

13. Guarnerio, p. 98, cites Fraccaroli; Levi, p. 490; Pernicone, p. 308.

14. There is much dispute over the text of this Inscription; of the two versions I have chosen the B text as given in *Early Italian Texts*, ed. C. Dionisotti and C. Grayson, 2nd ed. (Oxford, 1965), pp. 30–33; Burger, p. 25, gives a different reading. On the Inscription, see the discussion in Dionisotti-Grayson and in A. Monteverdi, "I primi endecasillabi italiani," *Studi Romanzi*, 28 (1939), 141–54.

15. Leon Battista Alberti (1406–72) and Leonardo Dati (1408–72) made the first (of many) attempts to introduce classical meters into modern verse by adapting or conserving the quantity and rules of classical prosody. Alberti and Dati wrote hexameters on the theme of friendship for a contest sponsored by Piero de'Medici on 22 October 1441, a contest meant to prove Italian capable of sustaining exalted themes. The theme was more exalted than the verse; there was no winner. In 1539, the humanist and poet Claudio Tolomei (1492–1555) published *Versi e regole della nuova poesia italiana* and expounded classical prosody for Italian use. Italian syllables were to be considered long or short, regardless of grammatical accent. Tolomei illustrated his principles with poems by himself and nine others. Tolomei's precepts found some followers, but in the seventeenth century, Gabriello Chiabrera, and in the nineteenth, Giosuè Carducci, sought to recognize the natural grammatical accents of Italian by limiting themselves to classical meters that seemed to present metrical forms analogous to traditional Italian schemes. Carducci, the most famous exponent of classical meters, published his *Odi barbare* (*Barbarian Odes*) from 1877 to 1889 as well as a historical study, *Poesia barbara dei secoli XV e XVI* (1881), and precipitated furious polemics. No one seems certain why Carducci called his verses "barbarian"; *E.I.*, p. 110, suggests he was following the spirit of Plautus (*Trinummus*, 19: "Philemo scripsit, Plautus uortit barbare"); E. H. Wilkins, *A History of Italian Literature* (Cambridge: Harvard University Press, 1954), p. 442, suggests he took the term from Tommaso Campanella's line: "Musa latina, è forza che prendi la barbara lingua." Perhaps Carducci took a hint for the title from Leconte de Lisle's collection, *Poèmes barbares* (1862, 1872, 1878). Pernicone, p. 340, cites Carducci as saying in effect his meters are "barbarian" because classical meters transposed into Italian would surely strike Greek and Roman ears as rude and approximate. On the "metrica barbara" and *Odi barbare*, see D'Ovidio's basic study, *Versificazione romanza*, pp. 291–357, and the discussions and bibliography in Guarnerio, pp. 240–74; Bickersteth, pp. 53–80, and Pernicone, pp. 338–42. For the classicizing impulse elsewhere, see R. A. Swanson, "Classical Meters in Modern Languages," *E.P.P.*, pp. 126–28.

16. For early instances and for the development of the *verso sciolto*, see Guarnerio, pp. 205–97; Pernicone, pp. 330–32; and Maruffi, pp. 79–81. For the influence on English verse, see the two entries under "Blank Verse" in *E.P.P.*, pp. 78–81, and F. T. Prince, *The Italian Element in Milton's Verse* (Oxford, 1954; rpt. and rev. 1962), esp. Ch. viii on the prosody of Milton's blank verse and Appendix A: "Specimens of Sixteenth-Century Italian Epic Blank Verse."

17. On the development of *settenari doppi* in the Middle Ages, see Guarnerio, pp. 86–87, and Federzoni, p. 42 n.; Burger, pp. 47–53, discusses the alexandrine; for the line in Italy, and its different forms, see pp. 49, 52–53.

SELECTED BIBLIOGRAPHY

*Bickersteth, G. L. *Carducci.* London: Longmans, Green, 1913.

*Boyde, P. "Note on Dante's Metric and Versification." In *Dante's Lyric Poetry.* Ed. K. Foster and P. Boyde. 2 vols. Oxford: Clarendon, 1967.

*Burger, M. *Recherches sur la structure et l'origine des vers romans.* Société de Publications Romanes et Françaises, 49. Geneva and Paris: Libraire E. Droz, 1957.

D'Ovidio, F. *Versificazione italiana e arte poetica mediovale.* Milano, 1910. Rpt. *Versificazione romanza: poetica e poesia mediovale.* Napoli, 1932.

E. I. *Enciclopedia Italiana.* "*Metrica.*" Vol. XXIII. Roma: Bestetti and Tumminelli, 1929–39.

**E. P. P.* *Encyclopedia of Poetry and Poetics.* Ed. A. Preminger with F. Warnke and O. B. Hardison, Jr. Princeton: Princeton Univ. Press, 1965. "Romance Prosody," "Classical Meters in Modern Languages," "Blank Verse."

Federzoni, G. *Dei versi e dei metri italiani.* Bologna: Nicola Zanichelli, n.d.

Fubini, M. *Metrica e poesia, lezioni sulle forme metriche italiana.* Milano, 1962.

Guarnerio, P. E. *Manuale di versificazione italiana.* Milano, 1893.

*Levi, A. "Della versificazione italiana." *Archivum Romanicum,* 14 (1930), 449–526. I cite this article. Professor Dante Della Terza kindly informs me that Levi recognized only the independent book-length study, *Della versificazione* (Genova, 1931). I have not been able to see this study.

Mari, G. *Riassunto e dizionarietto di ritmica italiana.* Torino, 1911.

Maruffi, G. *Piccolo manuale di metrica italiana.* Palermo, Torino: Carlo Clausen, 1893.

Meregazzi, M. C. *Stilistica e metrica.* Milano: Antonio Vallardi, 1940.

*Pernicone, V. "Storia e svolgimento della metrica," In *Tecnica e teoria letteraria,* Vol. II of the collection *Problemi e orientamenti critici di lingua e di letteratura italiana,* Ed. A Momigliano. Milano: Carlo Marzorati, 1951.

Though I have not been able to see them, the following items should be mentioned:

D'Arco Avalle, S. *Preistoria dell'endecasillabo.* Milano, Napoli, 1963.

Beccaria, G. L. "Appunti di metrica dantesca." Mimeo. Torino, 1969. [Forthcoming as a larger book.]

Contini, G. "Innovazioni metriche italiane fra Otto e Novecento." *Forum Italicum,* 3 (1969), 171–85.

Elwert, W. Th. *Italienische Metrik.* München, 1968.

Leonetti, P. *Storia della tecnica del verso italiano, Parte* I: *gli elementi della tecnica.* Roma, 1933.

——— *La tecnica del verso dialettale popolaresco dei primordi.* Napoli, 1934.

Pazzaglia, M. *Il verso e l'arte della Canzone del* De Vulgari Eloquentia. Firenze, 1968.

Spongano, R. *Nozioni ed esempi di metrica italiana.* Bologna, 1966.

*Contains a bibliography.

SPANISH

By LOWRY NELSON, JR.

Introduction

Spanish poetry has a rich and continuous history stretching from the recently discovered Mozarabic poems (eleventh century) to the present—a span of more than nine hundred years.[1] During that time the language has evolved continuously, but not radically, and the stress principle of versification has, though with wide latitude, remained constant. In a rough way it is possible to distinguish two main modes of Spanish poetry, the popular or traditional and the learned. Popular poetry of the Middle Ages is referred to as the *mester de juglaría* (*mester* > Lat. *ministerium* 'practice'; *juglaría* > Old Sp. *juglar* 'poet-performer'), and includes the epic poems, the ballads (*romances*), and various popular lyric forms such as the *zéjel* and the *cosante*. Learned poetry of the Middle Ages is referred to as the *mester de clerecía* (*clerecía* > *clérigo* 'religious,' 'man of learning'), and includes poetry based on syllable count as well as stress and written in a tradition that derives from medieval Latin hymnography and goliardic verse. The popular tradition allows a certain latitude in length of verse, whereas the learned tradition is fairly strict. Since the Middle Ages both popular and learned kinds have persisted, often practiced by the same poet. An extreme example would be Luis de Góngora (1561–1627), who throughout his life wrote both light and racy popular poetry and also the most Latinate poetry ever written in the vernacular. Dialect plays relatively little part in the main tradition of Spanish poetry, which is governed by Castilian, the regional speech that became the basis of standard Spanish. Still, it is a fact that in its earlier development Spanish poetry participated in many of the practices evolved in other parts of "Romania"—in France, Provence, Galicia, Portugal, and Italy. Besides, Arabic poetry had some part in influencing language, theme, and form—not surprisingly, since the Moors were not finally expelled from Spain until 1492, more than seven centuries after their invasion. Chief among the losses in living poetic tradition are the popular epic and ballad. The former did not survive the Middle Ages; the prime monument is the *Poema de mío Cid* (ca. 1140). The latter persisted in popular oral tradition that was widespread until the sixteenth or seventeenth century in Spain and has survived until the present in provincial Spain, Spanish America, and among the Sephardic Jews who were expelled from Spain in 1492 and settled elsewhere. At the same time the popular ballad has been imitated by such modern "learned" poets as Francisco de Quevedo (1580–1645) and Federico García Lorca (1898–1936).

In brief, then, it can be said that the long evolution of Spanish poetry is characterized by its use of standard Spanish, its use of both popular and learned elements, and its use of meter based on stress and syllable count. Exceptions to such a generalization, for example, dialectal elements, literary imitations of popular forms, old and modern "ametrical" verse, and free verse, are all felt to be distinct exceptions.

Some Special Phonological Features

The phonic wealth of the Spanish language has changed since the Middle Ages in two salient ways: an increase in the number of vowel sounds and a decrease in the number of consonantal sounds. These are both important for the study of Spanish versification.

Since the time when Spanish definitively evolved from spoken Latin, quantity in vowels has not been a distinctive feature of the language. Stress, however, has been operative and has helped to enrich the vocalic range by creating out of the five primary vowels fourteen diphthongs and four triphthongs, all of which may be either contained within word boundaries or, significantly for versification, formed between a word ending in a vowel and a word beginning with one. Diphthongs and triphthongs are usually treated by grammarians as monosyllabic, but occasionally by poets as dissyllabic. Either way they are prosodically significant.

Medieval Spanish was richer in consonantal sounds than Spanish since the Renaissance. The following sounds have disappeared from the standard language: *ts*, spelled either *ç* or *z*; *z*, the intervocalic pronunciation of the letter *s*; *dzh* and *zh* represented by the letter *j*; *sh*, the pronunciation of *x* until the latter sixteenth century; and the sounds of *b* and *v*, formerly about the same as in English but now merged in one sound, somewhere in between the two original sounds. Besides, in many parts of Spain and in most places outside of Spain, *c* before *e* and *i* is no longer pronounced unvoiced *th* as in standard Castilian Spanish, but rather *s*. Likewise, *ll*, pronounced like *lli* in English "million" in standard Castilian Spanish, is in many places, in Spain and elsewhere, pronounced like the *y* in "yet" or as *zh*. The result is that in modern Castilian Spanish we are left with roughly twenty-two consonantal sounds, not including allophones or nasalization.

Elements of Versification

A. *Rhyme and assonance.* Rhyme and assonantal rhyme have always played a conspicuous role in Spanish verse, not only as "ornaments" but also as means of signifying the end of a line of verse, the unity of a stanza or an assonantal "verse paragraph."

Rhyme in Spanish poetry is used largely as in other languages. It is to be found in the earliest Spanish popular stanzaic forms, such as the *jarcha*, the *zéjel*, and the *cosante*, as well as in the "learned" *cuaderna vía*, a sequence of four-line monorhymed stanzas in the *alejandrino* (a line of fourteen syllables divided seven-seven). Even though the grammarian Antonio de Nebrija (1444–1522) quite early condemned the use of rhyme as being a fetter, both it and assonance have vigorously survived the challenge of *versos sueltos* (unrhymed hendecasyllables) introduced in the Renaissance and, more recently, of free verse.

Assonantal rhyme is characteristically employed both in the popular epic and in the traditional ballad. It works according to the following rules: (1) With words stressed on the penultimate syllable (*palabras llanas* or *graves*) any set pair of vowels may serve. The following words, for example, would be in *i-a* assonance: *tranquila*, *ida*, *hija*, *caballería*. (2) With words stressed on the ultimate or final syllable (*palabras agudas*) the final vowel must be the same, as in the series: *cazar*, *palomar*, *brial*, *más*, *pagará*. In the oldest use of assonance, words whose stressed penultimate vowel was the same as that of end-stressed words in a series could terminate in unstressed *e* with or without a following consonant. Thus, the following are in assonantal rhyme: *llegar*, *padres*, *están*, *heredad*, *linaje*. (3) In the case of words with stress on the antepenult (*palabras esdrújulas*) the vowels considered to be in assonantal rhyme are those in the antepenultimate and in the ultimate or final syllable. Thus, in an *e-a* series the following would be in assonantal rhyme: *pérdida*, *sean*, *alameda*, *mudéjar*, *acémila*. Clearly the possibilities of assonantal rhyme as an organizing principle in Spanish verse are immense. No other European language seems to make such important use of assonance in poetry.

B. *Synalepha and dieresis.* Synalepha and, to some extent, dieresis are important in Spanish prosody. Somewhat in contrast to French and Italian, spoken Spanish tends to shun elision (complete assimilation of one vowel into another), but favors synalepha (the blending of two or even three contiguous vowels into a diphthong or a triphthong), which in verse counts as one syllable. In fact, in counting syllables the poet usually considers synalepha mandatory. Thus, these lines are to be counted as hendecasyllabic, that is, as containing eleven syllables:

> Y‿en este mismo valle donde‿agora
> me‿entristezco‿y me canso‿en el reposo . . .

In a way contrary to Italian and French usage, two contiguous occurrences of the same vowel, in separate words, as in *me entristezco*, are felt to produce a blending into a diphthong and not simple elision.

In certain words, however, diphthongs, usually treated by grammarians as monosyllabic, are sometimes treated by poets, invoking dieresis, as dissyllabic. Sometimes the choice reflects uncertainty early in the development of the language, as in words like *creer*, *dió*, and *fué*. (Only recently did the Royal Spanish Academy declare the latter two words monosyllabic and therefore in no need of the written accent.) Two typical instances of dieresis in verse appear in the following lines, the first octosyllabic and the second hendecasyllabic:

> y armonïosas se abrazan (Bécquer)
> armó de crüeldad, calzó de viento (Góngora)

Words containing contiguous occurrences of the same vowel, such as *poseer* and *azahar* (the *h* is not pronounced), when used in verse maintain dieresis or hiatus.

C. *Meter and rhythm.* Meter in Spanish, as in other languages, is a theoretical concept like the line in geometric figures and the phoneme in linguistics. It may be either closely or distantly approximated in given lines of verse, but it can never be absolutely realized. Thus, actual stressed and unstressed syllables are only relatively so (there is no absolute stress or absolute lack of stress), and two syllables are of the same duration only with reference to the duration of some other syllable. Any given line of verse, therefore, is in counterpoint to the ideal meter either in approaching it or in drawing away from it. Empirically, if a number of verse lines written in the same meter are averaged according to stressed and unstressed positions and according to syllable count, the averages should point quite closely to the absolute conditions of the ideal meter. The actualized phonic effect of the counterpoint between the meter and a given line is the rhythm. Even if the given line departs notably from the ideal meter, it must still be read (or better, performed) with the ideal meter in mind and not as prose. The distance between the ideal meter and a given line may be described as substitution of feet, hypermetry, or hypometry, or more generally and simply as variation. If the word "irregular" is used it should not be felt as pejorative, since it is precisely the poet's task to vary and to be "irregular." Otherwise he would produce either non-poetry or monotonous, and therefore bad, poetry.

D. "*Ametrical*" *verse*. Before we take up metrical verse, it will be chronologically sound to consider the "ametrical" verse of the popular epic, whose main exemplar is the *Poema de mío Cid* (ca. 1140). We may accurately describe this as a poem of about 3,735 extant lines, which range in length from ten to twenty syllables and are usually divisible into hemistichs. The lines are grouped in sequences or verse paragraphs that employ assonantal rhyme. For instance, the first few extant lines are in assonance according to the vowels *a-o*; the next six according to *e-a*; the next seven according to *o-e*; the next forty-three according to *a-a*; and so on. With all these variables the *Poema de mío Cid* may seem highly irregular in a pejorative sense. It is, however, only just to the poem to point out that most of its lines are of fourteen, fifteen, and thirteen syllables, in that order of frequency, and that the most common combinations of hemistichs are, in syllable count, seven-seven, seven-eight, and six-seven, also in that order of frequency. It is likewise noteworthy that the hemistichs are coterminous with whole grammatical phrases. (These approximations to "regularity" have encouraged at least two scholars in highhanded attempts to impose strict syllabism on the poem by chopping and padding.)[2]

The following is a fairly typical passage from the poem:

1689 Essora dixo el Çid: "de buena voluntad."
El día es salido   e la noch es entrada,
nos detardan de adobasse   essas yentes cristianas.
A los mediados gallos,   antes de la mañana,
el obispo don Jero*me*   la missa les cantava.

Here the relative "regularities" just mentioned are well illustrated. We may add that at a minimum it would seem that each hemistich has a major stress on its penultimate or ultimate syllable and a secondary stress preceding it. In some hemistichs of the poem a second or even third secondary stress may have to be posited, as in line ninety: "quando en Burgos me vedaron compra   y el rey me a ayrado." Experimental readings can perhaps enhance an impression of "regularity." The possibility that an accompanying instrument supplied "missing" stresses or phonic "lacunae" has hardly been explored. At all events, the "ametrical" verse of the *Poema de mío Cid* will stand fairly high on a scale of verse ranging from strictness to looseness. Thus: metrical verse (including hypometry and hypermetry), "ametrical" verse, free verse, rhythmical prose, prose.

E. *Metrical verse: syllabism and stress.* Given the fundamental elements of syllabism and stress, modern Spanish prosody proceeds empirically to describe the meter of given lines. It is assumed that no principle of organization or recurrence can begin to be established until the first major stress is perceived. Therefore, if any syllable or syllables precede the first such stress, they are considered to constitute the anacrusis. In most cases the second stress, whether major or secondary, occurs either on the second or on the third syllable following the first major stress. The upshot, then, is that the meter is duple or triple or mixed in several ways. Let us consider for example the octosyllabic line which has been commonly used in Spanish poetry. The following line of verse may be described as trochaic with anacrusis of two syllables and with two major stresses:

en el aire conmovido o o ó o ò o o o

Through the prevailing rhythm of the line, the fifth syllable may be said to take on a secondary stress, which we may represent as ò, that is, with a grave as distinct from an acute accent. It should be noted that to read the first three syllables as an anapest would be to contravene the convention of anacrusis and to upset the "elegance" of the whole system of descriptive Spanish prosody. With its stresses on the first and seventh syllables, the following line may be read as dactylic:

mueve la luna sus brazos ó o o ò o o ó o

Here again, because of the prevailing rhythm, the fourth syllable may be said to carry a secondary stress. Two kinds of "mixed" octosyllables occur, both with a single syllable of anacrusis and thus with the first major stress on the second syllable. What distinguishes them is that A has secondary stress on the fourth syllable and B has it on the fifth. Compare:

```
                                    /   \    /
A:  La luna vino‿a la fragua   o   o o  o o o  o o
                                  /    \    /
B:  sus senos de duro‿estaño   o  o o o  o o  o o
```

In all cases what is called the internal rhythmical period (*período rítmico interior*) is constituted by the part of the line from the first major stress to the syllable before the last major stress. The remaining unstressed syllables, together with the pause (*pausa*) at the end of the line and any unstressed syllables (that is, the anacrusis) at the beginning of the next line, constitute the linking rhythmical period (*período de enlace*). Each period is made up of feet (*cláusulas* or *pies*) which have less importance as a concept than they are granted in traditional English versification. The feet are called also tempos (*tiempos*), which may be either strong or weak, depending on whether they contain a principal or a secondary stress. A line is usually divided by a caesura (*cesura*), a pause of lesser duration and importance than that at the end of the line.

The first part of García Lorca's "Romance de la luna, luna" may be taken as an example for analysis. I present it first as it would normally be printed and then with a rhythmical analysis.

Romance de la luna, luna	Ballad of the Moon, the Moon
La luna vino a la fragua	The moon came to the forge
con su polisón de nardos.	with her bodice of spikenard.
El niño la mira mira.	The boy looks and looks at her.
El niño la está mirando.	The boy is looking at her.
En el aire conmovido	In the agitated air
mueve la luna sus brazos	the moon moves her arms
y enseña, lúbrica y pura,	and, voluptuous and pure, shows
sus senos de duro estaño.	her breasts of hard tin.
Huye luna, luna, luna.	Run away, moon, moon, moon.
Si vinieran los gitanos,	If the gipsies should come
harían con tu corazón	they would make of your heart
collares y anillos blancos.	white necklaces and rings.
Niño, déjame que baile.	Boy, let me dance.
Cuando vengan los gitanos,	When the gipsies come
te encontrarán sobre el yunque	they will find you on the anvil
con los ojillos cerrados.	with your little eyes closed.
Huye luna, luna, luna,	Run away, moon, moon, moon,
que ya siento sus caballos.	for now I sense their horses.
Niño, déjame, no pises	Boy, let me be, don't step
mi blancor almidonado.	on my starched whiteness.

Abbreviations: M.A. = mixed A P = pause
M.B. = mixed B ‿ = synalepha

	Anacrusis	Principal	Secondary	Principal		Secondary	
		/	\	/			
	o	o o	o o o	o o		o o	
1	La	luna	vino‿a la	fragua	P	con su	M.A.
		/	\	/			
		o o	o o	o o		o	
2		poli-	són de	nardos.	P	El	Tro.
		/	\	/			
		o o o	o o	o o		o	
3		niño la	mira	mira.	P	El	M.B.
		/	\	/			
		o o o	o o	o o		o o	
4		niño la‿es-	tá mi-	rando.	P	En el	M.B.
		/	\	/			
		o o	o o	o o			
5		aire	conmo-	vido	P		Tro.
		/	\	/			
		o o o	o o o	o o		o	
6		mueve la	luna sus	brazos	P	y‿en-	Dac.
		/	\	/			
		o o	o o o	o o		o	
7		seña,	lúbrica‿y	pura,	P	sus	M.A.
		/	\	/			
		o o o	o o	o o		o o	
8		senos de	duro‿es-	taño.	P	Huye	M.B.
		/	\	/			
		o o	o o	o o		o o	
9		luna,	luna,	luna.	P	Si vi-	Tro.
		/	\	/			
		o o	o o	o o		o	
10		nieran	los gi-	tanos,	P	ha-	Tro.

11	/ o o o rían con	\\ o o o tu cora-	/ o zón	P	o co-	M.B. (fluctuating?)
12	/ o o o llares y‿a-	\\ o o nillos	/ o o blancos.	P	o o Niño,	M.B.
13	/ o o déja-	\\ o o me que	/ o o baile.	P	o o Cuando	Tro.
14	/ o o vengan	\\ o o los gi-	/ o o tanos	P		Tro.
15	/ o o o te‿encontra-	\\ o o o rán sobre‿el	/ o o yunque	P		Dac.
16	/ o o o cón los o-	\\ o o o jillos ce-	/ o o rrados	P	o o Huye	Dac.
17	/ o o luna,	\\ o o luna,	/ o o luna,	P	o o que ya	Tro.
18	/ o o siento	\\ o o sus ca-	/ o o ballos.	P	o o Niño,	Tro.
19	/ o o déja-	\\ o o me no	/ o o pises	P	o o mi blan-	Tro.
20	/ o o cor al-	\\ o o mido-	/ o o nado			Tro.

The above is a nearly adequate description of Lorca's octosyllabic lines. Still, two of them need further comment, since they do not wholly conform to any of the four types. In line two the first stressed syllable is not strictly stressed (it would not be in prose) and, even if we grant it to be stressed, it cannot be said to have a principal stress. Nonetheless, by its position in the metrical scheme it takes on sufficient rhythmical stress and in doing so creates a kind of counterpoint or syncopation. Line eleven brings up two special matters. Ordinarily, if a line ends in a stressed syllable, an additional non-existent syllable is counted to make up the requisite number of syllables—eight in the case of the octosyllable. But in this case Lorca adds an actual syllable (internally), thus making the line in a sense "hypermetric" or "fluctuating" (*fluctuante*). Or, more simply, the *ía* in *harían* may be considered an instance of syneresis, in which the line may be described as regular M.B. (with its additional non-existent syllable).

For the most part octosyllabic lines can be explained in terms of the schemes just elaborated. Lines of other syllabic length can also be accommodated to a few patterns, generally consisting of trochaic, dactylic, or various kinds of mixed meter. In longer lines it often seems a simplification to deal with the varieties of hemistichs first and then to show how they are used in variable combinations in given lines.

F. *Stanzaic and Other Large Forms.* The *Poema de mío Cid* seems to have some meaningful organization in its groups of lines in assonantal rhyme; the same is not necessarily true in the ballads. Other types of poetry in Spanish show various kinds of broad organizational principles and relatively complex stanzaic forms according to line length, line recurrence, rhyme, assonantal rhyme, and rhetorical structures also common to prose. Such frequent forms as the *zéjel*, *jarcha*, *cosante*, *villancico*, *letrilla*, *redondilla*, *silva*, and *octava real*, are described in the "Indice de estrofas" in Tomás Navarro, *Métrica española: Reseña histórica y descriptiva* (Syracuse: Syracuse Univ. Press, 1956) and under separate articles in Alex Preminger, ed., *Encyclopedia of Poetry and Poetics* (Princeton: Princeton Univ. Press, 1965). The use of verse forms in Spanish drama is well illustrated in a particular case in S. Griswold Morley and Courtney Bruerton, *The Chronology of Lope de Vega's Comedias* (New York: MLA, 1940). Structural use of verse, parallelism, and correlation as in *versus reportati* is discussed in numerous places by Dámaso Alonso, including: "Versos plurimembres y poemas correlativos," *Revista de la Biblioteca, Archivo y Museo*, Ayuntamiento de Madrid, 13, No. 49 (1944); "Versos correlativos y retórica tradicional," *Revista de filología*, 28 (1944), 139–53; and *Estudios y ensayos gongorinos* (Madrid: Gredos, 1955).

Earlier Bibliography

The first accounts of Spanish versification date from the fifteenth century and are based upon Provencal models. In the *Gramática castellana* (1492) of Antonio de Nebrija we find the first emphasis on the importance of stress in Spanish versification in his discussion of the relation between Latin and Spanish poetry. Concern for new modes imported from Italy (such as *versos sueltos* and the sonnet) is shown in such works as Fernando de Herrera's *Anotaciones a las obras de Garcilaso de la Vega* (1580) and Juan Díaz Rengifo's *Arte métrica española* (1592). In Chapters lxxxiv–xcv of the *Arte de la lengua española castellana* by Gonzalo de Correas (1625; manuscript definitively and diplomatically edited by Emilio Alarcos García in 1954) sensible analyses are made of poetic texts according to prevailing duple and triple rhythm (trochaic and dactylic) with recognition of the occurrence of the amphibrach. In 1737 Ignacio Luzán published his *Poética*, which propounded a quantitative scheme that had some echo in the earlier nineteenth century, but which represents only an oddity in the history of the theory and practice of Spanish verse. In the early nineteenth century Andrés Bello (1781–1864) established firm principles for prosodic inquiry through the whole range of Spanish poetry. He showed the basic importance of stress and explored its workings. He also concerned himself with the principles of syllabism and with "ametrical" verse, as well as with other elements such as consonantal and assonantal rhyme. His principal treatise is the *Principios de ortología y métrica de la lengua castellana* (1835), now definitively edited along with related studies in *Obras completas de Andrés Bello* (Caracas: Ministerio de Educación, 1955), Volume VI edited by Samuel Gili Gaya. Later in the century the notes in the *Antología de poetas líricos castellanos* edited by Marcelino Menéndez y Pelayo (Madrid, 1890–1916) are of value because of their historical breadth and awareness. Numerous special studies of older Spanish poetry from a metrical point of view were published by Federico Hanssen, mostly in the *Anales de la Universidad de Santiago de Chile* roughly between 1896 and 1916. For the study of popular prosody the many works of Ramón Menéndez Pidal on the *Poema de mío Cid* and the ballads are authoritative: the principal studies are the *Cantar de mío Cid* (Madrid, 1908, and subsequent editions) and *Poesía juglaresca* (Madrid, 1924, and subsequent editions).

Recent Bibliography

A number of recent works stand out, foremost among them is *Métrica española: reseña histórica y descriptiva* by Tomás Navarro (Syracuse: Syracuse Univ. Press, 1956). Here we find principles succinctly argued, along with an elaborate repertory of verse forms and stanzas treated exhaustively in the precise terms of their historical development in poetic practice. Navarro pays proper tribute to the work of Pedro Henríquez Ureña, which first appeared as *La versificación irregular en la poesía española* (Madrid, 1920) and now is available in revised and definitive form as *Estudios de versificación española* (Buenos Aires: Universidad de Buenos Aires; Departamento

Editorial, 1961). Other recent treatises of general use and interest are: Dorothy Clotelle Clarke, *A Chronological Sketch of Castilian Versification Together with a List of its Metric Terms* (Berkeley and Los Angeles: Univ. of California Press, 1952); Joaquín Balaguer, *Apuntes para una historia prosódica de la métrica castellana* (Madrid: Consejo Superior de Investigaciones Científicas, 1954); Rafael de Balbín, *Sistema de rítmica castellana* (Madrid: Editorial Gredos, 1962); and Rudolf Baehr, *Spanische Verslehre auf historischer Grundlage* (Tübingen: Max Niemeyer, 1962). The fundamental bibliography from the beginnings to 1937 is: Dorothy Clotelle Clarke, *Una bibliografía de versificación española*, Univ. of California Pubs. in Modern Philology, xx, No. 2, 57–116 (Berkeley: Univ. of California Press, 1937). Relevant articles can usefully be consulted in: *Diccionario de literatura española*, third edition (Madrid: Revista de Occidente, 1964); *Encyclopedia of Poetry and Poetics*, edited by Alex Preminger and others (Princeton: Princeton Univ. Press, 1965).

NOTES

1. See S. M. Stern, *Les Chansons mozarabes* (Palermo: U. Manfredi Editore, 1953), and Emilio García Gómez, *Las jarchas romances de la serie árabe en su marco* (Madrid: Sociedad de Estudios y Publicaciones, 1965).

2. H. R. Lang, "Contributions to the Restoration of the Poema del Cid," *Revue Hispanique*, 66 (1926), 1–509; Charles V. Aubrun, "La Métrique de Mío Cid est regulière," *Bulletin Hispanique*, 49 (1947), 332–72.

FRENCH

By JACQUELINE FLESCHER

Versification is a complex texture, involving grammar and stylistics. It is the grammatical backbone that we are here concerned with. Its historical evolution can be seen as a gradual convergence towards the strict alexandrine form, which was firmly established in the seventeenth century, and a subsequent divergence from it. Because the basic structure of French verse is syllabic, in contrast, say, to the Germanic stress patterns, the relative importance of the various components of versification differs. A syllabic structure based on a fixed number of syllables is in itself a weaker framework than the stress pattern. Hence the importance in French verse of rhyme as a basic element strengthening the syllabic framework, in contrast to the auxiliary function of rhyme in English, where the stress pattern provides a sufficient framework in itself. The function of rhyme is moreover highly dependent on the fixed stress falling on the last syllable. It is the combined effect of the two that strengthens the rhythmic pattern. To determine adequately the interaction of these elements at different points in the historical evolution, it is necessary to take a synthetic view of the problem, rather than the traditional approach that views each component of metrics separately.

The Classical Alexandrine

The alexandrine came into its own in the middle of the sixteenth century with the poets of the Pléiade and was firmly established in the seventeenth century. Two factors determine its specific nature: its perfectly symmetrical pattern and its coincidence with syntax. The basic pattern of the alexandrine is defined by a fixed caesura (*césure fixe*) in the middle, which divides the line into two parallel *hémistiches*, each ending with a fixed accent on the last syllable. The rhythm is marked by a combination of accent and pause. Secondary accents are freely distributed (*accents mobiles*) and provide flexibility within firmly defined limits, but are marked by a weaker pause than the medial caesura. In the seventeenth century the secondary accents most frequently fell after the third and ninth syllables, thus creating a perfectly balanced four-part line:

> Sont-ce là ces projets || de grandeur et de gloire
> Qui devaient dans les cœurs || consacrer ma mémoire?
>
> (Racine, *Bérénice* IV.iv.1027–28)

Many other combinations are, however, possible and, as the following passage shows, a high degree of rhythmical variety can be obtained:

> Oui, je viens dans son temple || adorer l'Eternel;
> Je viens, selon l'usage || antique et solennel,
> Célébrer avec vous || la fameuse journée
> Où sur le mont Sina || la loi nous fut donnée.
>
> (Racine, *Athalie* I.i.1–4)

The rule of metrical coincidence was laid down by Malherbe and confirmed by Boileau:

> Que toujours dans vos vers le sens coupant les mots
> Suspende l'hémistiche, en marque le repos.
>
> (*Art poétique* I.105–06)

The stylistic exceptions in no way overshadow the perfect balance of sound and meaning where the metric pattern reinforces the syntax and the syntax sustains the metric pattern:

> Et là vous me verrez, soumis ou furieux,
> Vous couronner Madame, ou le perdre à vos yeux.
>
> (Racine, *Andromaque* III.vii.975–76)

The second verse is typical of the recurrent antithetic verses found in Corneille and Racine:

> S'il ne meurt aujourd'hui, je puis l'aimer demain.
> (*Andromaque* IV.iii.1200)
>
> Elle est veuve d'Hector et je suis fils d'Achille.
> (*Andromaque* II.v.662)

These examples show clearly the interaction of verse and syntax, the medial caesura marking the strong dividing line between the two antithetic clauses. The same pattern may be found between verses in the lines of Corneille that read like maxims:

> Je suis jeune, il est vrai, mais aux âmes bien nées
> La valeur n'attend pas le nombre des années.
> (*Le Cid* II.ii.405–06)

Because the end of the verse marks a pause in meaning and often corresponds with the end of a sentence, the auxiliary question of overflow (*enjambement*) is naturally raised. Boileau expressed his opinion vigorously on this point:

> Les stances avec grâce, apprirent à tomber,
> Et le vers sur le vers n'osa plus enjamber.
> (*Art poétique* I.136–37)

Exceptions occur, notably in La Fontaine, who frequently used overflow to highlight a comic effect:

> Mais, après certain temps, souffrez qu'on vous propose
> Un époux beau, bien fait, jeune et tout autre chose
> Que le défunt.
> (*La Fontaine, Fables* VI.xxi, *La Jeune Veuve*)

Though exceptions are also found in the classical dramatists, the difference in genre is not irrelevant to their frequency. Neither the fixed accent, nor the pause, nor even their combined effect would suffice in themselves to consolidate the unity of the alexandrine. Rhyme is essential to this end.

As a tighter metric pattern evolved, a need for greater rigor in the rhyme scheme began to seem important, and the quality of rhyme became a major preoccupation. A determining factor in the choice of rhyme was the rule of alternation between masculine rhymes (those ending without a mute *e*) and feminine rhymes (those ending with a mute *e*). The distinction was completely independent of grammatical gender. This rule of alternation, which had already been applied by certain poets at the end of the fifteenth century, was firmly established by Ronsard in the sixteenth century and rigorously decreed by Malherbe in the seventeenth.

> Maître Corbeau, sur un arbre perché,
>   Tenait en son bec un fromage.
> Maître Renard, par l'odeur alléché,
>   Lui tint à peu près ce langage.[1]
>
> (La Fontaine, *Fables* I.ii, *Le Corbeau et le renard*)

This rule was qualified by a secondary consideration: the distinction between *rime riche* and *rime banale,* the former a parallel strengthening of sound identity and syntactic divergence. Hackneyed or insipid rhymes and rhymes of the same grammatical category were to be avoided. This desired divergence in meaning derived its value from its reinforcement of the sound analogy which ran counter to it. A *rime riche* required identity of two sounds in each word: the last accented vowel and the consonant preceding it.[2]

> Enfin n'en pouvant plus d'effort et de dou*leur*,
> Il met bas son fagot, il songe à son ma*lheur*.
>
> (La Fontaine, *Fables* I.xvi, *La Mort et le bucheron*)

The question of syllable counting was of some importance, since the gradually widening rift between colloquial pronunciation and prosody affected the metrical value of particular syllables. The discrepancy began to be felt acutely with the disappearance of the mute *e* in colloquial pronunciation, precisely at the time when the alexandrine reached its purest form. Thus Malherbe declared that the mute *e* no longer counted as a syllable and must be elided. He rejected hiatus, namely the juxtaposition without elision of the final vowel of a word with the initial vowel of a word that followed it.[3] Malherbe made certain concessions to the evolution of pronunciation. The force of archaic pronunciation, however, continued strong. Literary tradition in a sense resisted classicism. Classical poets observed Malherbe's rules but allowed many exceptions, particularly in popular or comic contexts.

Though the pattern of the classical alexandrine was somewhat rigid as laid down in the rules of Malherbe and Boileau, in the hands of the classical poets it reached a degree of balance and harmony which earned the designation *le grand vers*. This term referred both to the dignity of style to which it lent itself and to the frequency of its use. It is interesting to see how this pattern had been gradually shaped.

Towards the Alexandrine

It is necessary to mark a dividing line between earlier verse forms where looseness of structure cannot always be clearly distinguished from variety, and a versification which begins to work out consciously its metric pattern in relation to context and aesthetic standards. The dividing line occurs roughly in the middle of the sixteenth century. Setting aside sporadic efforts, or even collective but excessive preoccupation with form at the expense of content, such as that of the *Grands Rhétoriqueurs*,[4] we can discern the beginning of prescriptive theory with the Pléiade. A conscious groping towards a stable poetic form and the awareness of a new direction begin with these poets.

The texture of French poetry until this time is somewhat difficult to define. Its various elements cannot easily be assembled into a coherent framework, although certain striking features appear. Among these, the isosyllabic character of French verse stands out clearly until the end of the Middle Ages. Hiatus of vowels inside a verse is accepted. Mute *e* inside a word, or at the end of a word, retains its full metric value and may even precede an initial vowel. In contrast to the later metric pattern, where elision of syllables tends to shift the rhythmic effect to syllabic groups, the pattern of this earlier verse is established by the individual syllables. Hence the likeness at this stage between French poetry and the poetry of other Romance languages.

The choice of verse length in early French poetry would seem to be linked partly to the oral and more particularly to the musical tradition. It is generally believed that syllables were more heavily stressed in Old French. The later need for a firmer structure may therefore have been influenced by stress attenuation.

Instances of the alexandrine occurred as early as the middle of the twelfth century, and the form received its name from its use in the *Roman d'Alexandre* towards the end of the century. But the shorter verse lengths continued to be dominant until the second half of the sixteenth century. The gradual victory of one over the other did not follow a linear evolution. Although the eight-syllable line is the oldest type of French verse and appears for the first time in the tenth century with the *Vie de Saint Léger*, it is used concurrently with the ten-syllable line from the eleventh century to the middle of the sixteenth. Each type of verse tends to be used in specific genres, but changes also occur within the same genre: for instance, decasyllabic verse is used until the thirteenth century in the *chansons de geste*, after which it is supplanted by the alexandrine. The octosyllabic verse is used in spoken narrative genres like the *lai* or the romance, and in the romance it is often supplanted by prose during the thirteenth century.

The dominance of the alexandrine by the second half of the sixteenth century likewise corresponds to a shift from epic, lyric, and narrative verse to the more cerebral *discours*. The octosyllabic line is too short to have a fixed caesura and therefore has a more flexible rhythm. The ten-syllable line is nearer to the alexandrine pattern in that it is the only other verse length having a fixed caesura. It cannot, however, reach perfect symmetry, since the caesura after the fourth, or occasionally after the sixth, syllable, divides the line into *hémistiches* of unequal length. Only the alexandrine corresponds to the syntactic unity of a sentence and to a symmetrical rhythmic structure.

Rhyme followed a similar evolution. As the sound identity gradually increased, so the function of the rhyme in the strengthening of the verse structure gained in emphasis and became an integral element of prosody. As rhyme became destined for the eye as well as for the ear, it had to be reinforced. In the early *chansons de geste* assonance was used. This consisted in the identity only of the final accented vowel:[5]

> Oliver sent qu'il est a mort nasfret
> De lui venger ja mais ne li ert lez.
> En la grant presse or i fiert cume ber,
> Trencher cez hanstes e cez escuz buclers
> E piez e poinz e seles e costez.
>
> (*Chanson de Roland* III.528–32)

This partial sound analogy, however, lost ground and during the twelfth century was gradually superseded by rhyme, namely the identity of the final accented vowel and the sounds that follow it:

> Je plains le temps de ma jeunesse
> Auquel j'ai plus qu'autre galé,
> Jusqu'à l'entrée de la vieillesse
> Qui son partement m'a celé.
>
> (Villon, *Le Testament* XXII)

Increasingly from the high Middle Ages to the beginning of the sixteenth century rhyme was sought as an end in itself. From the looseness of assonance, poets tended to fall into the artifice of rhetorical ornament, as in the *rimes équivoquées*:

> En m'esbalant je fais rondeaulx en rithme,
> Et en rithmant bien souvent je m'enrime;
> Brief, c'est pitié qu'entre nous rithmailleurs,
> Cas vous trouvez assez de rithme ailleurs,
> Et quand vous plaist, mieulx que moy rithmassez,
> Des biens avez et de la rithme assez.
>
> (Marot, *Epître au roi* VII.1518)

Such playing on words was rejected by Ronsard and DuBellay, who prepared the way for *rime riche*, though they did not themselves strictly observe their rules. The alternation of masculine and feminine rhymes was suggested by the Pléiade but not strictly enjoined until Malherbe.

In spite of Malherbe's and Boileau's harsh judgments of the Pléiade, the passage to the classical alexandrine can be attributed on the theoretical level to their codification of poetic craftsmanship and on the artistic level to the verse *Discours* of Ronsard, which came close to the antithetic pattern of classical verse:

> Madame je serai ou du plomb ou du bois
> Si moi que la nature a fait naître François
> Aux races à venir je ne contais la peine
> Et l'extrême malheur dont notre France est pleine.
>
> (*Continuation du discours des misères de ce temps*, ll. 1–4; 1562)

The Break from the Classical Alexandrine

The break from the traditional alexandrine begins with the romantics and develops in three main stages: the weakening of the alexandrine, the dislocation of the alexandrine in the *vers libéré*, and the complete liberation in the *vers libre*. This movement is, however, very complex. For one thing, the alexandrine in its strictest form persists side by side with the most revolutionary innovations.

The romantics, and more particularly Hugo, began the process of loosening the classical structure.[6] The breakdown of the symmetrical pattern was accomplished mainly by a free use of the ternary alexandrine (*alexandrin ternaire*). In effect the strong medial caesura was replaced by two caesuras, thus creating a ternary division of syllables, the most frequent being four plus four plus four:[7]

> J'avais vingt ans, ‖ j'étais criblé ‖ de coups de lance
> On me porta ‖ sanglant et pâle ‖ à l'ambulance.
> (Hugo, *Légende des siècles* IV, *La Sœur de charité*, ll. 1–2)

The medial caesura was, however, weakened more often than suppressed. Moreover, the ternary alexandrine was used by the romantics in combination with the classical alexandrine:

> C'est le duel effrayant ‖ de deux spectres d'airain,
> Deux fantômes ‖ auxquels le démon ‖ prête une âme.
> (*Légende des siècles* I, *Le Mariage de Roland*, ll. 14–15)

And the weakening of the internal structure was compensated for by a vindication of *rime riche*. Statistics show an increase from fifty-six to eighty-six per cent in rhymes of different semantic category between the classical and romantic poets.[8] The attention given to meaning tended to favor the use of unusual words; hence, the frequency too of *rimes rares*, which had previously been avoided. Emphasis was placed on oral quality at the expense of *rime pour l'œil*. Thus Hugo recommended *rime sonore*, showing a greater interest in the consonant preceding the last accented vowel than in the vowel itself. The oral emphasis also entailed an attempt to liberate verse from the alternation of masculine and feminine rhymes. The effectual responses in this direction were nevertheless limited.

The dislocation of the alexandrine was well under way by the middle of the nineteenth century; it worked in a variety of ways. Rhyme, caesura, verse length, and syntax were all important factors, but as the emphasis on specific elements of versification tended to differ with individual poets, so the dissolution of the classical pattern was an intricate process. In the case of Verlaine, it took the form of violent reaction against rhyme:

> Oh! qui dira les torts de la rime!
> Quel enfant sourd ou quel nègre fou
> Nous a forgé ce bijou d'un sou
> Qui sonne faux et creux sous la lime?
> (Verlaine, *Jadis et naguère*, *Art poétique*)

He frequently transgressed the rule of alternation between masculine and feminine rhymes and re-introduced assonance as a stylistic device:

> Quant à souffrir, quant à mourir, c'est nos affaires
> Ou plutôt celles des toc-tocs et des tic-tacs
> De la pendule en garni dont la voix sévère
> Voudrait persévérer à nous donner le trac
>
> De mourir le premier ou le dernier. Qu'importe,
> Si l'on doit, ô mon Dieu, se revoir à jamais?
> Qu'importe la pendule et notre vie, ô Mort?
> Ce n'est plus nous que l'ennui de tant vivre effraye!
>
> (Verlaine, *Chair*, *Vers sans rime*)

In a definite break with traditional metrics, shorter verse lengths were sometimes combined with unusual syntactic breaks at the end of a line, as in *Chant d'automne*, or a weakened rhyme scheme was combined with an asymmetrical verse length as in *Mandoline* (heptasyllable and exclusive use of feminine rhymes).

The process is most striking in a poet such as Mallarmé, because of the peculiar interaction of classical and modern elements. The basic metric structure of his verse is perfectly traditional. He often adheres closely to the twelve-syllable line, yet we partially lose sight of the metric pattern because of the unusual degree of grammatical distortion, which creates a counter-pattern to the verse. Overflow is effective in creating this disruption:

> Aimai-je un rêve?
> Mon doute, amas de nuit ancienne, s'achève
> En maint rameau subtil, qui, demeuré les vrais
> Bois mêmes, prouve, hélas! que bien seul je m'offrais
> Pour triomphe le faute idéale de roses. . . .
>
> (*L'Après-midi d'un faune*)

Each sentence runs on for several lines with unexpected ruptures and inversions and a minimum use of punctuation. The end of a verse often creates a break at a difficult grammatical juncture; for instance, after the personal pronoun:

> Quel sépulcral naufrage (tu
> Le sais, écume, mais y baves)
> Suprême une entre les épaves
> Abolit le mât dévêtu.
>
> (*Autres poèmes et sonnets*)

As the unity of the line is broken by overflow, so the internal unity of the syntactic group is frequently stretched across the normal place of the caesura:

> Réfléchissons . . .
> ou si ‖ les femmes dont tu gloses
>
> (*L'Après-midi d'un faune*)

The sixth syllable tends to occur in an unstressed word, or, as in the above example, in a word with a purely grammatical function, such as an article or a conjunction. Mallarmé does not, however, go to the extreme of other symbolists, who make the sixth syllable coincide with an unstressed *e* in the middle of a word.

Syntactic divergence, overflow, and caesura undermine the traditional alexandrine. Why then do we never feel a complete liberation from its hold in Mallarmé? Rhyme is doubtless the answer. In this respect, he works in the opposite direction from Verlaine, marking the end of the line distinctly with a *rime riche* and respecting the alternation of masculine and feminine rhymes. In *Le Cygne*, within a closely knit rhyme pattern heavily underlined by the assonance of the vowel *i*, Mallarmé manages to vary the grammatical category with each rhyme, thus creating an extreme degree of tension between grammar and metrics.

Several aspects of *vers libéré* are already present in Mallarmé. But the notion itself is difficult to define. *Vers libéré* occurs essentially in opposition to traditional versification and can therefore be established only in negative terms. According to Michel Décaudin, "Chaque groupe propose son propre jeu de règles nouvelles, ou plutôt de licences codifiées."[9] Theodor Elwert characterizes it as: greater flexibility in syllable counting owing to differences in the value given to obsolete *e*; violation of the rules of hiatus; flexibility or suppression of the caesura; overflow; preference for line lengths previously unused or unknown; liberation from traditional principles concerning the quality and alternation of rhymes; possibility of assonance instead of rhyme.[10]

These tendencies pushed to the extreme became *vers libre*: rejection of syllable counting, complete freedom in verse length, suppression of rules concerning rhyme—in other words, a dissolution of the regular structure of verse. One can hardly talk of a metrical pattern in free verse; still its rhythmic composition does stand out clearly in relation to prose. What distinctive features regulate this new verse form?

Let us examine two examples:

> Je t'ai prise contre ma poitrine comme une colombe
> qu'une petite fille étouffe sans le savoir
> Je t'ai prise avec toute ta beauté ta beauté plus
> riche que tous les placers de la Californie
> ne le furent au temps de la fièvre de l'or
> J'ai empli mon avidité sensuelle de ton sourire
> de tes regards de tes frémissements
> J'ai eu à moi à ma disposition ton orgueil même
> Quand je te tenais courbée et que tu subissais
> ma puissance et ma domination
> (Apollinaire, *Ombre de mon amour, L'Amour, le dédain et l'espérance*)

> Flèches fleurs saluant d'une scène sans fond les spectateurs invisibles
> Flèches fleurs qui font le geste d'échine des martyrs
> Flèches fleurs fers sûrs que fiche au flanc du silence
> L'enfant Liberté poêle prophète des aubes
> Phares d'un seul naufrage étoiles filantes
> Feux follets de l'immense cimetière en fête
> Sain foin nocturne des fusées
> Que votre volonté soit faite
> (Aragon, *Brocéliande, La Nuit d'août*)

In both these poems, rhyme, verse length, and caesura are ignored. Traditional verse is completely dislocated. Yet a rhythmic structure is restored by a new framework of repetition, based on a shift from metrics to stylistics. The elements common to both poems are: repetition of the same word, expression, or sentence, particularly at the beginning of a verse; parallelism of construction; free use of assonance and alliteration; absence of punctuation. Although the verse is much looser in texture than classical verse, these tendencies act as a compensation for the breakdown of metric regularity. Assonance and alliteration replace rhyme. The beginning of a line is more strongly marked than the end, with word repetition and grammatical parallelism fulfilling the function of rhyme. Internal word repetition and assonance serve as regulators, preventing the total loss of the marked rhythm formerly provided by fixed accents and caesura. The absence of punctuation softens distortion of word order and, therefore, aids semantic parallelism. Though these stylistic features are by no means peculiar to free verse and cannot pretend to retain the force of metric regulation, their orchestration nevertheless establishes a frontier between verse and prose.

The end of the nineteenth century marks a turning point in the creation of new verse forms. Yet the alexandrine remains on the poetic scene. Valéry uses it with almost Malherbian rigor, and even more striking is the persistence of the classical meter in surrealist poetry. In Eluard's *Capitale de la douleur* we find it in the very midst of free verse:

> Et l'ombre qui descend des fenêtres profondes
> Epargne chaque soir le cœur noir de mes yeux.
> (Eluard, *Capitale de la douleur*, *La Parole*)

Aragon himself is interesting in this respect, since on the one hand he covers the full range of metric and stylistic innovations, and on the other he reinforces the classical tradition. Statistics show that the prevalent verse forms in Aragon are the alexandrine, the octosyllable, and free verse in the following proportions: alexandrine, 30.5 per cent; octosyllable, 30 per cent; free verse, 18 per cent.[11] The alexandrine is moreover observed with all its traditional components and stands as a clear example of that curious phenomenon, classical symmetry intruding upon the most personal innovations of the twentieth century:

> Je n'oublierai jamais l'illusion tragique
> Le cortège les cris la foule et le soleil
> Les chars chargés d'amour les dons de la Belgique
> L'air qui tremble et la route à ce bourdon d'abeilles
> (Aragon, *Le Crève Cœur*, *Les Lilas et les roses*)

Critics and theorists of versification tend to be advocates either of the strict alexandrine form or of some form of liberated verse. Almost inevitably they take a firm stand for one or the other. Suberville and Grammont present any modernization as a breaking of the rules and speak in no uncertain terms: "Cette impuissance ne trahirait-elle pas en définitive un vice d'origine, qui est la confusion des genres, le refus de se soumettre à la nature des choses et aux règles qu'elle impose, d'un mot, l'individualisme anarchique?"[12] Jean Cohen, inversely, tries to show that authentic French poetry necessarily breaks from traditional form. To restore the balance, let us simply state the undeniable occurrence of a dialectic in twentieth century verse between tradition and innovation. We cannot arbitrate a battle still in progress.

The obstinacy of classical forms points to a strong aesthetic tradition and, perhaps, to inherent characteristics of the language which appear to call for a particular framework. The relatively small number of prose poems in French literature would seem to confirm this hypothesis. There is, however, no doubt that the technical innovations of the twentieth century are intimately bound to the content of its poetry. The alexandrine corresponds to a poetry where statement tends to dominate over suggestion. Historically it points to a loss of naïveté and a movement away from the lyrical and popular poetry of the preclassical period. A deliberate effort has been made in the twentieth century to break the static forms of the *discours* and reattain the dynamic quality of lyrical and popular verse. In the orchestration of sound and syntax regulating *vers libre*, song even gives way to incantation.

NOTES

1. This strict succession of masculine and feminine rhymes is called *rimes croisées*. There are other possible combinations, the most current being *plates* or *suivies* (two masculine and two feminine rhymes) and *embrassées* (two masculine separated by two feminine rhymes). The subject of rhyme is treated with finesse by Pierre Guiraud in *La Versification*, pp. 30–32, 86–92, 113–17. For full reference for all works cited in these notes, see selected bibliography at the end.
2. The rule concerning the final consonant in the seventeenth century was one of graphic, not phonetic identity (*rime pour l'œil*).
3. The rules concerning elision and hiatus had previously been determined by etymology: dissyllabic pronunciation in the original word resulted in *diérèse*, i.e., two syllables were counted; monosyllabic pronunciation resulted in *synérèse*, i.e., one syllable was counted.
4. A school of poets at the end of the fifteenth century and beginning of the sixteenth who were concerned exclusively with form, i.e., ornate refinements in style, virtuosity in versification, and artificial play on rhymes.
5. Assonanced verse was grouped in *laisses* of varying numbers of verses. Rhyme patterns introduced a prosodic element which was impossible in assonanced verse.
6. With the loosening of the classical structure comes the reinstatement of shorter verse

lengths, namely the decasyllabic and more particularly the octosyllabic line. Although a variety of verse lengths is used in the post-classical period, the prevalent forms are, in order of frequency, the twelve, eight, and ten syllable.

7. The ternary alexandrine had already been used by Racine, Molière, and La Fontaine, but generally speaking, the use of this division was rare among classical poets.

8. Jean Cohen, *Structure du langage poétique*, p. 85.

9. "Le Vers d'Apollinaire," in Monique Parent, ed., *Le Vers français au 20e siècle*, p. 163.

10. *Traité de versification française*, p. 165.

11. P. Polovina, "Le Rythme, la phrase et la rime, dans deux mille vers d'Aragon," in *Le Vers français au 20e siècle*, p. 197.

12. Jean Suberville, *Histoire et théorie de la versification française.*

SELECTED BIBLIOGRAPHY

Cohen, Jean. *Structure du langage poétique*. Paris: Flammarion, 1966.

Duhamel, G., and Ch. Vildrac. *Notes sur la technique poétique*. 2nd ed. Paris: Champion, 1925.

Elwert, W. Theodor. *Traité de versification française, des origines à nos jours*. Paris: Klincksieck, 1965. (French trans. of *Französische Metrik*, Max Hueber Verlag, 1961.)

Grammont, Maurice. *Petit Traité de versification française*. Paris: Armand Colin, 1965. (Collection U.)

Guiraud, Pierre. *La Versification*. Paris: Presses Univs. de France, 1970. (Que Sais-je? N° 1377.)

Kastner, L. E. *A History of French Versification*. Oxford: Clarendon, 1903.

Lote, Georges. *Histoire du vers français*. Paris: Boivin, 1949.

Parent, Monique, ed. *Le Vers français au vingtième siècle*. Paris: Klincksieck, 1967.

Suberville, Jean. *Histoire et théorie de la versification française à l'usage des classes de lettres*. Paris: Editions de "L'Ecole," 1946.

ENGLISH

I. HISTORICAL

By PAUL FUSSELL, JR.

The word meter comes from the Greek term for measure, and a convenient way to distinguish various metrical systems is to ascertain what is being measured or counted in each.[1] In English four metrical systems or kinds of meter are distinguishable: the syllabic, the accentual (sometimes called "stress meter" or "strong stress meter"), the accentual-syllabic (sometimes called "syllable-stress"), and the quantitative.

Syllabic prosody merely counts the number of syllables per line without regard to the stress of the syllables relative to each other. Although stress does of course appear in lines of verse composed syllabically—in English it is impossible to utter two syllables without stressing one more than the other—ideally stress operates in this meter as a device of embellishment or rhetorical emphasis rather than as the criterion of the metrical form.

In the late nineteenth and early twentieth centuries Robert Bridges experimented with syllabic meter, and recent practitioners have included Auden, Marianne Moore, Dylan Thomas, Donald Hall, and Thom Gunn. The syllabic meter has been one of a number of contemporary devices used to de-emphasize metrical form without losing it entirely, and to permit the emergence of a greater variety of local rhythms. Some of Dylan Thomas' most successful poems are syllabic, e.g., "Fern Hill," "Poem in October." Despite sporadic successes, however, modern English poetry has tended to show that syllabism is not a sufficiently marked measuring system in a language so Germanic and thus so inherently accentual as English.

When syllabic meter does create engaging effects in English, they will often be found to result from a pattern of stress emergent along with the simply syllabic. In Bridges' "Cheddar Pinks," for example, the poet's design of writing alternating five- and six-syllable lines with stress used nonstructurally seems to be modified by the accentual character of the

English language. The Anglo-Saxon inclination toward stress is such that despite our willingness to adopt the poem's convention of syllabism we cannot help noticing—or perhaps supplying—another more basic measuring system, an accentual system of two stresses per line:

> Mid the squander'd colour
>   idling as I lay
> Reading the Odyssey
>   in my rock garden
> I espied the cluster'd
>   tufts of Cheddar pinks
> Burgeoning with promise
>   of their scented bloom.

A similar duality, apparent in Marianne Moore's syllabic "In Distrust of Merits," can be illustrated in the quatrains that conclude each stanza. For most of the poem these terminal quatrains are largely syllabic, with stress falling apparently at random. For example:

> '. . . his ground in patience patience
>   patience, that is action or
> beauty,' the soldier's defence
>   and hardest armor for . . .

Here the scheme for the syllable count is seven, seven, seven, six. This syllabic system seems adequate to the poem until the climactic ending, where a strong personal assertion rather than gentle rumination is called for. The stresses now rise to take over the metrical structure:

> I inwardly did nothing.
>   O Iscariotlike crime!
> Beauty is everlasting
>   and dust is for a time.

In English it is as if stress, like passion and murder, will out, and it will out the moment the poet, arrived at a climax, seizes all the techniques of prosodic reinforcement offered by the nature of the English language. In longer syllabic lines, however, and in stanzas of mixed long and short syllabic lines—for instance, in Thomas' "Over Sir John's Hill" and in

Miss Moore's "Poetry"—the accentual emergence may be more difficult to detect.

While in syllabic verse only the syllables are counted, in accentual verse only the stresses are, and both accentual and accentual-syllabic systems work on the principle that, prosodically viewed, syllables are of two kinds only: stressed and unstressed. These systems do not require the complication of theories of "medial stress." In the accentual system syllables may vary greatly in number per line, and three or four brief syllables may be uttered in the same time as one or two lengthy ones. Accentual verse is timed verse. In the following accentual lines of Yeats's "The Cat and the Moon" we find three stresses per line, although the number of syllables varies from four to nine and the number of syllables between stresses diminishes in the last line to zero:

> Minnaloushe runs in the grass
> Lifting his delicate feet.
> Do you dance, Minnaloushe, do you dance?
> When two close kindred meet,
> What better than call a dance?
> Maybe the moon may learn,
> Tired of that courtly fashion,
> A new dance turn.

And in these accentual and alliterative lines of Auden's *The Age of Anxiety* we find four stresses, with the number of syllables varying from six to ten, and the number of syllables between stresses zero in a few instances.

> Now the news. Night raids on
> Five cities. Fires started.
> Pressure applied by pincer movement
> In threatening thrust. Third Division
> Enlarges beachhead. Lucky charm
> Saves sniper. Sabotage hinted
> In steel-mill stoppage. Strong point held
> By fanatical Nazis. Canal crossed. . . .

In our third metrical system, the accentual-syllabic, both stresses and syllables are counted, and the meter is conceived in terms of feet, or groups of stressed and unstressed syllables. In the accentual-syllabic system variations in stress position are more readily accepted than variations in the number of syllables per line.

The accentual-syllabic system is the one employed by Renaissance and neoclassic verse writers like Spenser, Shakespeare, Milton, Dryden, Pope, Swift, and Johnson. Accentual-syllabism seems especially popular during ages interested in classical rhetoric and committed to the sense of human limitation. The accentual-syllabic system makes possible the closed couplet and also the very precise kind of number control that appears in the recurrence not only of lines but of stanzas of equal or precisely varied length and in the recurring contrast of varied rhyme schemes. Thus the flourishing in the Elizabethan and Jacobean eras of sonnets, both Petrarchan and English, of various lyrical inventions such as those of Donne and Herbert, and of odes, such as Milton's "On the Morning of Christ's Nativity," the complex stanza of which is patterned $aa_6b_{10}cc_6b_{10}d_8d_{12}$:

For if such a holy Song
Enwrap our fancy long,
  Time will run back, and fetch the age of gold,
And speckl'd vanity
Will sicken soon and die,
  And leprous sin will melt from earthly mould,
And Hell it self will pass away,
And leave her dolorous mansions to the peering day.

Of the four English metrical systems, the accentual-syllabic is the most hostile to impulse, grandiosity, or hysteria: a weighty but interesting judiciousness is the tone most commonly associated with accentual-syllabism. The following lines, from Swift's "The Beasts' Confession to the Priest," exemplify not only the accentual-syllabic meter but also the kind of poetic material which seems suited to its most exacting use in the Augustan era. The stresses per line are four, the syllables eight:

Creatures of ev'ry Kind but ours
Well comprehend their nat'ral Powers;
While We, whom *Reason* ought to sway,
Mistake our Talents ev'ry Day.

The presence of syncope (the omission of presumably supernumerary syllables: *ev'ry, nat'ral*) is generally a signal that a strict accentual-syllabism is the prosodic vehicle. For this reason, if for no other, it is obvious that none but authoritative texts should be used in prosodic study.

Quantitative meter, finally, measures—as if English were Greek, Latin, or Sanskrit—durational rather than accentual feet: each foot, that is, is conceived to consist of a certain combination of "long" and "short" rather than stressed and unstressed syllables. Many learned poets, especially during the Renaissance, have attempted to structure the English line on principles of duration rather than stress. Spenser, for example, in his "*Iambicum Trimetrum*," imitates the iambic trimeter (i.e., hexameter) of the classical literatures:

> Vnhappie Verse, the witnesse of my vnhappie state,
> Make thy selfe fluttring wings of thy fast flying
> Thought, and fly forth vnto my Loue, whersoeuer she be:
> Whether lying reastlesse in heauy bedde, or else
> Sitting so cheerelesse at the cheerfull boorde, or else
> Playing alone carelesse on hir heauenlie Virginals.

But just as the syllabic poet's quest for novelty seems to solicit defeat from the sheer force of English accent, attempts to organize English lines according to quantitative feet established *a priori* risk a severe unnaturalness. As Harvey Gross has said, "English quantity is too faint an element of linguistic structure, and too unstable—so often a matter of individual pronunciation—to set up a pattern of expectation."[2] The English language is so heavily accented by nature that no other characteristic but accent seems to furnish an abiding basis for meter. Robert Bridges, inspired by the theorizing of William J. Stone, author of *On the Use of Classical Metres in English* (1898), experimented with quantitative English verse (see, for example, his "Wintry Delights"). But Bridges has testified to the strenuous difficulty of feeling in quantities rather than in stresses, and his experience implies that a meter customary in a given language has become customary precisely because it is based on the most conspicuous rhythmic characteristic of that language.

But to speak of English as a single language is somewhat misleading, for, prosodically speaking, there have been several English languages. It is thus more accurate to speak of English prosodies than of one English prosody: considered historically, the phenomena of English versification are too complex and multifold to be contained by any single system of explanation or description, even a "linguistic" one. Perhaps only a very few generalizations can hold true for all English poetry from, say, "The Battle of Maldon" in the tenth century to *Four Quartets* in the twentieth:

1. Because English is a Germanic and thus an accentual language, stress has played a more important part in the prosodic structure of English verse than it has in many other—especially Romance—prosodies.

2. When it is poetically organized, the English language appears to tend towards rising rhythms: that is, the main instinct in English prosody is for iambic or occasionally anapestic movements rather than for trochaic or dactylic.

3. Most English poetry seems to shape itself in lines of moderate length, with a tendency towards an uneven number of distinguishable metrical units (for example, five per line). A suggestion of something like a norm seems to be implied by the fact that about three-quarters of English poetry is written in blank verse. It seems characteristic of the ear trained to English usages that, presented with a series of six- or seven-foot lines, it tends to break them down into smaller units (two threes, or the fours and threes of ballad stanza). A long series of twelve-syllable lines is significantly the prosodic mode of the French drama rather than the English.

Apart from sharing in these few common characteristics, English meters of various historical ages manifest few similarities. The characteristics of English meters are best seen when they are distinguished according to the nature of the language in various periods of its history.

Old English (ca. A.D. 500–ca. 1100)

The powerful Germanic stresses of the Old English language provide a basis for a heavily accentual prosody in which the rhythm of sense (or natural word-emphasis) rather than any very abstract metrical imperative seems to support the meter. The customary line in Old English poetry consists of four strongly stressed syllables arranged, together with a varying number of unstressed ones, in two hemistichs (half-lines) of two stresses each. The stressed syllables alliterate systematically, and the alliteration emphasizes even further the force of the accent. The two half-lines composing the line are separated by an invariable medial caesura. Counterpoint or syncopation (that is, the pleasurable frustration of absolute expectation) is achieved both by varying the position of the stress within the half-line, and by frequently replacing the first stressed syllable of one of the half-lines with a "rest." Variation also appears in the alliterative pattern.

The following, from *Beowulf* (lines 8–11), exemplifies the four-stress line structure (in the first two lines) and shows two instances of replacing a stress with a rest (at different positions in the last two lines). In the second half-line of both four-stress lines, the position of the second stress varies from that in the first half-line. The "normal" half-line is seen in the first half of the first and second lines, the second half of the third, and the first of the fourth.

Wēox under wolcnum weorðmundum þāh,
oð þæt him ǣghwylc ymbsittendra
𝄽 ofer hronrāde hȳran scolde,
gomban gyldan; 𝄽 þaet wæs gōd cyning!

John C. Pope argues that in recitation each stress and each rest was signalled by a sound struck on a harp, at equal time intervals.

Some modern metrical critics and theorists (among them C. S. Lewis and Northrop Frye) have suggested that even beneath the iambic pentameter line of blank verse or the heroic couplet of Modern English we still catch a faint echo of the four-stress Old English line. And some have suggested that what we are talking about when we speak of "metrical variations" is really the modern line's apparent indecision about whether to adopt a four- or a five-stress structure—an indecision, as it were, about whether to "grow up" historically. As Joseph Malof says, "There is a significant tendency in the [iambic pentameter] line to lead a double life, to qualify for strict iambic pentameter through such devices as 'promotion' of a medial stress to the rank of a full one, and yet to assert beneath the surface the four strong beats of our native meter."[3] But there are several difficulties with such theories. They tend to neglect the fact that in the Old English line structural alliteration and strong medial caesura are as characteristic as the four stresses. Modern English poetry has had no difficulty in casting off completely these other equally marked characteristics of Old English verse. Perhaps the occasional resemblance of the later line to the Old English one is less a matter of a direct forgotten ancestry than of coincidence. For although Old English verse can be recalled and imitated (as in Auden's *Age of Anxiety*), nothing really like it can be recovered: the language has changed, and each significant linguistic change projects us into an altered prosodic world in which the meters of the past can perhaps be understood but never again commonly practiced.

Middle English (ca. 1100–ca. 1500)

After the Norman Conquest, rapid language changes (loss of inflection, multiplication of dialects, Romance accretions on what had been primarily a Germanic vocabulary) quickly complicated and diversified the former stable and unitary prosody. Although it persisted for a time in the greatly changed language of Middle English, the old four-stress accentual line, with its varying number of unstressed syllables, was gradually laid aside in favor of a line in which, for the first time in English, syllabic numeration becomes an important structural criterion. The strongly Germanic accentual quality of the language seems to weaken slightly, and instead of a prosody based on emphatic pressures at approximately equal times we find one expressive of a new consciousness of the numerical equivalence of stressed and unstressed syllables.

The linguistic complexities of the Middle Ages created a situation in which several distinctive prosodic systems were in use simultaneously. Thus we find, as if competing for pre-eminence:

1. An adaptation of the Old English four-stress accentual prosody to the requirements of an increasingly less inflected language: rhyme and assonance begin to appear, the strong medial caesura falls gradually into disuse, and syllabic numeration becomes more predictable. Thus *Sir Gawain and the Green Knight:*

> After, the sesoun of somer with the soft windes,
> When Zeferus sifles himself on sedes and erbes;
> Wela-winne is the wort that waxes theroute,
> When the donkande dewe dropes of the leves . . .

2. Accentual-syllabic rhyming verse in lines of four stresses and eight syllables (derived from French octosyllabic verse), and lines of ten syllables (from the Italian hendecasyllable), as in Chaucer's rhymed couplets written after his Italian journeys. His early *Romaunt of the Rose*, a highly successful rendering of the original French *Roman*, is written in the eight-syllable line:

> Ful gay was al the ground, and queint,
> And powdred, as men had it peint,
> With many a fressh and sondry flow'r,
> That casten up ful good savour.

A masterpiece of the ten-syllable line is the Prologue to his *Canterbury Tales*.

3. A highly accentual lyric prosody—sometimes overstressed until it resembles Hopkins' sprung rhythm—found especially in songs and other pieces set to music. An example is the anonymous fifteenth-century "I Sing of a Maiden":

> I sing of a maiden
>   That is makeless;
> King of alle kinges
>   To here sone she ches.
>
> He cam also stille,
>   Ther his moder was,
> As dew in Aprille
>   That falleth on the grass.

(By rhetorically appropriate compressions of medial and final *e*, the lines may be read as alternately of six and five syllables.)

Out of all this prosodic complication and variety, as the language moved toward greater stability, one tradition did gradually succeed in establishing pre-eminence: the accentual-syllabic. With the final relative stabilization of language and dialects long after the initial linguistic shock of the Conquest, the five-stress, decasyllabic line of Chaucer emerged. It is this line—the line that Chaucer can be said to have discovered for English poetry—that furnishes the base for Renaissance and later developments in Modern English.

Modern English (ca. 1500–)

Sixteenth and Seventeenth Centuries: Three facts are important in Renaissance prosody: (1) the language attained a state of relative stability; (2) the widespread admiration of the Greek and Latin classics invited imitation, and not merely of their themes and spirit but of their technical finish: this imitation helped to detect and expose the apparent coarseness or haphazardness of earlier English prosodies; and (3) rhetorical and metrical criticism, in the manner of the Ancients, began to be written and to be read.

The Renaissance admiration for Greek and Latin meters impelled one school of prosodists and poets to attempt to import classical quantitative usages into English practice; theorists, dilettantes, and poets like Ascham, Sidney, Spenser, and Campion labored to imitate quantitatively the classical heroic hexameter or the Greek lyric measures.

Alongside this neo-classical impulse to "refine" English verse occurred the more central and much more successful exploitation of the accentual-syllabic pentameter line as a vehicle for narrative and drama. One impulse was to urge the line toward a new regularity in stress placement; Chaucer's meter was thought rough in the later sixteenth century. Wyatt and Surrey had recovered English accentual-syllabic poetry directly from the Italian model, Surrey imposing a high degree of accentual regularity. Sackville was another regularist. A little later a more subtle instinct for expressive variation made itself felt. Gradually there was a recovery of nerve as poets of skill began to see what could be done without the line's blowing up in their hands. Marlowe and Shakespeare and even the lesser dramatists of the Elizabethan age reveal, through their instinctive comfort with a more flexible iambic pentameter line, that this is going to become, for whatever reason, the staple line of the Modern English period. (The terminology of this versification involves an in some ways unfortunate adaptation of the language of classical quantitative verse to the English accentual-syllabic.)

In lyric verse the song writers, most often obliged to fit words to pre-existing airs, produced free accentual-syllabic lines; and lyric practitioners like Donne, Crashaw, Herbert, and Marvell made various accentual-syllabic stanzaic patterns the vehicles for wit, shock, and ecstasy by a bold shifting or addition of stresses.

In the midst of all this inventiveness, we find, however, a renewed impulse toward greater prosodic regulation. As early as the first decade of the seventeenth century, in Samuel Daniel's *Defense of Rhyme* (?1603), we find a theoretical anticipation of the practice of such later seventeenth-century masters of the closed heroic couplet as Denham and Waller. In *Paradise Lost* Milton adheres to a fixed decasyllabic rule, though with Italianate syllabic compressions and accentual variations that differentiate him from the couplet writers. By the time of Dryden, English prosody reaches, in both theory and practice, an ideal of strict syllabic limitation in the line and even a relative predictability of stress positions.

Eighteenth Century: English prosody after the Restoration reveals a strong French influence. Metrical theorists and dogmatists like Edward Bysshe, Richard Bentley, and Henry Pemberton advocated a perfect regularity in the heroic line, and minor poets like Richard Glover responded by composing as far as they were able in a strictly fashioned accentual-syllabic verse without any expressive variations. The absence of variations—or any use of "substitute feet" for iambic—is what George Crabbe is pointing to (in *The Village*, 1) by the word *altérnate*:

No shepherds now, in smooth, alternate verse,
Their country's beauty or their nymphs' rehearse.

Although the major talents of the late seventeenth and early eighteenth centuries—Dryden, Prior, Gay, Swift, Pope—largely maintained the Renaissance tradition of expressive variation, even they responded to the regularist pressures of their age: they carefully observed a uniformity in the number of syllables per line (though sometimes invoking elisions or syncopes: "o'er th' unbending," "e'er," "ev'ry"), which is to say that they were careful to "substitute" duple feet only. Perhaps even more important, they tightened the grammatical structure of couplet rhetoric, the parallels, antitheses, and end-stopping, thus greatly increasing the effect of verse regularity.

Soon after 1740, however, a new reaction set in—this time against the very metrical stability that Pope and his school had labored to refine. This reaction expressed itself in the prosodic writings of Samuel Say, John Mason, and Joshua Steele, who pointed out that monotony might easily be the cost of iambic lines long continued without trisyllabic substitution, and who argued that bold shifting and omission of stress are expressive techniques which the English poet aspiring to exploit all the resources of metrical language cannot do without. Rejecting the more arbitrary syncopes (e.g., *nat'ral*) often involved in a strict accentual-syllabism, the later eighteenth-century prosodic revolutionaries (Blake, Wordsworth, Coleridge) created a line swelling or diminishing according to the dynamics of its rhetoric.

Nineteenth Century: The characteristic meter of nineteenth-century English poetry is a modification of strict accentual-syllabism. The use of trisyllabic substitution in lines otherwise composed of dissyllabic feet becomes the technical hallmark of nineteenth-century poetry. In addition, there is fairly widespread experimentation with anapestic and other trisyllabic meters, and with accentual meters. Coleridge speaks of the meter of *Christabel* (1816) as "being founded on a new principle: namely, that of counting in each line the accents, not the syllables." When, however, he speaks of the latter as varying "from seven to twelve," while the number of accents is always four, we realize that the description could fit a range of variation, from the headless traditional iambic tetrameter to the full anapestic tetrameter; and this is in fact the range we find. It is a broad range, and the effect is certainly unusual, though it may not be fully the effect of accentual verse.

In prosodic theorizing the impulse toward accentualism manifested itself in the development of musical analogies to verse and in musical methods of scansion and notation: Sidney Lanier was a pioneer in this dubious work. The cause of accentualism was strengthened also by the rise of Germanic philology to academic fashion: both prosodists and poets were now reminded that English was solidly a Germanic tongue whose metrical basis must be primarily some arrangement of strong stresses. Indeed, the transfer of British intellectual allegiance from France to Germany during the nineteenth century can be deduced in part from the British rediscovery of the charms of accentual prosody. It was in the 1870's that Hopkins experimented with his techniques of overstressing and produced some extraordinary (often extraordinarily fine) illustrations of the accentual vogue as well as of the Victorian admiration for things Germanic.

But an impatience with inherited prosodic "restraints" is probably the clearest motive underlying the metrical choices of nineteenth-century poets; and the development of "free verse" around the middle of the century can be seen both as an expression of nineteenth-century Liberalism and as an extension of the primitivist strain in Romanticism.

Despite the general atmosphere of moderate experimentation, many of the most prominent practitioners, like Tennyson and Arnold, continued to work, for the most part, in what is essentially the accentual-syllabic system bequeathed them by the sixteenth, seventeenth, and eighteenth centuries, its strict syllabic limitation only slightly, if at all, relaxed, and its disposition of stresses as conservative as ever.

Twentieth Century: Most of the prosodic experiments of the twentieth century have been associated with the United States rather than with Britain; perhaps one reason is the greater accessibility to American poets of the fructifying nineteenth-century example of Walt Whitman. During the 1920's and 1930's Ezra Pound and William Carlos Williams tightened the freely cadenced long line of Whitman and made of it a witty, informal instrument for suggesting—laconically in Pound, more volubly in Williams—the rhythms of American speech. The same poets and others experimented with various momentarily emergent patterns of accent, immediate textures of meter, in poems which were on the whole so free as to be non-metrical. See, for example, William Carlos Williams, "The Widow's Lament in Springtime" and "Spring and All." We can conjecture, incidentally, that one cause of the new American prosodic tonality in the twentieth century is the marked secession of the American from the British dialects.

But even such initially refreshing experiments as the "spatial cadences" of E. E. Cummings and the syllabism of Marianne Moore have inspired no large school of followers and exploiters. T. S. Eliot's poetic dramas have shown what can still be done with a muted accentualism, and Auden has produced accentual, accentual-syllabic, and syllabic verse with equal facility. Many of the best American and British poets exploit the possibilities both of looser forms and of a more or less stable sort of accentualism or even accentual-syllabism: Frost, the Wallace Stevens of "Sunday Morning," Graves, Richard Wilbur, Randall Jarrell, and W. D. Snodgrass have all turned from the metrical radicalism of the 1920's to something very like the system of accentual-syllabism which, for over four hundred years, has been the staple system for poetry in Modern English. Still, these writers and others, W. S. Merwin, Ted Hughes, and Charles Tomlinson, for example, exhibit so much variety of versification, both loose and strict, that we can safely say that no resurgence of classicism or triumphant return of tight control is in the offing. At least one poet, Robert Lowell, has clearly turned, not *from* metrical radicalism, but *to* it. *Lord Weary's Castle* is strikingly metrical; *Life Studies* and later volumes are more and more subtly free.

When we stand well back and survey the whole course of English poetry over almost fifteen centuries, we perceive even through the linguistic upheavals a large recurring pattern of action and reaction. Prosody veers now towards ideals of tight control and unitary domination, now towards relaxations of control—now towards the measurable norms of a public domain, now towards a recognition of the private world. Prosodic history exhibits no long-term unlimited "progressive" tendency. Freedom in meter is not a virtue identical with expressiveness. The imperative underlying the rhetoric of a Yeats poem—or of Lowell's "Skunk Hour"—is not less formal, though it is less conventional, than that underlying the rhetoric of "The Dream of the Rood" or of Chaucer's *Hous of Fame*. A degree of tolerance in the underlying imperative, allowing variations from the expected, has made metrical expressiveness possible throughout the history of English verse.

NOTES

1. This article was written in consultation with Edward Weismiller and W. K. Wimsatt. Some of the materials derive from Paul Fussell, Jr., *Poetic Meter and Poetic Form* (New York: Random House, 1965). © 1965, by Random House, Inc.; rpt. by permission.
2. *Sound and Form in Modern Poetry* (Ann Arbor: Univ. of Michigan Press, 1964), p. 33.
3. "The Native Rhythm of English Meters," *Univ. of Texas Studies in Lit. and Lang.*, 5 (1964), 586.

ENGLISH
II. BIBLIOGRAPHICAL

By RAE ANN NAGER

In compiling this list, I have given a certain preference to recent works, works that might be overlooked, and works that include extensive references. Only published works have been included; dissertations have been omitted. I have not been able to examine all 1969 titles and only some 1970 ones. I am particularly grateful to Professor Craig La Drière of Harvard for assistance and advice.

I. BIBLIOGRAPHICAL GUIDES

1. Bailey, Richard W., and Sister Dolores Marie Burton. *English Stylistics: A Bibliography*. Cambridge, Mass.: M.I.T. Press, 1965. See section on "Structures of Sound in Poetry," 137–58.

2. Goetze, Alfred, Wilhelm Horn, and Friedrich Maurer, eds. *Germanische Philologie: Ergebnisse und Aufgaben: Festschrift für Otto Behagel*. Heidelberg: Carl Winter, 1934. Kurt Wagner, "Phonetik, Rhythmik, Metrik," 3–18; Hans Kuhn, "Die altgermanische Verskunst," 19–28.

3. Lafourcade, Françoise. "Contribution à une bibliographie chronologique pour l'étude des théories sur la versification anglaise de 1550 à 1950." In *Hommage à Paul Dottin. Caliban*, No. 3, Spec. Issue, Annales publiées trimestriellement par la Faculté des Lettres et Sciences Humaines de Toulouse, N. S. II, Fasc. 1 (1966), 271–317. 772 entries in chronological order.

4. Omond, Thomas Stewart. *English Metrists. Being a Sketch of English Prosodical Criticism from Elizabethan Times to the Present Day*. Oxford: Clarendon 1921. Rev. and expanded version of a work first pub. 1903. Still the best general guide to ca. 1920.

5. Shapiro, Karl. *A Bibliography of Modern Prosody*. Baltimore: Johns

Hopkins Press, 1948. 71 annotated entries, covering the period 1892–1947; over half the items listed were published 1920–39. Fuller and more recent is the selected bibliography in Item 6.

6. ———, and Robert Beum. *A Prosody Handbook.* New York: Harper, 1965. The bibliography (pp. 203–12) is probably the most useful introd. for the student. 171 entries, beginning with Aristotle and running to 1963; more than 130 entries from the 20th century.

7. Thompson, John. "Bibliography." In *The Founding of English Metre.* New York: Columbia Univ. Press, 1966. Pp. 167–77. 224 entries; 90 directly related to English prosody or phonology, particularly in its earlier historical development.

II. THEORETICAL AND ANALYTICAL STUDIES

8. Abercrombie, Lascelles. *Principles of English Prosody. Part 1, The Elements.* London: Martin Secker, 1923. A lucid presentation of what the author (a very good critic) considered the essentials of English prosody, but far more inclusive than what today would be called a primer.

9. Barkas, Pallister. *A Critique of Modern English Prosody, (1880–1930). Studien zur englischen Philologie LXXXII.* Halle: Max Niemeyer, 1934. A critical survey of prosodic theories (Abercrombie, Alden, Bridges, Mayor, Omond, Stewart, et al.) classified as temporalist and non-temporalist, with various sub-classifications.

10. Chatman, Seymour. *A Theory of Meter.* The Hague: Mouton, 1965. An extensive survey of rhythm and meter based on modern psychological, phonological, and linguistic investigation. Ch. vi analyses 11 recorded versions of Shakespeare's Sonnet 18.

11. Erlich, Victor. "Verse-Structure: Sound and Meaning." In *Russian Formalism: History-Doctrine.* The Hague: Mouton, 1955. Pp. 182–98. A survey of the critical views of the Russian formalists. See also Item 35.

12. Fraser, G. S. *Metre, Rhyme, and Free Verse.* London: Methuen, 1970. Concise, elementary account of varieties of verse in English, with a view to practical analysis; makes some use of modern linguistics.

13. Frye, Northrop, ed. *Sound and Poetry.* (English Institute Essays.) New York: Columbia Univ. Press, 1957. Essays by Edward T. Cone, Frederick W. Sternfeld, John Hollander, Craig La Drière, Ants Oras, and Harold Whitehall, with an introd. on rhythm in poetry and music by Frye.

14. International Conference on Work-in-Progress Devoted to Problems

of Poetics, in Warsaw, 1960. *Poetics.* The Hague: Mouton, 1961. See the sections "Poetics and Linguistics," 3–70, "Versification and Sound-Texture," 75–199, and esp. the suggestive typological study contrasting varieties of English and Czech versification by Jiří Lévy, 178–88.

15. Joos, Martin. *Acoustic Phonetics.* Baltimore: Linguistic Society of America, 1948. See also Items 26 and 27.

16. Kemball, Robin. "English and Russian Versification. A General Comparison." In *Alexander Blok: A Study in Rhythm and Metre.* The Hague: Mouton, 1965. Pp. 55–156. See also Items 11 and 23.

17. Keyser, S. Jay. "The Linguistic Basis of English Prosody." In *Modern Studies in English: Readings in Transformational Grammar.* Ed. David Reibel and Sanford A. Schane. Englewood Cliffs, N.J.: Prentice-Hall, 1969. Pp. 379–94. A more general presentation by the same author of the generative principles is Item 82. For a contrasting generative view, see Item 21.

18. La Drière, Craig. "Prosody." In *Encyclopedia of Poetry and Poetics.* Ed. Alex Preminger, Frank J. Warnke, and O. B. Hardison, Jr. Princeton: Princeton Univ. Press, 1965. See also the entry "Prosodic Notation." Concise, comprehensive treatment of prosody in general, including generalizations applicable to and exemplified from the prosody of English.

19. ——— "Prosody." In *Dictionary of World Literature.* Ed. Joseph T. Shipley. New York: Philosophical Library, 1943. A briefer, earlier article than Item 18. It deals more directly with English versification.

20. Lewis, C. S. "Metre." *Review of English Literature* (Leeds), 1 (1960), 45–50. Perceptive criticism of both the teaching of prosody and the neglect of it.

21. Magnuson, Karl, and Frank G. Ryder. "The Study of English Prosody: An Alternative Proposal." *College English,* 31 (1970), 789–820. A response to Item 82; other articles generated by Item 82 are listed on p. 789, n. 2, of this article.

22. McAuley, James. *Versification: A Short Introduction.* East Lansing: Michigan State Univ. Press, 1966. (Also pub. as *A Primer of English Versification.* Sydney: Univ. Press, 1966.) In addition to giving an account of metrical patterning and its relation to the natural prosody of speech, notes "other elements contributing to variety" in English versification (Ch. v).

23. Nabokov, Vladimir. *Notes on Prosody.* (Bollingen Series 82.) New York: Pantheon, 1968. Orig. pub. as App. 2 in N's translation of Pushkin's *Eugene Onegin.*

24. Omond, Thomas Stewart. *A Study of Metre.* London: Alexander

Moring, 1920. Often suggestive account from a temporalist point of view.

25. Pace, George B. "The Two Domains: Meter and Rhythm." *PMLA*, 76 (1961), 413–19. "Specifically I shall attempt to establish the respective domains of traditional and linguistic metrics, the one as meter, the other as rhythm" (p. 413).

26. Pike, Kenneth. *Phonetics.* Ann Arbor: Univ. of Michigan Press, 1943; rpt., 1966. See also Items 15 and 27.

27. Pulgram, Ernst. *Introduction to the Spectography of Speech.* (Janua linguarum 7.) The Hague: Mouton, 1959.

28. Schramm, Wilbur Lang. *Approaches to a Science of English Verse.* Iowa City: Univ. of Iowa, 1935. Univ. of Iowa Studies, Series on the Aims and Progress of Research, No. 46. Schramm's attempt to relate a "survey of phonetic measurements to" the analysis and description of verse is analogous for 1935 to what Chatman attempts with the linguistics of his time in Item 10. For more recent spectographic analysis, see Items 15 and 27. For phonetic reinstatement of the syllable, still problematical for Schramm in 1935, see Item 26.

29. Schwartz, Elias, W. K. Wimsatt, and Monroe C. Beardsley. "Rhythm and 'Exercises in Abstraction'." *PMLA*, 77 (1962), 668–74.

30. Stewart, George R. *The Technique of English Verse.* New York: Holt, 1930. Perhaps the best of the generally temporalist accounts of English verse structure.

31. Taig, Thomas. *Rhythm and Metre.* Cardiff: Univ. of Wales Press, 1929. Many acute and original observations on historical developments of English verse and theory and analysis, and on the rhythmic relations of music and poetry; much use of musical analogy, but conceived in terms broader than current musical analysis.

32. Verrier, Paul. *Essai sur les principes de la metrique anglaise.* Paris: H. Welter, 1909. Although temporalist in orientation, V's book reflects the fullest application to English versification of developments in late 19th- and early 20th-century experimental phonetics.

33. Wimsatt, W. K. "The Rule and the Norm: Halle and Keyser on Chaucer's Meter." *College English,* 31 (1970), 774–88. See Item 82.

34. ———, and Monroe C. Beardsley. "The Concept of Meter: An Exercise in Abstraction." *PMLA,* 74 (1959), 585–98. Argues the primacy of metrical patterns as against features of individual oral performance. For further debate, see Items 25 and 29.

35. Zhirmunski, Viktor. *Introduction to Metrics: The Theory of Verse.* The Hague: Mouton, 1966. Trans. C. F. Brown. (Orig. pub. as *Vvedenie v*

Metriku. Leningrad, 1925.) For comparative studies of Russian and English metrics, see Items 16 and 23.

See also Items 57, 59, 61.

III. SPECIAL ASPECTS

Phonology. 36. Crystal, David. *Prosodic Systems and Intonation in English*. Cambridge: Univ. Press, 1969.

37. Dobson, E. J. *English Pronunciation 1500–1700*. Vol. I: *Survey of the Sources*. Vol. II: *Phonology*. Oxford: Clarendon, 1957.

38. Halle, Morris, and Noam Chomsky. *The Sound Pattern of English*. New York: Harper, 1968.

39. Kaiser, Louise, ed. *Manual of Phonetics*. Amsterdam: North-Holland Publishing Co., 1957. This standard work has been completely revised and extended by Bertil Malmberg. Amsterdam: North-Holland Publishing Co., 1968.

40. Kökeritz, Helge. *Shakespeare's Pronunciation*. New Haven: Yale Univ. Press, 1953.

41. ——— *A Guide to Chaucer's Pronunciation*. Stockholm: Almquist & Wiksell, and New Haven: Whitlock's, 1954.

42. Lieberman, Philip. *Intonation, Perception, and Language*. Cambridge, Mass.: M.I.T. Press, 1967. See esp. "Prominence, Stress, and Emphasis in American English," 144–61.

43. Trager, George L., and Henry Lee Smith, Jr. *An Outline of English Structure*. Washington, D.C.: American Council of Learned Societies, 1956.

Linguistics and Verse. 44. Epstein, Edmund L., and Terence Hawkes. *Linguistics and English Prosody*. Studies in Linguistics: Occasional Papers, No. 7, 1959.

45. Fowler, Roger. "What Is Metrical Analysis?" *Anglia,* 86 (1968), 280–320.

46. ——— " 'Prose Rhythm' and Metre." In *Essays on Style and Language*. Ed. Roger Fowler. London: Routledge & Kegan Paul, 1966. Pp. 82–99.

47. Hawkes, Terence. "Problems of Prosody." *Review of English Literature* (Leeds), 3 (April 1962), 32–49.

48. Leech, Geoffrey N. *A Linguistic Guide to English Poetry*. London: Longmans, Green, 1969. Ch. vii deals with "metre"; the treatment is essentially temporalist, but non-temporal aspects are also considered.

49. Sebeok, Thomas, ed. *Style in Language*. Cambridge, Mass.: M.I.T. Press, 1960. See esp. "Part Five: Metrics."

50. Smith, Henry Lee, Jr. "Toward Redefining English Prosody." *Studies in Linguistics,* 14 (1959), 68–76.

Verse and Music. 51. Brown, Calvin S. "Can Musical Notation Help English Scansion?" *JAAC,* 23 (1965), 329–34. Outlines some cases where musical notation can help, but is skeptical of its usefulness as the normal method of scansion.

52. Hendren, Joseph W. "Time and Stress in English Verse, with Special Reference to Lanier's Theory of Rhythm." *Rice Institute Pamphlet* XLVI, No. 2, July 1959.

53. Mussulman, Joseph A. "A Descriptive System of Musical Prosody." *Centennial Review,* 9 (1965), 332–47. Argues that traditional musical prosody has been based on false premises, but that the employment of "broader concepts of rhythm, meter, and notation" (p. 346) can serve several valid purposes, among them the accurate recording of differences among various performances of a poem.

Prose Rhythm. 54. Classe, André. *The Rhythm of English Prose.* Oxford: Blackwell, 1939. A temporalist account of the physical elements of prose rhythm.

55. Saintsbury, George. *A History of English Prose Rhythm.* London: Macmillan, 1912. Rpt. 1965, Indiana Univ. Press, Bloomington. Equally a history of prose style.

56. Tempest, Norton R. *The Rhythm of English Prose: A Manual for Students.* Cambridge: Univ. Press, 1930. Still the best introduction to the study of prose rhythm.

See also Item 73.

IV. HISTORICAL STUDIES

General History. 57. Alden, R. M. *English Verse: Specimens Illustrating Its Principles and History.* New York: Holt, 1929. A valuable collection of examples. Two thoughtful essays are basically temporalist in orientation.

58. Allen, John D. *Quantitative Studies in Prosody: II. Elements of English Blank Verse.* Johnson City: East Tennessee State Univ. Press, 1968. A statistical study of nine "elements" in the blank verse of ten poets from

Spenser and Shakespeare to Auden and Frost. The second division of the work presents tables and "conclusions" concerning specific usages (placement of caesura, metrical variation, etc.).

59. Halpern, Martin. "On the Two Chief Metrical Modes in English." *PMLA,* 77 (1962), 177–86. Sees two major divisions in English verse: (1) the iambic tradition and (2) all other English verse, which he believes to be written in some variation of strong-stress meter, whether regular in syllable count or not.

60. Lehmann, W. P. *The Development of Germanic Verse Form.* Austin: Univ. of Texas Press and the Linguistic Society of America, 1956. The treatment will be useful to students of both earlier and later forms of English prosody.

61. Malof, Joseph. "The Native Rhythm of English Meters." *Texas Studies in Language and Literature,* 5 (1964), 580–94. Views the history of English versification as the continuous reassertion of predominant native rhythms following experimentation with foreign forms. Equates native with "rhythmic"; foreign with "metrical."

62. ——— *A Manual of English Meters.* Bloomington: Indiana Univ. Press, 1970. Organizes much historical information under topical heads.

63. Saintsbury, George. *A History of English Prosody.* 3 vols. London: Macmillan, 1906–10. Still the fullest treatment of the entire history of English versification.

64. ——— *A Historical Manual of English Prosody.* London: Macmillan, 1910. Same material as Item 63, more concise form.

65. Schipper, Jakob. *Grundriss der englische Metrik.* Wien und Leipzig: W. Braumuller, 1895. *A History of English Versification.* Oxford: Clarendon, 1910. "Book I: The Line" (analyses "native" and "foreign" meters); "Book II: The Structure of Stanzas."

Old English. 66. Baum, Paull F. "The Meter of the Beowulf." *MP,* 46 (1948), 73–91, and 46 (1949), 145–62. ". . . *Beowulf* is composed of metrical units (which for the most part correspond with grammatical units), consisting of short verses of two, and sometimes three, stresses each, united by alliteration to form a so-called 'long-line' . . . the two-stress verses, or dipodies, are generally trochaic, with occasional anacrusis and with frequent use of additional light syllables" (p. 162).

67. Bliss, Alan Joseph. *The Metre of Beowulf.* Oxford: Blackwell, 1958. A re-examination and vindication of Sievers (Item 74), with a further application of his methods; Chs. xv and xvi offer brief analyses of OE verse, both

earlier (*Caedmon's Hymn, Bede's Death Song, The Leiden Riddle*) and later (*The Battle of Maldon, The Battle of Brunanburh*).

68. Creed, Robert P. "A New Approach to the Rhythm of *Beowulf*." *PMLA,* 81 (1966), 23–33. Describes six different patterns of stress within measures, a normal line consisting of four theoretically isochronous measures ("theoretically isochronous" because the time of the measures would actually vary with performance). A modification of J. C. Pope, Item 72. Folkways Records FL 9858 (1964), *Lyrics from the Old English,* is a demonstration of the thesis, read by Burton Raffel and Robert Creed.

69. Isaacs, Neil D. "Afterword on the Scansion of Old English Poetry." In *Structural Principles in Old English Poetry.* Knoxville: Univ. of Tennessee Press, 1968. Pp. 167–90. Offers "a pragmatic approach to scanning Old English poetry (not including expanded verses)" (p. 168) in the form of "ten amendments" to Creed, Item 68.

70. Le Page, R. B. "A Rhythmical Framework for the Five Types." *English and Germanic Studies,* 6 (1957), 92–103. A criticism of certain aspects of J. C. Pope's musical notation (Item 72), partially based on the results of a frequency and amplitude trace recording, showing that "equal" rhythmical units varied considerably in actual duration.

71. Malone, Kemp. "Lift Patterns in Old English Verse." *ELH,* 8 (1941), 74–80. Attempts to classify OE lines "in terms of the sequences of rhythmical high points which these lines exhibit" (p. 74).

72. Pope, John C. *The Rhythm of Beowulf.* New Haven: Yale Univ. Press, 1942. Describes the rhythmic structures as isochronous measures with, however, a varying number of syllables and varied stress-patterns. Catalogues 107 varieties of Sievers' Type A verse, 58 of Type B, 39 of Type C, 58 of Type D, 17 of Type E.

73. ——— "Aelfric's Rhythmical Prose." In *Homilies of Aelfric: A Supplementary Collection.* (EETS 259.) New York: Oxford Univ. Press, 1967. Pp. 105–36.

74. Sievers, Eduard. *Altgermanische Metrik.* Halle: Max Niemeyer, 1893. Classification of OE verses into "types" (determined by position of stresses). A model for most subsequent studies.

75. Slay, D. "Some Aspects of the Technique of Composition of Old English Verse." *Transactions of the Philological Society* (London), 1952, pp. 1–14. Catalogues the priorities of stress in OE words: nouns and adjectives, finite verbs and adverbs, pronouns and function words.

76. Stevick, Robert D. "The Meter of *The Dream of the Rood.*" *Neuphilologische Mitteilungen,* 68 (1967), 149–68. "The best guide to reconstructing

the meter is the syntax in conjunction with alliteration. The meter itself consists of the regularized interval of incidence of stressed syllables in an ultimately duple rhythm" (p. 166).

77. Taglicht, Josef. "*Beowulf* and Old English Verse Rhythm." *Review of English Studies,* 12 (1961), 341–51. Discusses the effects of preconception upon the treatment of OE verse by Sievers, Heusler, Pope, Bliss, et al.; ends with "a new rhythmical interpretation," which the author says will accommodate comfortably at least 95% of the verses in *Beowulf* (p. 351).

Middle English. 78. Baum, Paull F. *Chaucer's Verse.* Durham, N. C.: Duke Univ. Press, 1961. Argues "Chaucer's line is a series of five iambs" (p. 10), and that "modern English versification starts with Chaucer" (p. 11).

79. Borroff, Marie. *Sir Gawain and the Green Knight: A Stylistic and Metrical Study.* New Haven: Yale Univ. Press, 1962. An extensive treatment of the meter of *Gawain* includes a survey of theories held about the alliterative tradition and their application to the text. See also "Bibliography: Language and Meter," 279–80.

80. Christopherson, Paul. "The Scansion of Two Lines in Chaucer." *English Studies,* 45 (1964), Suppl., 146–50. Demonstrates the metrical regularity of "two apparently awkward lines in Chaucer" to support his contention that the iambic-decasyllabic theory should not be abandoned until the contemporary pronunciation has been reconstructed by the best means available.

81. Donaldson, E. Talbot. "Chaucer's Final *-e.*" *PMLA,* 63 (1948), 1101–24.

82. Halle, Morris, and Samuel Jay Keyser. "Chaucer and the Study of Prosody." *College English,* 28 (1966), 187–219. Proposes a theory of Chaucerian prosody formalized as a branching rule with substitution transformations, following the methods of contemporary linguistics.

83. Lewis, C. S. "The Fifteenth-Century Heroic Line." *Essays and Studies by Members of the English Association,* 24 (1938), 28–41. The 15th-century heroic line consists of hemistichs, each containing either two or three ictuses, with an indefinite number of stressed syllables.

84. Malone, Kemp. "Chaucer's 'Book of the Duchess,' A Metrical Study." In *Chaucer und seine Zeit: Symposion für Walter F. Schirmer.* Ed. Arno Esch. (Buchreihe der *Anglia,* Zeitschrift für englische Philologie, 14.) Tübingen: Max Niemeyer, 1968. Pp. 71–96. Analysis of *BD* according to Germanic

verse patterns; includes catalogue of all lines by Sievers' types "with certain additional symbols affixed" (p. 81).

85. Manzalaoui, Mahmoud. "Lydgate and English Prosody." *Cairo Studies in English* (1960), pp. 87–104. "A generalized theory of prosody" (p. 87) with Lydgate's versification used as a focal point.

86. Mustanoja, Tauno F. "Chaucer's Prosody." In *Companion to Chaucer Studies*. Ed. Beryl Rowland. Toronto: Oxford Univ. Press, 1968. Pp. 58–84. Surveys the scholarship; 115-item Bibliography.

87. Oakden, James Parker. *Alliterative Poetry in Middle English.* 2 vols. Manchester: Univ. Press, 1930, 1935. See "The Metrical Survey," I, 131–241.

88. Ramsay, Robert Lee. "Versification." Introd. to R's ed. of John Skelton, *Magnyfycence,* EETS (E.S. 98, 1908), pp. li-lxxi. Summarizes and develops earlier views (Schipper, Luick) in a careful account of Skelton's dramatic practice.

89. Skeat, Walter W. "Versification." In *The Complete Works of Geoffrey Chaucer*. Oxford: Clarendon, 1894. VI (General Introd., Secs. 98–117), lxxxii–xcvii. Summary of Chaucer's practice, with observations on English versification generally, applying a theory of metrical structure based on breath-groups or "monopressures." See also Item 4, p. 315, and Item 24, pp. 25–29. This theory is further elaborated by Skeat in *Transactions of the Philological Society* (1895–98), pp. 484–503.

90. Southworth, James G. *Verses of Cadence.* Oxford: Blackwell, 1954. Contends that Chaucer's verse is a modification of the native English rhythmic tradition.

91. ——— *The Prosody of Chaucer and His Followers: Supplementary Chapters to Verses of Cadence.* Oxford: Blackwell, 1962. Organizes supporting evidence, with great stress on the punctuation of MSS, for the thesis presented in Item 90.

Renaissance. 92. Burke, Brother Fidelian. *Metrical Roughness in Marston's Formal Satire.* Washington, D. C.: Catholic Univ. of America Press, 1957.

93. Hendrickson, G. L. "Elizabethan Quantitative Hexameters." *PQ*, 28 (1949), 237–60. Concludes, from examining English verses constructed according to Latin patterns, that the poets were more successful than critics have allowed. Probably the most useful single treatment of English experimentation with classical meters.

94. Ing, Catherine. *Elizabethan Lyrics: A Study in the Development of English Meters and Their Relation to Poetic Effect.* London: Chatto & Windus, 1951.

Ch. ii, "Renaissance Theories of Metre," and Ch. iii, which contains a glossary of Elizabethan prosodic terms, are of particular interest.

95. Oras, Ants. *Pause Patterns in Elizabethan and Jacobean Drama: An Experiment in Prosody.* (Univ. of Florida Monographs in the Humanities, 3.) Gainesville: Univ. of Florida Press, 1960. Statistically based, with graphs; includes all major Renaissance dramatists, useful for tracing the positional shift of the caesura.

96. Ringler, William. "Master Drant's Rules." *PQ*, 19 (1950), 70–74. On Sidney and quantitative verse.

97. Sipe, Dorothy L. *Shakespeare's Metrics.* New Haven: Yale Univ. Press, 1968. A study of Shakespeare's choice among available lexical variants as indicative of his concern for metrical regularity. Treats the syllabic structure of the word-unit as a determinant of the meter of the line.

98. Stein, Arnold. "George Herbert's Prosody." *Language and Style,* 1 (1968), 1–38.

See also Item 7.

Milton. 99. Bridges, Robert. *Milton's Prosody with a Chapter on Accentual Verse.* Oxford: Clarendon, 1921. Rpt. 1965. Rev. and enlarged version of a work that first appeared in 1893. Greatly influenced modern prosodic study.

100. Evans, Robert O. *Milton's Elisions.* (Univ. of Florida Monographs in the Humanities, 21.) Gainesville: Univ. of Florida Press, 1966.

101. Kellog, George A. "Bridges' *Milton's Prosody* and Renaissance Metrical Theory." *PMLA,* 68 (1953), 268–85. Relates antecedent Italian theory to Milton's practice and Bridges' observations.

102. Oras, Ants. *Blank Verse and Chronology in Milton.* (Univ. of Florida Monographs in the Humanities, 20.) Gainesville: Univ. of Florida Press, 1966.

103. Prince, F. T. *The Italian Element in Milton's Verse.* Oxford: Clarendon, 1954. Milton's indebtedness to Della Casa and Tasso and the structure of Miltonic verse.

104. Shawcross, John T. "The Prosody of Milton's Translation of Horace's Fifth Ode." *Tennessee Studies in Literature,* 13 (1968), 81–89. Argues that Milton's translation is in "quantitative" verse, and that "quantitative" verse may also occur in the choruses of *Samson Agonistes.*

105. Sprott, S. Ernest. *Milton's Art of Prosody.* Oxford: Blackwell, 1953.

106. Weismiller, Edward. "The 'Dry' and 'Rugged' Verse." In *The Lyric and Dramatic Milton.* Ed. Joseph H. Summers. (Selected Papers from the

English Institute.) New York: Columbia Univ. Press, 1965. Pp. 115–52. Shows the relationship between certain difficult rhythms in 17th-century English poetry and their source in Italian syllabic verse; relates the choral odes of *Samson Agonistes* formally to Cowley's *Pindarique Odes* (1656); and sees the odes of *Samson* as perhaps written in "that ultimate form of seventeenth-century English irregular verse, the blank or near-blank Italianate Pindaric" (p. 150). The study of which this essay is a part, Weismiller's *The Prosody of Milton's English Poems,* will be published as the final volume of *A Variorum Commentary on the Poems of John Milton* (editor-in-chief, Merritt Y. Hughes; Columbia Univ. Press and Routledge, Kegan Paul; in preparation).

Eighteenth Century. 107. Adler, Jacob H. "Pope and the Rules of Prosody." *PMLA,* 76 (1961), 218–26. Examines "the rules laid down in Pope's letter on prosody and the critical statements upon prosody to be found elsewhere in his works." Compares "Pope's views with the general critical opinion of the century concerning prosody" and "with Pope's practice throughout his career" (p. 218).

108. ——— *The Reach of Art: A Study in the Prosody of Pope.* Gainesville: Univ. of Florida Press, 1964. A study of Pope's general metrical and rhetorical technique and its variation throughout his career.

109. Audra, Emile. "Libre v: L'Art de Pope, Chapitre III: La Versification." In *L'Influence française dans l'œuvre de Pope.* Paris: Librairie Ancienne Honoré Champion, 1931. Pp. 581–610. First to notice that the French treatise of Lancelot was direct source of rules presented by Bysshe (pp. 589–93), a fact later independently discovered and noted by Culler, Item 112.

110. Bysshe, Edward. *The Art of English Poetry 1702.* English Linguistics 1500–1800: A Collection of Facsimile Reprints, No. 75. Sel. and ed. R. C. Alston. Menton, Eng.: Scolar Press, 1968.

111. ——— *The Art of English Poetry 1708.* Introd. A. Dwight Culler. Augustan Reprint Society, Pub. No. 40, 1953. Rpt. Part I, "Rules for Making Verses." Introd. material is largely from Item 112.

112. Culler, A. Dwight. "Edward Bysshe and the Poet's Handbook." *PMLA,* 63 (1948), 858–85. Discusses the background and enormous influence of Bysshe's work.

113. Fussell, Paul, Jr. *Theory of Prosody in Eighteenth-Century England.* New London: Connecticut Coll., 1954.

114. Piper, William Bowman. *The Heroic Couplet.* Cleveland: Case Western Reserve Univ., 1969.

Since 1800. 115. Barry, Sister M. Martin. *An Analysis of the Prosodic Structure of Selected Poems of T. S. Eliot.* Washington, D. C.: Catholic Univ. of America Press, 1948. Rev. ed., 1969.

116. Baum, Paull F. "Sprung Rhythm." *PMLA,* 74 (1959), 418–25. Discusses Hopkins' statements about sprung rhythm and illustrates the difficulties of applying them to the scansion of some of Hopkins' shorter poems.

117. Berg, Sister M. Gretchen. *The Prosodic Structure of Robert Bridges' "Neo-Miltonic" Syllabics.* Washington, D. C.: Catholic Univ. of America Press, 1962. Bridges' theories and his "syllabic" practice.

118. Beum, Robert. *The Poetic Art of William Butler Yeats.* New York: Frederick Ungar, 1969.

119. ——— "Syllabic Verse in English." *Prairie Schooner,* 31 (1957), 259–75. Surveys the practitioners and conditions of syllabic verse-writing in English.

120. Fuller, Roy. "An Artifice of Versification." *Wascana Review,* 4 (1969), 5–20. On syllabic verse, chiefly that of Marianne Moore.

121. Holloway, Sister Marcella Marie. *The Prosodic Theory of Gerard Manley Hopkins.* Washington, D. C.: Catholic Univ. of America Press, 1947.

122. Jankowsky, Kurt R. *Die Versauffassung bei Gerard Manley Hopkins, den Imagisten und T. S. Eliot: Renaissance altgermanischen Formgestaltens in der Dichtung des 20. Jahrhunderts.* München: Max Hueber, 1967.

123. Lightfoot, Marjorie J. "*Purgatory* and *The Family Reunion:* In Pursuit of Prosodic Description." *Modern Drama,* 7 (1964), 256–66. Yeats stays closer to the iambic norm in his four-stress lines, while Eliot often moves toward free verse.

124. Patmore, Coventry. *Coventry Patmore's "Essay on English Metrical Law": A Critical Edition with a Commentary.* Ed. Sister M. Augustine Roth. Washington, D. C.: Catholic Univ. of America Press, 1961. Patmore incorporates ideas from antecedent, esp. temporalist, theory and anticipates a great deal of subsequent temporalism.

125. Pick, John, ed. *A Hopkins Reader.* New York and London: Oxford Univ. Press, 1953. See "Poetic Theory," 69–124, and "Practical Criticism," 127–69.

126. Schneider, Elisabeth W. "Sprung Rhythm: A Chapter in the Evolution of Nineteenth-Century Verse." *PMLA,* 80 (1965), 237–53. Chiefly on the historical context of Hopkins' metrical experiment "The Wreck of the Deutschland."

ENGLISH
III. THE IAMBIC PENTAMETER

By MORRIS HALLE and SAMUEL JAY KEYSER

> What, then, exactly is Prosody? Our English word is not carried over from the Greek word with its uncertain and various meanings, but it must have come with the French word through the scholastic Latin; and like the French term it primarily denotes the rules for the treatment of syllables in verse, whether they are to be considered as long or short, accented or unaccented, elideable or not, etc., etc. The syllables, which are the units of rhythmic speech, are by nature of so indefinite a quality and capable of such different vocal expression, that apart from the desire which every artist must feel to have his work consistent in itself, his appeal to an audience would convince him that there is no chance of his elaborate rhythms being rightly interpreted unless his treatment of syllables is understood. Rules must, therefore, arise and be agreed upon for the treatment of syllables, and this is the first indispensable office of Prosody.
>
> Robert Bridges "A Letter to a Musician on English Prosody"

When a poet composes metrical verse, he imposes certain constraints upon his choice of words and phrases that ordinary language does not normally obey.[1] The poet and his readers may not be able to formulate explicitly the nature of the constraints that are operative in a given poem; there is little doubt, however, that neither the poet nor the experienced reader would find great difficulty in telling apart wildly unmetrical lines from lines that are straightforwardly metrical. Thus few people familiar with the canon of metrical English verse from Chaucer to Yeats would disagree with the proposition that (1*b*) and (1*c*) are lawful embodiments of the iambic pentameter, whereas (1*a*) is not, even though (1*a*) has the same number of syllables as (1*b*), but (1*c*) does not.

(1) (*a*) Ode to the West Wind by Percy Bysshe Shelley
(*b*) O Wild West Wind, thou breath of Autumn's being
(*c*) The curfew tolls the knell of parting day

In addition, readers of verse possess the ability to categorize metrical lines as more or less complex. Thus, most readers would no doubt judge (1*b*) as a more complex iambic pentameter line than (1*c*).

We shall look upon these readily observable abilities of experienced poetry readers as crucial facts that must be accounted for by an adequate theory of prosody. A good theory, however, would be expected to do more than that; it would also help us to understand the nature of metrical verse and illuminate the relationship between a speaker's everyday linguistic competence and his ability to judge verses as metrical or unmetrical, as complex or simple. We restrict this study to the favorite meter of English poets, the iambic pentameter. The approach used here can readily be extended to other meters; see, for example, Halle "On Meter and Prosody" and Halle and Keyser, *English Stress*.

We propose that the ability of readers and poets to judge verse lines as metrical or unmetrical, and as more or less complex, is due to their knowledge of certain principles of verse construction. This knowledge—much like the average speaker's knowledge of his language—is tacit rather than explicit. People when questioned may be unable to give a coherent account of the principles that they employ in making the above judgments of verse lines. It is, therefore, the task of the metrist to provide a coherent and explicit account of this knowledge, just as it is the task of the grammarian to make explicit what it is that the fluent speaker of a language knows about it.

We shall assume that this knowledge consists of two distinct parts: one concerns the abstract pattern underlying the meter; the other, the rules that relate the abstract pattern to concrete lines of verse. We regard this assumption as a working hypothesis to be justified by showing that insightful and important results can be obtained with its help.

The sequences of abstract entities that underlie the meter are symbol strings such as those in (2):

(2) (*a*) XXXXXXXXXXXX
(*b*) WSWSWSWSWS(W(W)) where parenthesized entities are optional.

These abstract patterns are related to concrete lines of verse by correspondence rules such as those illustrated in (3):

(3) (*a*) Each abstract entity (X, W, S) corresponds to a single syllable.[2]
(*b*) Stressed syllables occur in S positions only and in all S positions.[3]

We scan particular lines by establishing a correspondence between the syllables of the line and the abstract entities in the abstract pattern such as those in (2). Lines are judged metrical if such a correspondence can be established exhaustively without violating the applicable correspondence rules. In (4) we illustrate the scanning of a line from Robert Bridges' "Testament of Beauty," a poem written in the pure syllable-counting meter defined by the abstract pattern (2*a*) and the correspondence rule (3*a*):

```
(4) Long had the homing bees plundered the thymy flanks
     |    |   | | |   |    | |     | | | |
     X    X   X X X   X    X X     X X X X
```

In (5) we illustrate the scanning of an iambic pentameter line which is defined by the pattern (2*b*) and the correspondence rules (3*a*) and (3*b*). It should be noted that (3*a*) and (3*b*) together imply that an unstressed syllable must occur in each W position. We shall see below that the somewhat indirect formulation adopted here is actually required in order to characterize the full variety of stress patterns that may lawfully actualize the iambic pentameter pattern.

```
         /      /         /      /      /
(5) The curfew tolls the knell of parting day
     | | |  |    |    | |  | |    |
     W S W  S    W    S W  S W    S
```

The characterization of the iambic pentameter that has been given here with the help of the pattern (2*b*) and the correspondence rules (3*a*) and (3*b*) is essentially a more formal statement of the description to be found in many of the standard treatises. Thus in Robert Bridges' important *Milton's Prosody* we are told that the normal iambic pentameter line can be defined as

(6) a decasyllabic line on a disyllabic basis and in rising rhythm (i.e. with accents or stresses on the alternate even syllables); and the disyllabic units may be called *feet*. (p. 1)

We discuss the question of feet below (p. 222). At this point we wish only to note that the normal iambic line defined by (6)—or equivalently by (2*b*), (3*a*), and (3*b*)—does not characterize (1*b*) or any of a huge number of lines that appear commonly in iambic pentameter verses, e.g.,

(7) As ook, firre, birch, aspe, alder, holm, popler,
Wylugh, elm, plane, assh, box, chasteyn, lynde, laurer,
Mapul, thorn, bech, hasel, ew, whippeltree—
(Chaucer, Knight's Tale, ll. 2921–23)

(8) Batter my heart, three-person'd God, for you
As yet but knock, breathe, shine, and seek to mend;
That I may rise, and stand, o'erthrow me, and bend
Your force to break, blow, burn, and make me new.
(Donne, "Holy Sonnet 14")

(9) O Wild West Wind, thou breath of Autumn's being
Thou from whose unseen presence the leaves dead
Are driven like ghosts from an enchanter fleeing, . . .
(Shelley, "Ode to the West Wind")

(10) Speech after long silence; it is right,
All other lovers being estranged or dead, . . .
(Yeats, "After Long Silence")

The existence of such lines has not escaped the attention of Bridges or of any other serious student of prosody. In fact, immediately below the definition (6) Bridges notes that in Milton one may find three types of exception to the norm:

I Exceptions to the number of syllables being ten,
II Exceptions to the number of stresses being five,
III Exceptions in the position of the stresses.

In other words, each of the three properties of the line that are specifically regulated in the definition (6) is violated on some occasion in the iambic pentameter of Milton's *Paradise Lost*.

To account for these exceptions Bridges and many other metrists supplement the definition of the norm with a list of allowable deviations, which commonly includes the items below:

(11) 1. unstressed foot (pyrrhic)
2. heavy foot (spondee)
3. initial foot inverted (trochee)
4. verse-medial foot inverted (trochee)
5. extra slack syllable inserted verse-medially
6. dropping of verse-initial slack syllable (headless)

We shall refer to the account based on the norm (6) and the allowable deviations (11) as the standard theory of the iambic pentameter. We examine next the lines in (7)–(10) in order to illustrate the functioning of the standard theory.

The lines from Chaucer (7) are metrical by a liberal invocation of allowable deviation (11.2), for heavy feet abound in (7). Moreover, there is an initial trochee (11.3) in the last two lines, and an extra slack syllable (11.5) in the second line.

The first line of Donne's Sonnet (8) has an initial trochee (11.3) as well as a verse medial heavy foot (11.2) in the phrase *three-person'd God.* The second line contains a spondee (11.2), as does the fourth line; whereas the third line has an initial pyrrhic foot (11.1) and an extra slack syllable (11.5) *me and.*

The first line of Shelley's poem (9) exhibits two spondees (11.2). The second line contains an initial trochee (11.3) and the pyrrhic foot (11.1) *-ence the,* and a verse final spondee (11.2). The third line has an extra slack syllable *en* in *driven* (11.5) and a pyrrhic (11.1).

In the Yeats verses (10) the first line is headless (11.6) and contains one verse medial spondee (11.2) and a pyrrhic foot (11.1). The second line begins with a spondee (11.2) and includes an extra slack syllable in *being* (11.5).[4]

Although the standard theory consisting of the abstract pattern (2*b*), the correspondence rules (3), and the list of allowable deviations (11) correctly establishes the lines in (7)–(10) as metrical, it has a number of inadequacies that suggest rather fundamental revisions. Consider first the line (1*a*) which we have been using as our prime example of an unmetrical line:

```
/                 /        /      /       /
Ode to the West Wind by Percy Bysshe Shelley.
```

The line contains an inverted first foot (11.3), a heavy foot (11.2), and two verse-medial trochaic substitutions (11.4). Since all these are admissible deviations, the line must be judged metrical by the standard theory. But this surely is an unacceptable consequence.

The difficulty arises from the fact that the standard theory expresses allowable deviations in terms of feet. (In fact, it is only in this domain that the entity *foot* plays a significant role.) Implicit in this view is the notion that deviations in one foot are independent of deviations in adjoining feet. Deviations in one foot, however, are not independent of deviations in adjoining feet. Thus the line just scanned was unmetrical because it had two consecutive trochaic feet, and such lines are ruled out in iambic meters. It is, of course, possible to modify (11.4) so as to take account of this possibility. But if adjoining feet are not independent, there is a serious question as to the sense of setting up feet as entities intermediate between the line and the weak and strong positions that constitute the line. We shall propose below an account that does not make use of the concept *foot*, and we shall attempt to show that such an account is superior to the standard theory even where the latter is patched up to handle cases like the one just discussed.

We have already noted that an important shortcoming of the standard theory is that it deals with allowable deviations by means of a list, thus implying that there is nothing in common among the allowable deviations, for in the standard theory there are no qualifications for membership in this list. By characterizing the allowable deviations with the help of a list, the standard theory renders itself incapable of explaining certain facts about English verse which an adequate theory would be expected to explain. It was noted many years ago by Jespersen (p. 262) that whereas an iambic line could tolerate a trochee in the first two syllables,[5] a trochaic line could not tolerate an analogous iambic substitution in the first two syllables. He cites the following lines from Longfellow:

(12) Tell me not in mournful numbers
Life is but an empty dream

and observes that the second line may not be replaced by:

(13) A life's but an empty dream

There is no explanation for this phenomenon in the standard theory.

There is a further systematic correlation which is suggested by Jespersen's observation. If iambic verse permits the dropping of an initial slack syllable (see the first line of (10)), trochaic verse admits of an extrametrical slack syllable at the beginning of a line. The following trochaic couplet is illustrative:

(14) All the buds and bells of May
From dewy sward or thorny spray

(Keats, "Fancy")

Indeed, if one did not know that "Fancy" was written in trochaic meter the above couplet would be metrically ambiguous since it can easily have occurred in an iambic tetrameter poem. This second correlation between iambic and trochaic verse also remains unexplained in the standard theory.

Thirdly, Jespersen (p. 255) notes that major syntactic breaks—what he refers to as pauses—appear to play an important role in the metrical behavior of a line. This break is commonly indicated orthographically by a comma, semi-colon, colon, or period. It is noteworthy that two of the categories on the allowable deviation list are commonly associated with major syntactic breaks. These two are internal trochaic substitution, which often occurs after a major syntactic break (see 28*c–d*), and the heavy foot, which is composed of two positions separated by a major syntactic break (see (7)). Once again a deeper generalization is hinted at here which the standard theory does not capture.

To meet the objections just sketched we propose to replace the standard theory by the account below:

(15) (*a*) *Abstract metrical pattern* (cf. (2*b*))
*(W)SWSWSWSWS(x)(x)
where each x position may only be occupied by an unstressed syllable and where elements enclosed in parentheses may be omitted.

(*b*) *Correspondence rules* (cf. (3))
(i) A position (S or W) corresponds to either a single syllable, or
a sonorant sequence incorporating at most two vowels (immediately adjoining to one another, or separated by a sonorant consonant).

Definition: When a stressed syllable is located between two unstressed syllables in the same syntactic constituent within a line of verse, this syllable is called a *stress maximum*.

(ii) stressed syllables occur in S positions and in all S positions;
or
stressed syllables occur only in S positions, but not necessarily in all S positions;
or
stress maxima occur only in S positions, but not necessarily in all S positions.[6]

The order of alternatives of the correspondence rules is significant. Each earlier alternative is subsumed by each later alternative and the later alternatives can be viewed as enlarging the class of lines which are deemed metrical. For example, in (15*b*i) the first alternative allows only ten- to twelve-syllable lines to realize the abstract metric pattern whereas the second alternative increases to twenty the number of syllables in lines which realize the abstract metrical pattern. At first sight the correspondence rules given here with their several alternatives may appear to differ but little from the list of allowable deviations incorporated in the standard theory. This, however, disregards the very important fact that while in the standard theory there is no limitation as to what is to be included in the lists, the alternative statements of the revised theory are subject to the limitation that later statements must subsume—and hence be generalizations of—earlier statements. In addition, we propose that the order of statements in the correspondence rules reflects the complexity of a line. The order is, therefore, our formal device for capturing the important concept of tension. The intuitive basis for this is reasonably straightforward. If the means whereby a given abstract pattern is actualized are narrowly restricted, the pattern is readily perceived as being present in the data. On the other hand, when the means whereby a pattern is actualized are allowed to be of a great variety, it becomes correspondingly difficult to discern that the pattern is encoded in a given sequence of words. Thus no one can miss the iambic pentameter pattern in

/ / / / /
The curfew tolls the knell of parting day

whereas, it takes considerable sophistication to see that the same pattern is present in Donne's line

/ / / /
Yet dearly I love you and would be lovèd fain

This increased difficulty in perception of the pattern which results from utilizing more complex correspondence rules explains also why there are no lines in which all and only the most complex correspondence rules are utilized. Such lines exceed the threshold of the reader's ability to perceive the pattern. We return to questions of this type in the last part of the paper.

To begin our discussion of the revised theory let us simply see how the theory permits a line to be scanned. The procedure is as follows: in each line we first establish position occupancy by numbering the different syllables in the line from left to right.[7] If the number is ten, a one-to-one occupancy of positions by syllables is assumed, in accordance with the first alternative of (15*b*i). If the number is one less than ten, a check is made to determine if a one-to-one syllable-to-position assignment can be made by assuming a headless line. If the number of syllables is more than ten, a check is made to determine whether the line contains any extra-metrical syllables, or whether two adjacent syllables may be assigned to a single position in accordance with the second alternative of (15*b*i). (See also below p. 227).

Having established the syllable-to-position assignments, we next locate stressed and unstressed syllables in the line. We then check to see if the location of stressed and unstressed syllables satisfies one of the three alternatives of (15*b*ii). We begin by checking the first alternative and underlining all positions in which this alternative is not satisfied; i.e., we underline each position where an S is occupied by an unstressed syllable or a W by a stressed syllable. Next we examine the line by means of the second alternative of (15*b*ii) and underline all positions where it is violated; i.e., a W occupied by a stressed syllable now receives a double underline. Finally, we check out the third alternative; if any position violates this alternative—i.e., if any W is occupied by a stress maximum—the line is judged unmetrical. Below we illustrate the procedure just outlined:

(16) The cúrfew tólls the knéll of párting dáy

W S W S W S W S W S

This line satisfies in its entirety the first alternative of both (15*b*i) and (15*b*ii).

(17) And léaves the wórld to dárkness and to mé

W S W S W S W S W S

In line (17) the fourth S violates the first but not the second alternative of (15*b*ii).

```
       /            /         /    /           /          /
(18) Batter my heart, three-person'd God, for you
      | |    |  |         |    |  |     |   |   |
      W S    W  S         W    S  W     S   W   S
```

In (18) the first S violates the first alternative of (15*b*ii) but not the second, and the first and third W violate the second alternative, but are allowed by the third alternative. An example of cases where all three alternatives are violated is provided by the triply underlined and barred position in the unmetrical line (19*a*).

```
        /                 /      /          /      /
(19a) Ode to the West Wind by Percy Bysshe Shelley[8]
       |    |   |   |    |    |  |  |  |         | |
       W    S   W   S    W    S  W  S  W         S W
```

The revised theory provides a great deal of freedom within the iambic pattern while at the same time providing sufficient constraints to make the art form an interesting one for the poet to work in. It is for this reason that when one finds a poet moving outside of the constraints of the meter, one is tempted to search for some aesthetic reason for his doing so. Consider, in this regard, the following opening line from a sonnet by Keats:

```
        /              /      /        /        /
(19b) How many bards gild the lapses of time
       |    | | |      |     | | | | |
       W    S W S      W     S W S W S
```

This line is unmetrical since it contains a stress maximum in the fourth W position in violation of the last alternative of (15*b*ii). However, it seems quite clear that the poet is purposely moving outside of the meter in order to caricature metrically the sense of the line. The line is literally what it speaks of figuratively, a "lapse of time." This metrical joke requires that the line be treated as unmetrical.

Returning to metrical lines, we note Donne's line (20) as an instance where later alternatives of both (15*b*i) and (15*b*ii) apply;

(20) Yet dearly I love you and would be lovèd fain

W S W S W S W S W S

The second and third W in (20) violate the first alternative of (15*b*i) but not the second, while the third S violates the first but not the second alternative of (15*b*ii). Note that the assignment of two syllables to a single position has to be done in the way shown. If different syllables were to be assigned to a single position the line would be unmetrical because stress maxima would occupy W positions.

The assignment of syllables to positions is, of course, a strictly metrical assignment. It does not imply that the syllables assigned to a single position should be slurred or elided when the verse is recited. The correspondence rules are not instructions for poetry recitations. They are rather abstract principles of verse construction whose effect on the sound of the recital verse is much more indirect.

It is obvious that the second alternative of (15*b*i) subsumes the first alternative as a special case. Poets appear to differ a great deal as to the precise extension of the second alternative. For example, Chaucer not only makes use of elision, but allows for monosyllabic words to be assigned to a single position along with an adjacent syllable under certain special conditions.[9] Other poets seem to modify elision as defined in (15*b*i) by allowing it to operate on two vowels separated by an optional fricative consonant (s, f, v, etc.) as well as across an optional sonorant.[10] Still other poets allow for an extra-metrical syllable internally before a major syntactic break. Examples of the latter are:

(21) And as I past I worshipt: if those you seek

(Milton, *Comus,* l. 302)

From mine own knowledge. As nearly as I may

(Shakespeare, *Ant.* II.ii.91)

and Shelley as well (see (25) below).

Whatever the usages may be from one poet to another, they can readily be accounted for by suitable extensions of the correspondence rules, and, as they appear to have only limited general theoretical interest, we shall not attempt to deal further with these rules here.

We recall that in rejecting the standard theory we stressed the fact that the list of allowable deviations (11) was not otherwise restricted, and that there was no mechanism for excluding from this list such obviously absurd items as (21):

(21) 1. Insertion of a parenthetic phrase in a line
2. Trochaic foot followed by a dactyl
3. Elision of exactly three syllables verse finally.

We must now show that the allowed deviations of the standard theory (11) are in fact subsumed by the various alternatives of the revised theory advanced here, and that it excludes the absurdities collected in (21).

That the revised theory excludes (21) is really unnecessary to demonstrate in detail since there is no way in which even the last (i.e., most general) alternatives of (15*b*i) and (15*b*ii) can be stretched so as to include (21). It is equally self-evident that (11.5) which allows an extra slack syllable in the line and (11.6) which admits headless lines are included by the revised theory. The latter is specifically allowed by (15*a*), where the first W is marked as optional and parenthesized. It ought to be noted here that the omission of the line-initial W contributes to the complexity of the line, whereas the omission of the line-final, extra-metrical syllable leaves the complexity of the line unaffected. We have reflected this difference between the two parenthesized sub-sequences by supplying an asterisk to the first parentheses in (15*a*). We have, however, at this point no explanation for this difference. Examples of headless lines in iambic pentameter are given in (23):

/ / / / /
(23) (*a*)—Twenty bookes clad in blak or reed—
| | | | | | | | | | |
*(W) S W S W S W S W S

(Chaucer, *CT* Prol., l. 294)

/ / / /
(*b*)—Speech after long silence; it is right
| | | | | | | | | |
*(W) S W S W S W S W S

(Yeats)

Extra slack syllables in the line (11.5) are allowed by the later alternatives of (15*b*i), as we have already seen in our discussion of (20) above. The third line of (8), repeated here as (24), is an additional example:

```
                  /           /            /           /
(24) That I may rise and stand, o'erthrow me and bend
      |  |  |   |   |       |     |    |     V     |
      W  S  W   S   W       S     W    S     W     S
```

Turning now to the remaining allowable deviations, we recall that the unstressed foot (11.1), has already been illustrated in (17) above. The third line of (9), repeated here as (25), offers an additional example:

```
            /           /              /     /
(25) Are driven, like ghosts from an enchanter fleeing
      |    |      |      |     |  | |  | |  | |
      W    S      W      S     W  S W  S W  S W
```

Here the third S contains an unstressed syllable, a realization allowed by the second alternative of (15*b*ii). (For the assignment of *driven* to a single position, see above p. 227.)

The next allowable deviation (11.2), the heavy foot (spondee), requires invocation of the last alternative of (15*b*ii). We have already invoked it in our discussion of (18) above. Notice, however, that it is required to accommodate all of the lines of (7), the second of which is repeated here by way of illustration:

```
       /     /     /    /     /      /        /      /
(26) Wylugh, elm, plane, assh, box, chasteyn, lynde, laurer
       V     |     |    |     |     |  |      |      |  |
       W     S     W    S     W     S  W      S      W  S
```

In (26) the first W violates the first alternative of (15*b*i) and both the first and second alternatives of (15*b*ii). The second and third W's violate the first two alternatives of (15*b*ii) but are allowed by the last alternative.

The two final allowable deviations of the standard theory concern inverted feet; by (11.3) these are allowed verse-initially, by (11.4) they are allowed verse-medially. We have shown in (18) above how examples of the former type would be scanned by the revised theory. An additional example of a line beginning with an inverted foot is scanned in (27).

```
      /          /      /
(27) Silent upon a peak in Darien   (Keats)
     | |  | | | |   |   | | |
     W S  W S W S   W   S WS
```

Verse medially inverted feet may appear in two distinct positions, after stressed syllables (cf. (28 *a–b*)) and after a major syntactic boundary (cf. (28 *c–d*)).

```
                 /          /    /           /
(28) (a) The Millere was a stout carl for the nones (A. Prol. l. 545)

              /         /  /           /    /     /
     (b) The course of true love never did run smooth (MND I.i.134)

              /          /         /       /     /
     (c) Appeare in person here in Court. Silence. (WT III.i.10)
         |   |  |   | |  | |       |    | |
         W   S  W   S W  S W      [S    W S

            /         /  U     /    U U    /     U  U  /
     (d) Friends, Romans, countrymen, lend me your ears.
          |         | |    |    | |   |     |  |   |
          W         S W    S    W S   W     S  W]  S
                                                   (JC III.ii.78)
```

The occurrence of two stressed syllables back to back as in *stout carl* and *true love* may correspond to any verse internal W S or S W sequence by virtue of the last alternative of (15*b*). To illustrate this we scan (28*a*) and (28*b*) below:

```
                 /          /    /           /
(28) (a) The Millere was a stout carl for the nones
          | | |   | | |   |   |    | | |
          W S W   S W S   W   S    W S W

              /         /  /           /    /
     (b)The course of true love never did run smooth
         | |      |  | |   | |   | |      |
         W S      W  S W   S W   S W      S
```

Instances of two stressed syllables corresponding to a W S sequence were scanned in (18), (23*b*) and (26) above.

It is an interesting fact that inverted feet appear only under the following three conditions in an iambic pentameter line; verse initially, after a stressed syllable (see (18)), and after a major syntactic boundary (see p. 223 above), across which the stress subordination rules of English do not operate. In the standard theory this is just another fact, to be noted down, of course, but not to be endowed with any special significance. In the revised theory, on the other hand, these three environments are the environments where a stressed syllable will not constitute a stress maximum and hence where a stressed syllable may occupy a W position. Note, in particular, that line (28*d*) would be unmetrical, were there no major syntactic boundary before *lend*. Thus, in the light of the revised theory, the restriction of inverted feet to the above three environments is anything but a curious coincidence; it rather reflects a significant property of the meter. It is one of the reasons for our assertion that the revised theory is more powerful than, and hence to be preferred over the standard theory.

There is yet another odd fact noted by metrists that finds a ready explanation in the light of the revised theory, but is just a curiosity from the point of view of the standard theory. This is an asymmetry cited above between trochaic and iambic lines with regard to the admissibility of inverted feet in verse-initial position (see pp. 222–23 above.) The abstract metrical pattern for a trochaic line must be of the form

(29) SWSWSWS(W)

and its correspondence rules, those of (15*b*). If one allows an inverted foot (i.e., an iamb) at the beginning of a trochaic line, one places a stress maximum in a W position, thereby violating the last alternative of (15*b*ii). We illustrate this with the help of the line concocted by Jespersen on the model of Longfellow's "Psalm of Life":

```
                    /      /
(30) A life's but an empty dream
     |  |     | |  |    |  |
     S  W     S W  S    W  S
```

Here the second syllable violates all three of the alternatives of (15*b*ii), and hence renders the line unmetrical. As we have seen above the same does not happen when a trochee is substituted for the first iamb in an iambic line. Such lines (see (28*a*)) are allowed by the third alternative of (15*b*ii) and are therefore perfectly metrical lines.

Notice also that the introduction of an initial extrametrical syllable will have no effect on a trochaic line, but its inclusion in an iambic line will be limited to lines without inverted first feet since, otherwise, a stress maximum will be realized in a W position in violation of the last alternative of (15*b*ii).[11]

Once again the revised theory shows certain facts to be lawful consequences which are deducible from certain other facts, and thus provides a more adequate explanation for the phenomena than the standard theory.

The final argument in favor of the revised theory is that, as noted above, it is relatively easy to reconstruct the notion of metrical complexity or tension within the revised theory. In the standard theory it is possible to attribute increasing complexity to each succeeding item in the list of allowable deviations. This procedure, however, is quite *ad hoc*. There is no independent justification for ordering the allowable deviations as in (11); hence nothing can be deduced from that order. This does not hold for the order of the alternatives in the correspondence rules (15*b*): here the alternatives are ordered in increasing generality, beginning with the least general and ending with the most general. As already remarked above, the degree of difficulty that a reader will experience in discerning the abstract metrical pattern in a line can be plausibly assumed to be directly related to the richness and variety of the means that can be employed in actualizing the pattern. It should follow, therefore, that when a greater variety of correspondences is employed, the pattern is more difficult to perceive. The number of underlines in the different lines scanned in accordance with our procedure can then be taken as a measure of the complexity of the line. As demonstrated above this measure works properly in extreme cases. Whether it works properly in all cases cannot be determined at this stage in the progress of our science. Questions can naturally be raised about our decision to assign equal complexity to later alternatives regardless of source. It is perfectly conceivable that the increase in complexity due to the need to invoke the third rather than the second alternative of the correspondence rule (15*b*ii) should be a fraction of that resulting from the invocation of the second alternative of (15*b*i). Such questions, however, can be answered only when a massive body of verse has been subjected to the type of analysis proposed. The best that can be done at this point is to list in order of increasing complexity all the lines that have been analyzed above so as to show that the judgments made by our scheme are not totally implausible.[12]

		Complexity of
(31)	1. The curfew tolls the knell of parting day (16)	0
	2. Twenty bookes clad in blak or reed (23a)	1
	3. And leaves the world to darkness and to me (17)	2
	4. Are driven like ghosts from an enchanter fleeing (25)	2
	5. Yet dearly I love you and would be lovèd fain (20)	3
	6. Appears in person here in Court. Silence (28*b*)	3
	7. The Millere was a stout carl for the nones (27*a*)	4
	8. Speech after long silence; it is right (23*b*)	5
	9. Silent upon a peak in Darien (28*a*)	5
	10. Batter my heart, three-person'd God, for you (18)	5
	11. Friends, Romans, countrymen, lend me your ears (28*c*)	6
	12. Wylugh, elm, plane, assh, box, chasteyn, lynde, laurer (26)	7

It will be observed that the lines in (31) vary in complexity from zero to seven. Lines with considerably greater complexity can be readily invented (cf. (32) with the complexity of (17)), but such lines do not appear to be attested in the poets. The theory, thus, allows for a greater variety of line than anyone ever found use for. When faced with such a fact, one may attempt to revise the theory so as to restrict the number of unattested cases that are allowed by the theory. Alternatively one may attempt to explain the unattested cases in some plausible fashion leaving the theory intact. Since we are unable at this point to come up with a significant improvement over the revised theory, we must look for an explanation for the observed facts within the theory. If it is granted that the complexity of a line is directly related to the difficulty that the line in question poses for the reader, and if one further supposes that poets normally do not wish to turn their poems into difficult crossword puzzles the artistry of which cannot be appreciated without laborious pencil and paper calculations, then it is not unreasonable to assume further that there is an upper bound on the complexity that a given poet would ever wish to impose on his lines. A supposition of this sort is perfectly natural in the case of syntax: while clearly there is no upper bound on the number of nouns that can be conjoined in a noun phrase, it would surprise no one to learn that a perusal of the collected works of all American novelists from Hawthorne to Henry James did not reveal a single conjoined noun phrase composed of more than twenty-seven (or, for that matter, none of more than sixty-nine) nouns.[13]

The case of the iambic pentameter does not appear to us so dissimilar as to rule out an analogous explanation for the absence of lines such as (32) in verses written in iambic pentameter.[14]

(32) bíllows, bíllows, seréne mírror of the maríne bóroughs, remóte wíllows

W S W S W S W S W S

NOTES

1. This essay is a shortened version of a part of a larger study dealing with English metrics. The full study constitutes the third chapter of Halle and Keyser, *English Stress* (Harper and Row). (Permission to reproduce material from this book granted by publisher.) This work was supported in part by National Institute of Mental Health Grant No. MH-13390-02 and in part by National Science Foundation Grant No. GS-2005 at Brandeis University. We wish to acknowledge the extremely helpful comments of Edward Weismiller and W. K. Wimsatt. We are indebted to them for many improvements in the exposition which follows; responsibility for its imperfections is, of course, our own. For full reference for all works cited in these notes, see the selected bibliography at the end.

2. We use the term "syllable" here as the equivalent of "sequence of speech sounds consisting of one syllabic sound ('vowel') preceded and followed by any number of consecutive nonsyllabic sounds ('consonants')." In particular, we do not take a position on the vexing question of whether or not utterances can be unambiguously segmented into syllables.

3. By stressed syllable we mean here the syllable that has the main stress in the word; all other syllables in the word are subsumed under the term "unstressed." Thus in the word *instrumentality*, the antepenult syllable will be viewed as "stressed" and all other syllables lumped together as "unstressed." We regret this imprecise language, but we see no ready way out of this terminological embarrassment.

4. An example of a verse medial inverted foot (11.4) can be found in (28).

5. See W. K. Wimsatt (in Thomas A. Sebeok, *Style in Language*): ". . . it is not at all clear to me why the trochaic substitution in the first foot is so acceptable in the iambic line. I'm never able to make up my mind whether it is because it just happened, as Mr. Ransom, I think, suggests, sort of got established, or whether there is some peculiar reason" (p. 206).

6. In previous studies (see, e.g., Halle and Keyser, "Chaucer and the Study of Prosody,"

we proposed that a stress maximum is constituted by a stressed syllable located between two syllables with lesser stress. The definition of stress maximum given here limits more severely the syllables that can be stress maxima. Since in metrical lines, stress maxima may *not* correspond to W positions, an immediate consequence of the more restrictive definition of the stress maximum is to admit as metrical certain lines that previously had been judged as unmetrical; e.g.,
from Chaucer:

1. "With this quyksilver, shortly for to sayn" (C.Y., l. 1111); cf. "for quyksilver, that we it hadde anon" (C.Y., l. 1103);
2. "He was short-sholdered, brood, a thikke knarre" (A. Prol., l. 549);
3. "Ther nas quyk-silver, lytarge, ne brymstoon" (A. Prol., l. 629);

from Spenser:

4. "Ne let house-fyres, nor lightnings helplesse harmes" (Epithalamion xix.7);

from John Donne:

5. "Askt not of rootes, nor of cock-sparrows, leave" ("Progress of the Soule," l. 217);
6. "Th'hydroptique drunkard, and night-scouting thiefe" ("Holy Sonnet III," l. 9).

Though lines of this kind are clearly unusual, they do occur and thereby provide justification for "weakening" the theory in the manner outlined here. The need for a revision of the definition of the stress maximum given in Halle and Keyser, "Chaucer and the Study of Prosody," was noted independently by J. Meadors, "On Defining the Stress Maximum." Note, finally, that "unstressed" in (15*a*) means literally "without stress." This may not be invariant from one poet to another but seems correct for Chaucer and the major poets of the Renaissance.

7. It is important to keep in mind that extra-metrical syllables, both in verse initial and verse final position, are not included in the numbering.

8. Edward R. Weismiller (in a personal letter) has pointed out that lines which exhibit a violation of our rules do, in fact, occur in the work of many Renaissance poets; for example, in the metrically experimental poet Sidney's *Astrophel and Stella:*

```
              /        /   /                  /
With sword of wit, giving wounds of dispraise      (10.10)
 W     S   W   S   W S    W     S  W  S
```

It is Weismiller's belief that such lines are in imitation of an Italian model, the so-called "double trochee." Since we have no relevant statistical studies for the major poets of the Renaissance, we are not in a position to judge how common lines like the above are. A reading of the first thousand lines of the metrically conservative poet Spenser's *Faerie Queene* yielded three clear examples: I.i.12.9, I.ii.36.4, I.iii.7.9, which suggests that the so-called "double trochee" was far from common. They are, in any case, unmetrical in terms of (15) and, if Weismiller's contention is correct, we should expect few lines of this type to occur in poets and in periods known not to be influenced by the Italian model. For a fuller discussion of the term metricality see Halle and Keyser, "Illustration and Defense of a Theory of the Iambic Pentameter."

9. For a discussion of Chaucer's rule in some detail see Halle and Keyser, "Chaucer and the Study of Prosody," and for a criticism of the rule as given there see Hascall, "Some Contributions to the Halle-Keyser Theory of Prosody." Hascall's modification is based upon the observation that in the overwhelming number of instances in which a monosyllabic word is assigned with another syllable to a single position, the monosyllabic word is not a member of a major lexical category (i.e., not an adjective, noun, adverb, verb). This seems to us a correct observation and requires modification of the rule along the lines specified by Hascall.

10. Extensions of the class of consonants which participate in elision are suggested in Hascall

and in Freeman, "On the Primes of Metrical Style." It is one of the contributions of Bridges, *Milton's Prosody*, that the content of this rule actually changes in Milton between *Paradise Lost* and *Samson Agonistes*.

11. Notice that the occurrence of an extra-metrical syllable in verse-initial position in a trochaic line will have the same effect as a verse final extra-metrical syllable in an iambic line; namely, both may turn a main stress into a stress maximum. This suggests that stress maxima in these positions are not crucial to the meter, which would then be a purely internal matter. If this is so, the last position of an iambic line and the first position of a trochaic line would have to be given a rather different theoretical status. Bridges was aware of this: "Tyrwhitt is quoted as saying that one of the indispensable conditions of English blank verse was that the last syllable should be strongly accented. The truth seems to be that its metrical position in a manner exonerates it from requiring any accent.—Whether the 'last foot' may be inverted is another question.—A weak syllable can very well hold its own in this tenth place, and the last essential accent of the verse may be that of the 'fourth foot' " (p. 39).

12. Recent studies (see Beaver, "A Grammar of Prosody" and Freeman, "On the Primes of Metrical Style") have dealt with the question of metrical style in terms other than line complexity. They have taken into account such things as the number and position of stress maxima, the number and position of unactualized S positions, and so forth. For example, in a discussion of the following lines from Pope's "An Essay on Criticism":

1. When Ajax strives some rock's vast weight to throw
2. The line too labours, and the words move slow.

Freeman notes that the heavy stresses back to back contribute to the overall impression of slowness: "Stress neutralization is at work even more clearly in another of Pope's deliberately and exaggeratedly 'slow' lines:

(/)
And ten low words oft creep in one dull line
w s w s w s w s w s

The line is perfectly metrical, but the monosyllabic Adjective-Noun and Adverb-Verb combinations create so much stress neutralization that no stress maxima, or at most one, are actualized in the line" (p. 78).

It is perhaps worth noting that while the large number of heavy stresses back to back in this line is in part responsible for the impression of slowness, it is not in itself a sufficient condition. Thus, we can paraphrase this line by a simple permutation and while the complexity level remains the same, the line seems impressionistically quite different:

And ten low words in one dull line oft creep.

Conversely, note that (18) above can be made to seem much slower by performing a similar inversion which leaves the complexity level unchanged:

Batter my heart, for you, three-person'd God.

The precise relationship to a theory of metrical style of such factors as line complexity and the arrangement of syntactic structures within the line remains to be explored. The most that can be said at this juncture is that the revised theory, we hope, provides an adequate tool for such explorations.

13. We have tried to demonstrate the existence of an inverse relation between metrical complexity of a verse type and the frequency of this type by studying the statistics of different verse types in *Beowulf*; see Halle and Keyser, *English Stress*, pp. 153–55.

14. In May 1970 (see Bibl.), two articles appeared: Wimsatt: "The Rule and the Norm," and Magnuson and Ryder, "The Study of English Prosody," which take issue with the

theory of prosody in Halle and Keyser, "Chaucer and the Study of Prosody" and Keyser, "The Linguistic Basis of English Prosody." The theory presented above anticipates in certain instances the objections raised. A more detailed reaction to these critics, which touches also upon a number of points not treated above, appears in Halle and Keyser, "Illustration and Defense."

SELECTED BIBLIOGRAPHY

Beaver, Joseph C. "A Grammar of Prosody." *College English*, 29 (Jan. 1968), 310–21.

Bridges, Robert. *Milton's Prosody*. Oxford: Clarendon, 1921.

——— "A Letter to a Musician on English Prosody." Rpt. Gross (see below), pp. 86–101.

Freeman, Donald C. "On the Primes of Metrical Style." *Language and Style*, 1 (Spring 1968), 63–101.

Gross, Harvey S., ed. *The Structure of Verse: Modern Essays on Prosody*. Greenwich, Conn.: Fawcett, 1966.

Halle, Morris, "On Meter and Prosody." In *Progress in Linguistics*. Eds. Manfred Bierwisch and Karl Erich Heidolph. The Hague: Mouton, 1970. Pp. 64–80.

——— and S. Jay Keyser. "Chaucer and the Study of Prosody." *College English*, 28 (Dec. 1966), 187–219.

——— and S. Jay Keyser. *English Stress: Its Form, Its Growth, and Its Role in Verse*. New York: Harper, 1971.

Hascall, Dudley. "Some Contributions to the Halle-Keyser Theory of Prosody." *College English*, 30 (Feb. 1969), 357–65.

Jespersen, Otto. "Notes on Meter." *Linguistica*. Copenhagen: Levin & Munksgaard, 1933.

Keyser, S. Jay. "The Linguistic Basis of English Prosody." In *Modern Studies in English: Readings in Transformational Grammar*. Ed. David Reibel and Sanford A. Schane. Englewood Cliffs, N.J.: Prentice-Hall, 1969.

——— and Morris Halle. "Illustration and Defense of a Theory of the Iambic Pentameter." *College English*, 33 (Nov. 1971), 154–76.

Magnuson, Karl, and Frank G. Ryder. "The Study of English Prosody: An Alternative Proposal." *College English*, 31 (May 1970), 789–820.

Meadors, James. "On Defining the Stress Maximum." M.I.T., 1969. Unpub.

Sebeok, Thomas A., ed. *Style in Language*. Cambridge: M.I.T. Press, 1960.

Weismiller, Edward. "The 'Dry' and 'Rugged' Verse." In *The Lyric and Dramatic Milton*. Ed. Joseph H. Summers. New York: Columbia Univ. Press, 1965. Pp. 115–52.

Wimsatt, W. K. "The Rule and the Norm: Halle and Keyser on Chaucer's Meter." *College English*, 31 (May 1970), 774–88.

VERSE AND MUSIC

By MONROE C. BEARDSLEY

Among the aesthetic analogies that have tempted the parallelizer of the arts, that between poetry and music has perhaps proved the most rewarding. Many significant points of similarity have been found: in mode of existence (since in a sense the verbal inscription and the musical score are both sets of instructions for performance), in regional qualities (especially those that make lyric and melody seem predestined for each other in a successful song), in structure, and in features of sound texture.[1] Like most analogies, however, this one can be pushed beyond the bounds of legitimacy, where it encourages the discovery of pseudo-likenesses, or of superficial likenesses that mask profound differences.

The phenomenon of meter stands at precisely this boundary, a kind of Checkpoint Charlie that sharply challenges our understanding of the nature of verse and its relation to music. For it seems obvious that meter is one thing that verse and music share; not contingently, but as an essence of both. Yet whether we have here a deep affinity or a mere equivocation is a serious question, and one whose implications divide students of prosody into divergent and sometimes mutually uncomprehending camps.

I believe the safest way to the center of our topic is one that may appear to begin as a detour—namely, a brief review of certain fundamental features of music.

Rhythm in Music

Fortunately, Leonard Meyer and Grosvenor Cooper have clearly distinguished the concepts that we require.[2] They are *pulse, meter,* and *rhythm.*

"A pulse is one of a series of regularly recurring, precisely equivalent stimuli."[3] The term "stimuli" could be misleading here; we are concerned, not with such things as amplitude of sound wave, but with heard sounds. A series of pulses, whether or not other sounds occur between them, establishes what we may call "pulse," *tout court*; and once pulse is established, it may continue to be heard, even if some individual pulses are skipped, provided that the intervals between the ensuing sounds can be heard as multiples or simple fractions of the intervals between the original pulses. In dance music, pulse is most pronounced, being established and maintained by the beats of drums or other percussion instruments; but most Western music (save for passages of recitative, plain song, and improvisation) establishes pulse.

"Meter is the measurement of the number of pulses between more or less regularly recurring accents."[4] When in a series of pulses, some are accented—i.e., "marked for consciousness"—a contrast between strong and weak pulses appears. Conventional time signatures mark different musical meters: 2/4, 3/4, 5/4—the march, the waltz, the unusual meter of Tchaikovski's *Allegro con grazia,* in his B Minor Symphony (No. 6), which can also be analyzed as an irregular alternation of 2/4 and 3/4.

"Rhythm may be defined as the way in which one or more unaccented beats are grouped in relation to an accented one."[5] In music, meter is pulse plus accent, rhythm is accent plus grouping. When in a series of sounds, some are heard as accented, some not, the accented ones may command attention and serve to organize the rest: the unaccented ones gravitating to the accented ones and segregating themselves within the aural field. The units thus formed (which may be called "feet") are rhythmic units, each of which has its peculiar pattern of accented and unaccented elements. Cooper and Meyer easily appropriate the old prosodic terms for these foot patterns. When an unaccented sound forms a group with its succeeding accented sound, that group is iambic; when two successive unaccented sounds form a group with their succeeding accented sound, that group is anapestic—and so on for the other patterns. (By definition there are no pyrrhic or spondaic groups, since there is one and only one accented sound in a group.)

An important feature of the Cooper/Meyer analysis of musical rhythm is that it reveals not only the first-level rhythmic patterns, but also a hierarchy of rhythmic or pararhythmic patterns in which lower-order groups become elements in higher-order groups. For example, "The Star-Spangled Banner" opens with a sequence of twelve notes that divide into two groups with the same rhythmic pattern. Even this short passage has some rhythmic subtleties that are capable of being analyzed in different ways. A somewhat over-simple analysis will illustrate the Cooper/Meyer notation for up-beats and down-beats (which they extend to whole sections of movements.)

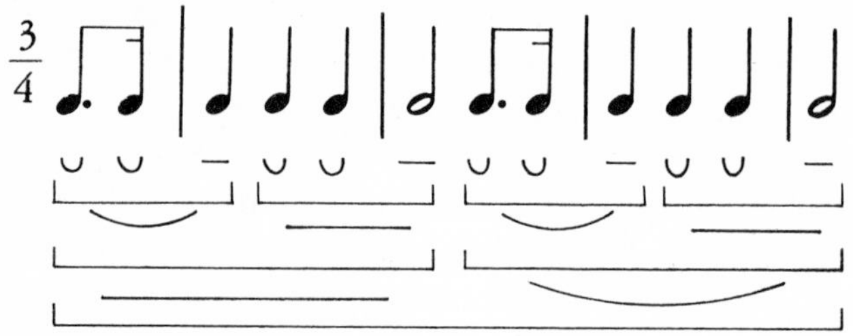

On this analysis, twelve notes form four anapestic groups; the first two anapests form an iambic group, which in turn becomes the stressed element in a trochee. Leonard Meyer has suggested (in a letter) a more complex analysis, involving the concept of overlapping or pivoted groups:

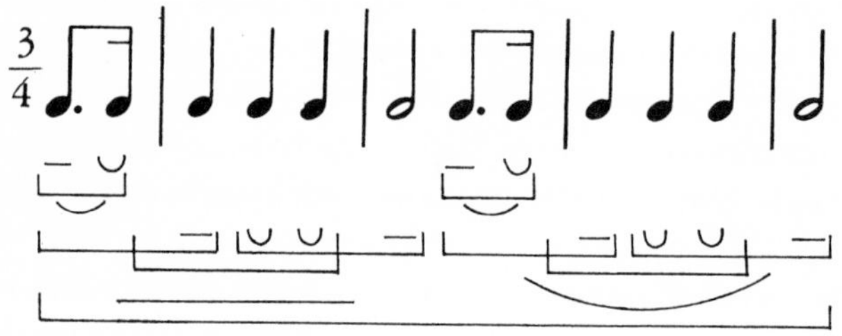

This brings out the continuity and thrust of the quarter-notes.

It is important to mark the relationships among these basic concepts. By definition, there can be no meter without pulse; but there can be rhythm without pulse—if, for example, the first clause of "The Star-Spangled Banner" were played in a free fashion that did not establish pulse but preserved its rhythmic patterns. It would be like recitative.

Meter in Verse

What Cooper and Meyer call a "rhythmic pattern" in music is what prosodists are wont to call a "metric pattern" in verse. Recurrence of metric pattern is meter.

One consequence of this usage had best be confessed at once: since metric patterns, as here defined, involve both more prominent and less prominent syllables, the arrangement of (syntactically ordered) words in lines solely on the principle that each line must contain a certain number of syllables ("syllabic meter") is not meter at all by my definition. It is certainly a sound pattern and may constitute the organization of certain kinds of verse, but I shall not be concerned with it here.

In discussing verse meter, certain distinctions are essential. Taking the script of a poem (the written or printed text) as a kind of verbal score, we may speak of a particular reading of it, whether vocal or subvocal, as a performance. The account of a performance will include the following points: (1) There is a continuing play of feelings on the part of the subvocal performer (reader) or of the audience of a vocal performer: for example, his expectations that certain patterns will continue. These belong to the phenomenally subjective aspect of the experience; but they are a response to (2) the phenomenally objective aspect of the experience. When a metrical pattern is repeated, it sets up its own inward momentum: its pushes and pulls. Even where the local pattern is momentarily weakened or disrupted, the quality of iambicity or trochaicity may still be present, and the line or passage as a whole can be characterized as iambic or trochaic on account of its pervasive quality. Let us call this the "metrical character." It is of course partly a function of (3) a prevailing metrical pattern. It is no tautology to say that a particular stanza has an iambic character, as a whole, because so many of its feet have an unmistakable iambic pattern. But at the same time the metrical character of a line or stanza as a whole may decide the metrical pattern of a particular foot, if there is metrical ambiguity.

Metrical patterns in verse depend on three fundamental features, still imperfectly understood. They are (i) syllabization, (ii) accent, and (iii) linkage.

(i) The problems of giving a satisfactory linguistic definition of "syllable," and of explaining how one syllable is distinguished from another, are well treated by Seymour Chatman,[6] and need not be reviewed here, since prosodists are quite securely in agreement (a) that syllables are the sound elements of which verse meter is a property and the measure, and (b) that, in all but a few cases, it is clear enough for prosodic purposes how many syllables a line possesses.

(ii) The problems involved in explaining accent, or the kind of prominence that one syllable has over others, are also well treated by Chatman;[7] the consensus is that it depends not only on loudness but also on other phonological factors—just as musical accent, according to Cooper and Meyer, is a function of more than one musical variable.[8] The much-vexed questions whether there is a fixed number of stresses in the repertoire of English speech, and (if so) what significance they have for metrical analysis, can be set aside here. Since the correct pronunciation of a word or phrase requires that certain syllables be accented vis-à-vis others, a series of words can be assembled in which certain syllables are more heavily accented than their neighbors. Following Chatman, we may call that accent "ictus." A relatively accented syllable of a word, or a one-syllable word, takes on ictus when it occurs in a series of words having a particular metrical character, and functions as the accented syllable in one of the feet.

(iii) I consider every syllable of a line as attaching itself to its predecessor or its successor—the one with which (or the one that is part of a word with which) it makes the more satisfactory and complete unit of sense. Thus in "the course of human events," "of" groups with "human" at least slightly better than with "course", and hence (in my terminology) is linked to "hu-"; but "hu-" is linked to "-man" as making with it a single word. In general, prepositions and adjectives link to what follows, verbs to their subjects, and, within words, root-syllables and etymologically associated syllables to each other. Linkage can be indicated by an arrow showing the direction of affiliation; two-headed arrows indicate symmetrical linkage. (There is some arbitrariness in this system—e.g., with syllables embedded in proper names—but I believe not much.)

Four score and se ven years a go

Consider each pair of adjacent syllables linked by an arrow: if the first syllable is (comparatively) stressed, the pair has what I shall call a "trochaic linkage" (e.g., "seven"); if the second, an "iambic linkage" (e.g., "ago"). When linkage appears in verse, it may conform to or cut across the prevailing meter, depending on its position. Thus:

Of man's | first dis|o bed|ience and | the fruit

Linkage within these foot-divisions (iambic linkages) works with the meter, reinforcing it; linkage across the foot-divisions (trochaic) works against the meter.[9] Note that "disobedience," which (being a double trochee) might be thought to work doubly against the meter, actually works half with the meter—in its position in this line—since its central syllables link to each other rather than to the affixes. The linkages in this line can then be characterized as six iambic and four trochaic (6I/4T).

A few more examples:

The sea | is calm | to night — 5I/1T

The tide | is full | the moon | lies fair — 6I/2T

Rough winds | do shake | the dar|ling buds | of May — 8I/2T

And sum|mer's lease | hath all | too short | a date — 6I/4T

By sea | girls wreathed | with sea | weed red | and brown — 5I/5T

Till hu|man voi|ces wake | us and | we drown — 4I/6T

He hangs | be tween | in doubt | to act | or rest — 10I/0T

In doubt | to deem | him self | a god | or beast — 10I/0T

When to | the ses|sions of | sweet si|lent thought — 3I/7T[10]

I sum|mon up | re mem|brance of | things past — 4I/6T

The last example shows that the iambic character of a line cannot be completely explained by a predominance of iambic linkages, though where less than half of the linkages are iambic, the iambicity of a line, considered by itself, is likely to be weak. I believe that any passage of iambic verse that consists of more than a couple of lines will be found to have considerably more iambic than trochaic linkages. (The total for the sonnet "When to the sessions" is, by my count, 93I/47T.) Trochaic verse (e.g., Part III of W. H. Auden, "In Memory of W. B. Yeats") has more trochaic than iambic linkages, though the difference is generally not great.

Since the first syllable of a line can link only to its successor, and the last syllable to its predecessor, initial and final feet have considerable weight in determining the character of the line. When a line starts off either iambically or trochaically, its metrical thrust overcomes a certain amount of contrary linkage—especially when the initial linkage goes both ways ("*Avenge* O Lord thy slaughter'd Saints, whose bones"; "*Werther* had a love for Charlotte such as words could never utter"). Hence it is rare to find verse whose lines begin with an up-beat and which is nevertheless trochaic ("The mountain sheep are sweeter/But the valley sheep are fatter./We therefore deemed it meeter/To carry off the latter"—but Peacock's "War-Song of Dinas Vawr" shortly becomes, and remains iambic), or a verse whose lines begin with a down-beat which is nevertheless iambic ("Take, oh take those Lips away / That so sweetly were forsworn"). And it is extremely difficult, if not impossible (as W. K. Wimsatt has pointed out to me), to find verse whose lines begin with an up-beat and have masculine endings and which is nevertheless trochaic, or verse whose lines begin with a down-beat and have feminine endings and which is nevertheless iambic.

The method I have been using has affinities to a proposal made many years ago by George R. Stewart, and recently revived by Charles Stevenson.[11] Stewart groups words into "phrases," counting as a phrase a single word or a word "together with its proclitic and enclitic words" (p. 64). To take an example from Stevenson:

> The hungry judges soon the sentence sign
>
> And wretches hang that jurymen may dine

He then classifies each group as "rising," "falling," or "neutral." Counting the phrases in samples of iambic and trochaic verse, he finds that rising groups predominate in both iambic and trochaic verse, but the ratio of rising to falling phrases is generally much higher in iambic verse. In my judgment, Stewart's method brings out part of the truth, but his classification of phrases is somewhat arbitrary, and since a high percentage of phrases in most verses turns out to be neutral, much relevant information is lost that the method of linkages takes into account:

> The hun|gry jud|ges soon | the sen|tence sign — 3I/7T
>
> And wretch|es hang | that ju|ry men | may dine — 6I/4T

Leonard Meyer has suggested that verse is also capable of higher-order metrical (or, better, parametrical) structures, like music. Some of these are embodied in stanza-forms that give certain lines, or groups of lines, the character of an up-beat to others that have the character of a down-beat. In the heroic couplet, the first line is the up-beat. In the ballad-form, we can discern at least three levels of metrical and parametrical relationship:

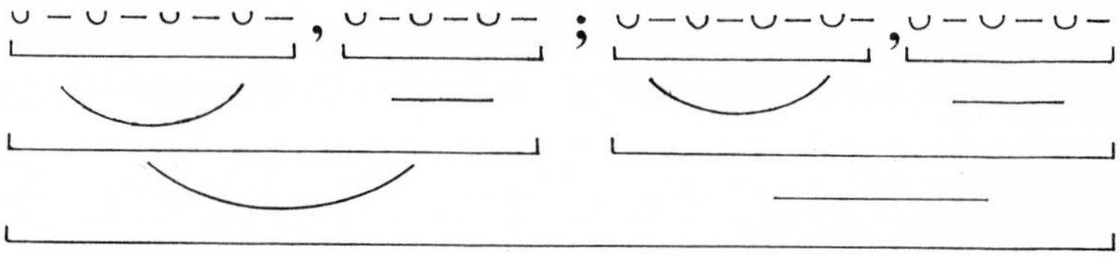

On a still higher level, in a Petrarchan sonnet the octave may be heard as an up-beat to the sestet. But even with stanzaic organization, verse cannot build such elaborate hierarchical structures as are found in music.[12]

Verse and Musical Notation

The score of a musical composition is written in a notation and serves to define that work, since performances that comply with it (at least within certain limits) are performances of the work, while those that do not comply are not. The script of a poem may be considered, in a looser sense, a kind of score for performing that work.[13] When works of art are defined by scores or scripts, there is always more in any performance than is prescribed in the score, so that there can be widely differing performances of the same work, some better than others from the aesthetic point of view. A poem-script leaves many options open; but, among other things, it ordinarily specifies the meter of the poem.

Those who employ musical notation in analyzing verse generally justify this notation by the claim that they are making explicit a part of what is somehow implicit in the script. The question of the legitimacy of this claim involves the basic issues concerning the relationship of verse and music. A typical analysis using musical notation is:

There has been a great deal of discussion about the propriety of this sort of analysis. Four principal objections have been advanced.

First, it is argued that musical notation for verse tends to "obscure the difference between rising and falling meters," since "musical rhythms are essentially falling rhythms."[14] But I think this argument misreads the notational convention that places the main beat at the beginning of the measure. The difference between iambic and trochaic musical rhythms—between up-beats and down-beats—can be represented exactly in musical notation.

Compare:

(*a*) (*b*)

The rhythm in Example *a* is falling, in Example *b*, rising: *a* is trochaic, *b* iambic, in the same way that the line "Falling, falling, falling, falling down" is trochaic, and "Arise, arise, arise, arise, arise" is iambic.[15]

Second, it is argued that musical notation, with a time-signature and bar-lines, calls for pulse, and this prescription goes beyond anything that can be contained in a script. The score for "Hot cross buns!" above specifies that the words shall be read with four pulses to the measure, with alternating accented and unaccented beats. That score can, of course, be performed. But the verbal script says nothing about pulse:

> Hot cross buns!
> Hot cross buns!
> If you have no daughters,
> Give them to your sons!

It is perfectly possible to read this verse with no pulse and yet preserve the metrical character of the lines; such a reading will comply with the script. Yet it is also true that we are strongly inclined to read it with a pulse; it seems natural to read nursery rhymes that way. Why this is so has not been satisfactorily explained. It may have something to do with the semantic thinness of such verses. When we are confronted with a verse script, and cast about for the best performance (i.e., the most satisfying one), we consider how much subtlety and complexity of meaning is there to be brought out. Generally speaking, the more meaning, the less a pulse is called for, or even permitted, in a good performance; but nursery rhymes would amount to very little without a strong pulse.

Third, it is argued that the prosodic use of musical notation rests on the false supposition that syllable-lengths are related in approximately fixed ratios. In writing a score for a pulsed performance of "Hot Cross Buns!" we specified that each syllable of "daughters" shall have exactly half the length of "Hot" or "cross," and that "Hot" and "cross" shall have half the length of "buns" (or it might be more easily performable if these half-notes were made into quarter-notes and followed by rests.) But these ratios are highly unlikely to occur in ordinary speech, where the first syllable of "daughters," for example, would be longer than "Hot." If English syllables could be divided into several fixed lengths, corresponding to half-notes, quarter-notes, eighth-notes, etc., then the script of a verse would indeed contain instructions about the timing of individual syllables and words, and musical notation could make this explicit. But they cannot.[16]

Fourth, it is argued that conventional musical notation, with its bar-lines, presupposes that the sounds it represents fall into equally-timed or isochronic groups, but that this is not true of verse-sounds. Against this it might be argued that even if the performance of a verse need not have pulse, and even if syllables are not of fixed lengths, it may still be the case that in all genuine performances the ictus will fall at what are perceived as equal intervals. A great many writers on prosody have held precisely this view, despite the objections of those who argue (1) that nothing in a script can prescribe such isochronism and (2) that there is no good aesthetic reason for regarding it as a necessary feature of verse-performance.[17]

The principle of isochronism—i.e., the principle that equal, or apparently or substantially equal, timing is necessary to the performance of verse—is sometimes regarded as self-evident.[18] It has also been defended. One argument is that a verse-script carries with it an implicit rule of performance (part of the relevant "language game") that it be read isochronically. But if this were so, one would expect expert readers of, say, Shakespeare's sonnets to follow the rule. The evidence is that they do not.[19] A second argument is that even if syllable-stress meter can occur without isochronism, since its metrical regularity is preserved by the occurrence of equal numbers of syllables between the ictus, nevertheless strong-stress meter, in which the number of intervening syllables may vary, would not be meter at all unless equally timed.

/ u / u u /
Waves of anger and fear
/ u u / u u /
Circulate over the bright
u / u / u u /
And darkened lands of the earth
u / u u / u /
Obsessing our private lives.[20]

There is a problem here, no doubt. If we reject the principle of isochronism, we have to say that Auden's meter consists in the regularity of three feet to a line, plus a kind of semantic equality, by which the extra unstressed syllable in a foot becomes of less weight if it is "and" or "the" or another comparatively unobtrusive monosyllable. A third argument is that prose speech is isochronic, as demonstrated by Pike and others, and "This tendency of our speech, abstracted and simplified into a pattern, becomes the rhythms of our verse."[21] The thesis may help to explain the performance of nursery rhymes, but not of Shakespeare's sonnets, where the metric pattern, as an expressive element, actually works against the isochronism of prose.

Setting Verse to Music

Though the phenomena of verse meter and musical rhythm are, as we have seen, identical, it does not, of course, follow that where verse and melody meet in song, the meter of the one and the rhythm of the other either must or should correspond. The significance of the relationships I have been discussing may appear more fully if we consider briefly the various features of the sound of verse that are taken into account by the composer in setting words to music. One thing he takes into account is the *meaning* of the words, and the problems here are both old and complex;[22] here we are concerned, however, only with the *sound* of the words, considered (no doubt somewhat artificially) apart from their sense. The composer faces a number of choices posed by the notable aspects of verbal sound.

First, in so far as a word may be said to have a special quality, or *timbre,* the composer must take it into account. For the word, when sung, contributes its quality to the note that the singer produces in singing it. And though the singer, if properly equipped, may vary the word's quality within a wide range (making liquid sounds harsh, and sibilants rough), the range has obvious limits ("La-la-la-la" can hardly be made very staccato, nor "kikikik" very legato).

Second, the composer must decide how far he wishes to respect the metrical patterns of given words and phrases, i.e., their distribution of accents. The melismatic style, which supplies several notes for a single syllable, necessarily introduces rhythms that correspond to nothing metrical. For special purposes, the composer may violate even the verbal accents. This is done by Stravinsky in *The Rake's Progress* (see, e.g., Tom's mad song, the Arioso in Act III, Scene iii).[23] The natural style of song keeps close to the rule of "one syllable, one note" (except occasionally for masculine rhymes set to feminine musical figures), and generally respects the prominent metrical patterns of words and phrases.[24]

Third, the composer must decide how far to respect the prevailing metrical character of the verse. Often he can achieve impressive effects by conforming the prevailing rhythms of his melody to the meter of the verse, but sometimes he can obtain more subtle effects by making, for example, regular iambic verse work with a melody of a quite different rhythm ("Drink to me only with thine eyes").

Fourth, the composer generally pays attention to the comparative length of syllables in the words he sets, though he is not bound to respect it. In deciding, for example, which syllables are to be maintained for several pulses, or are to appear in a series of rapid notes, or are to be set to a pair of notes that encompass a wide interval, he must be aware of limitations imposed by syllabic length.

Fifth, the composer must decide how far he wishes to respect the linkages of the verse. Composers who favor songs that are *durchkomponiert* often exhibit an extreme sensitivity to verbal linkages and are guided by it (for example, Hugo Wolf). But in a strophic song, linkage is bound to be overridden a good deal,[25] since the linkages of a musical phrase will not exactly match the linkages of the words in every verse. Both of these lines,

Das Wand-ern ist des Mül-ler's Lust (first verse)

O Wand-ern, Wand-ern mei-ne Lust (last verse)

(*Die Schöne Müllerin*) are set by Schubert to the same music, though in the first line "des" is linked to "Müller," and in the second, the corresponding syllable "-ern" is linked to its predecessor, "Wand-".[26] However, this contrast can be moderated in performance by elision and by slight displacements of the notes (anticipations or delays).

Sixth, the composer must decide how far to respect the parametrical (stanzaic) pattern. In some well-known folk-settings of ballads (e.g., "Barbara Allen"), there is a close correspondence of the musical stanza to the metrical stanza. But the composer may change the stanzaic pattern of the verse to build higher-level structures (as Sullivan does with the words of Gilbert, and Purcell with the words of Nahum Tate)—e.g., by repeating lines and phrases or adding "tra-la-la" or other nonsense syllables.[27]

The composer's freedom in all of these decisions reflects the extent to which music and verse are different artistic enterprises, with divergent virtues and achievements. It is always in order to inquire whether a particular musical setting is suited to a particular verse, or whether one setting is better than another. But such questions are not to be decided by the mechanical application of rules, and indeed they are sometimes very difficult to get at, precisely because—as Susanne Langer has emphasized in her "principle of assimilation"[28]—in a song all features of the verbal sounds are transformed into musical elements. Though their meaning is not lost, but becomes another stratum of the work, their sound bends sharply to the composer's will.

NOTES

1. See John Hollander, "The Music of Poetry," *JAAC*, 15 (Dec. 1956), 232–44; Bertrand H. Bronson, "Literature and Music," in James Thorpe, ed., *Relations of Literary Study* (New York: MLA, 1967); Calvin S. Brown, *Music and Literature: A Comparison of the Arts* (Athens: Univ. of Georgia Press, 1948); James E. Phillips and Bertrand H. Bronson, *Music and Literature in England in the Seventeenth and Eighteenth Centuries* (Los Angeles: Univ. of California, 1954); Edmund Gurney, *The Power of Sound* (London: Smith, Elder, 1880), Chs. xix-xxii; Donald F. Tovey, "Words and Music: Some Obiter Dicta," *The Main Stream of Music* (New York: Oxford Univ. Press, 1949); Tovey, "Rhythm," in *Musical Articles from the Encyclopaedia Britannica* (London: Oxford Univ. Press, 1937); Tovey, *Essays in Musical Analysis*, Vol. v, *Vocal Music* (London: Oxford Univ. Press, 1937); Susanne K. Langer, *Feeling and Form* (New York: Scribners, 1953), Chs. ix-x; Albert Wellek, "The Relationship between Music and Poetry," *JAAC*, 21 (Winter 1962), 149–56; M. C. Beardsley, *Aesthetics* (New York: Harcourt, Brace, World, 1958), pp. 339–52; *Comparative Literature*, 22 (Spring 1970), special number on music and literature.
2. See Grosvenor W. Cooper and Leonard B. Meyer, *The Rhythmic Structure of Music* (Chicago: Univ. of Chicago Press, 1960), Ch. i. Meyer had previously explained these basic distinctions in *Emotion and Meaning in Music* (Chicago: Univ. of Chicago Press, 1956), Chs. iii-iv, pp. 102–27, 143–49; see the rest of Chs. iii and iv for the underlying *Gestalt* principles involved.
3. Cooper and Meyer, p. 3.
4. Cooper and Meyer, p. 4.
5. Cooper and Meyer, p. 6.

6. *A Theory of Meter* (The Hague: Mouton, 1965), pp. 30–40, 101–14. Cf. Wilbur L. Schramm, *Approaches to a Science of English Verse* (Iowa City: Univ. of Iowa, 1935), Univ. of Iowa Studies, N.S. No. 297, Ch. iii.
7. *A Theory of Meter*, pp. 40–76, 119–27.
8. Cooper and Meyer, p. 7.
9. The generalization that, in iambic verse, linkages across the foot-divisions are trochaic has an interesting exception, which has been pointed out by W. K. Wimsatt: namely, the four-syllable "crescendo," in which each syllable is stressed more than its predecessor. In "-brance of things past," the pair "of things" is linked, and straddles the feet, but is in itself iambic. See Wimsatt and Beardsley, "The Concept of Meter: An Exercise in Abstraction," *PMLA*, 74 (1959), 593–94; and Wimsatt, "The Rule and the Norm: Halle and Keyser on Chaucer's Meter," *College English*, 31 (1970), 774–75.
10. The first foot being itself trochaic, its internal linkage counts as trochaic.
11. See George R. Stewart, "The Iambic-Trochaic Theory in Relation to Musical Notation of Verse," *JEGP*, 24 (1925), 61–71; cf. *The Technique of English Verse* (New York: Holt, 1930), p. 36; Charles L. Stevenson, "The Rhythm of English Verse," *JAAC*, 28 (Spring 1970), 339 ff.
12. Meyer has also applied his analysis to the relationships between verbal phrases, and finds rhythmic patterns of up-beats and down-beats on that level, as well. This work has not yet been published.
13. See Nelson Goodman, *Languages of Art* (Indianapolis, Ind.: Bobbs-Merrill, 1968), Chs. iv-v. Cf. Barbara H. Smith, *Poetic Closure: A Study of How Poems End* (Chicago: Univ. of Chicago Press, 1968), pp. 8–14.
14. Calvin S. Brown, "Can Musical Notation Help English Scansion?" *JAAC*, 23 (Spring 1965), 332, 331.
15. Cf. Cooper and Meyer, pp. 12–18.
16. This point has been made by Calvin S. Brown, "Can Musical Notation Help . . . ?" p. 332; cf. Warner Brown, *Time in English Verse* (New York: Science Press, 1908), Archives of Psychology, No. 10, pp. 21 ff. Calvin Brown shows that the use of musical notation cannot be justified on the grounds that there is an average ratio of 2:1 between "long" and "short" syllables in English, as argued by Joseph W. Hendren in reply to comments by W. K. Wimsatt and M. C. Beardsley on an earlier study by Ada Snell; see Hendren, "A Word for Rhythm," *PMLA*, 76 (1961), 302; Wimsatt and Beardsley, "The Concept of Meter," p. 589 n. (I want also to thank Wimsatt for several helpful comments on this essay.)
17. See Lascelles Abercrombie, *Principles of English Prosody, Part I* (London: Martin Secker, 1923), pp. 130 ff.; Calvin Brown, "Can Musical Notation Help ... ?" p. 332; Wimsatt and Beardsley, "The Concept of Meter," pp. 588–92. Martin Halpern, "On the Two Chief Metrical Modes in English," *PMLA* 77 (1962), 177–86, holds that iambic meter "will not usually lend itself to oral renderings in which equal time-intervals occur between each major syllable" (p. 186), but "the heavy stresses which occur every third syllable in regular anapestic or dactylic verse will naturally invite equal or nearly equal time-intervals between them in an oral rendering" (p. 183). There is some truth in this, though the nature of the "invitation" is not clear; in any case, like the nursery rhyme's invitation to a pulsed, and consequently isochronic, performance, it would not be part of what counts as a performance of the verse, but of what counts as a *good* performance of the verse.
18. "Like most metrists, I consider it axiomatic that meter is a species of rhythm," says Seymour Chatman (*A Theory of Meter*, p. 12), who defines rhythm as the recurrence of a marked temporal interval (see Ch. ii). In his view, the metric groups, or feet, are not exactly equal in performance, but have a "rough equality" that enables them to be treated, or accepted, as equal (pp. 114–19). Cf. Stevenson, "The Rhythm of English Verse," pp. 328 ff.: "the metrical stresses of verse correspond to the *beats* of music" (p. 332).

19. Schramm (*Approaches to a Science of English Verse*), who has studied this question, notes that the "rhythmic intervals [=feet] of the average poem may deviate from equality to the startling amount of 24 per cent [when the intervals are measured from peak to peak] without in the least degree impairing the rhythmical effectiveness of the reading" (p. 6); he denies that feet, in performance, are isochronous (p. 69). The significance of his figure is much increased when it is understood as the final result of *three* averagings: (a) He calculates the mean length of (a small sample of) feet in a performance of a particular poem (Gray's *Elegy*: .86 seconds). (b) He calculates the mean deviation from that mean (.35 seconds) and the mean deviation's percentage of the mean length (41%). This implies, of course, that in the *Elegy* performance many of the feet (both longer and shorter) must have deviated more than 41% from the mean, and that the difference between the longest and shortest foot was probably considerable. (c) He calculates the mean of the percentage of deviation for the eleven poems studied. The result: 24%. But since "The Congo" (with—not unexpectedly—only 9% deviation) pulls down this final figure, it should be noted that seven of the eleven poems (as performed) had a higher than 20% mean deviation from the mean length of the feet.

Schramm's experimental design no doubt leaves something to be desired, but it does offer some evidence against the isochronic principle, which is so frequently reiterated without any evidence at all.

20. See Paul Fussell, Jr., *Poetic Meter and Poetic Form* (New York: Random House, 1965), p. 11.

21. John Thompson, *The Founding of English Metre* (New York: Columbia Univ. Press, 1961), p. 13. Cf. David Abercrombie, "A Phonetician's View of Verse Structure," *Linguistics*, 6 (June 1969), 5–13: "the stress-timed rhythm of English is the basis of the structure of English verse" (p. 7).

22. They are discussed in the books and articles referred to in n. 1 above.

23. Cf. Handel's setting of the words "a thick darkness" (*Israel in Egypt*), commented on by D. F. Tovey, *Essays* (n. 1 above), v, 97.

24. Some changes in metrical pattern can, however, be made by the composer without violating the natural distribution of accents. A phrase like "go with," which might constitute an iambic foot in the verse, would adapt itself to becoming trochaic when set to music. Bronson (see above, n. 1) notes the "limitless flexibility" of iambic meter in musical settings. In "Where'er you walk," in Handel's *Semele*, "the composer has taken full advantage of the caesuras and given a smooth deliberation, almost spondaic, to the metrical foot" (p. 135; cf. p. 137).

25. Barbara Smith (*Poetic Closure*, p. 67) notes that some stanzaic poems that otherwise invite musical setting may resist strophic setting because of the great variation in linkage from stanza to stanza (e.g., George Herbert, "Vertue").

26. A melody like "The Battle-Hymn of the Republic," with its insistently rising (iambic) rhythm will inevitably force the singer to ignore the trochaic linkages: words like "coming," "trampling," "vintage," are torn apart by the music. Cf. what happens to iambic linkages in the heavily trochaic setting of "Fear no danger to ensue," in Purcell's *Dido and Aeneas*.

27. My fifth and sixth points (including the Schubert example) I owe to Leonard Meyer, to whom I am indebted for very helpful comments on this essay. I would also like to thank Alan Tormey for his helpful comments.

28. Langer, *Feeling and Form*, Ch. x.